1819–1900
Julia Robbins Barrett
Abolitionist, Artist, Suffragist

I0815863

In haste, Julia

Mary E. Keenan

ISBN 978-1-884186-47-9

Photo Credits:
Pages 8, 10, 13, 15, 30, 37, 41, 42, 57, 64, 80, 82, 88, 114, and Lexington maps courtesy of the Lexington Historical Society.

Page 22 courtesy of Ruth Wathen-Dunn.

Pages 33, 134, 147, and 163 courtesy of the Concord Free Public Library.

Page 92 courtesy of the National Park Service.

Page 94 courtesy of the New Hampshire Historical Society.

Page 154 courtesy of the Schlesinger Library.

Pages 127 and 141 courtesy of Mass Audubon.

Concord maps courtesy of Harvard University Press.

Printed by Puritan Press, Inc., Hollis, NH

Published by the Lexington Historical Society, PO Box 514, Lexington, MA 02420

CONTENTS

Introduction   1

The Robbins Family Tree   5

CHAPTER 1

July 4, 1824   7
   Both the Robbins and East Lexington flourish and remember
Late summer 1832—spring 1833   12
   Growing up in East Lexington and Montpelier
August 1835   23
   Julia—a student at Adams Female Academy
June 1836   24
   Julia surveys her belongings—books and a bonnet

CHAPTER 2

February 1839   31
   Financial ruin for the family and a new interest for Julia
March 25, 1844   35
   Local happenings fail to satisfy Julia's restless spirit
May 11, 1845   43
   Julia takes a serious look at a utopian community
October 12, 1847   49
   Loss, legal matters, and—perhaps—love
September 10, 1849   56
   A cause and a petition keep Julia occupied

CHAPTER 3

Autumn 1850   63
   Julia, alone amidst family, is disappointed with Davison
December 30, 1850   71
   Julia volunteers in the army of abolition
February 1851   76
   Shirts, a toothache, and an uncertain future

December 1851   82
    Finally, Julia sets her own course
September 5, 1852   87
    Early days in Lowell
August 1854   93
    Julia receives letters from a dangerous man
March 17, 1855   99
    Letters from a life-long friend and from a disconcerting cousin
June 3, 1856   104
    An attack on Senator Sumner shocks his supporters
April 24, 1857   107
    A loss in Lexington; letters and visitors to Lowell
March 30, 1860   113
    Julia feels alone against the world

CHAPTER 4

May 17, 1860   123
    Farewell to the single life and the city
September 29, 1863   128
    Concord, a town in time of war
March 12, 1874   135
    Securing a farm and mourning a senator
July 18, 1883   145
    The School of Philosophy—ideas for a summer day
November 23, 1886   148
    A bazaar and petitions, this time for municipal suffrage
January 14, 1891   159
    Life after two losses

EPILOGUE

1892–1900   165
    Julia's last years

Endnotes   171

List of Correspondence   191

Bibliography   197

Lexington and Concord maps follow page 122

ACKNOWLEDGMENTS

Gracious thanks are extended to those who lent their time and talent over the years as *In Haste, Julia* became a reality:

- the Lexington Historical Society, especially to S. Lawrence Whipple and Richard Kollen for their enthusiasm and knowledge in guarding Lexington's heritage
- Susan Bennett, Director of the Lexington Historical Society
- John Zilliax for continued wise counsel
- Jane Brox for thoughtful guidance
- Charles Butts for his excellent advice
- Leslie Perrin Wilson, Curator, and Connie Manoli-Skocay, William Munroe Special Collections, Concord Free Public Library, for their enthusiastic assistance
- Nancy and Reinier Beeuwekes of October Farm for their warm welcome
- Nancy Bivona, Mary Gillespie, Roberta Neuman, and Judith Wilson for their careful reading
- Catharina Slautterback of the Prints Department and Mary Warnement of the Reference Department at the Boston Athenaeum
- Faith Ferguson, who shared the history of Follen Church and knew Julia's pew number
- Florence Bartoskefsky at Baker Library; Victor A. Berch at Brandeis; Jennifer DeRemer at Arlington's Robbins Library; Joseph Dmohowski of Wardman Library at Whittier College, home to hundreds of Parker Pillsbury letters; Eric Frazier of the Rare Books Department of the Boston Public Library; Jean Marie Procious of the Phillips Library at the Peabody Essex Museum; David Smolen of the New Hampshire

Historical Society; and Diana Yount of the Franklin Trask Library at Andover Newton Theological School

- the librarians at the Belmont Public Library, Cary Library in Lexington, the Schlesinger Library, Houghton Library, and other institutions
- Don Trageser, Christyann Rothmel, Lindsey Valich, Janet Keefe, and the entire team at Puritan Press for their thoughtful shepherding of my manuscript into this book
- Jonna Sundberg for capturing Julia's world in the book cover
- my sister Ann—for all those days, months, and years when Julia was center stage

In Haste, Julia is based on the diaries and letters in the Robbins-Stone Papers of the Lexington Historical Society. All quotations from the Lexington (Massachusetts) Historical Society collections are with the permission of the Society.

INTRODUCTION

I met Julia Robbins by accident. At the time I had no inkling that the life of this nineteenth century woman (1819–1900) would be a major focus for years to come. It was 1964 and I was teaching U.S. History at William Diamond Junior High School in Lexington, Massachusetts, somewhat daunted at the responsibility of presenting April 19 to the young people of the town in the school named in honor of Captain John Parker's drummer boy. The town revolved around April 19—the day in 1775 that the Lexington militia faced British regulars on the Green and the first shot of the American Revolution was fired. Thus, I joined the Lexington Historical Society where I was welcomed by the ever-gracious Ruth Morey, the society's first woman president and Lexington's first female selectman.

In a subsequent conversation with Mrs. Morey, I asked about the women of Lexington; there had to be more to the history of the town than a single glorious April day. Mrs. Morey told me of Ellen Stone, a long-lived Lexingtonian (1854–1944) who, in 1881, was the first woman elected to the School Committee. Even though women suffrage was still decades away, women were allowed to vote for and serve on local school committees. After all, the education of the young was one of the tenets of Republican womanhood, a philosophy molding women's lives after the American Revolution.

Ellen Stone's papers are in the Historical Society's archives, then housed in a small brick building attached to the Hancock-Clarke House on the south side of Hancock Street. In the next decade the house would be returned to its original site on the north side of the street and the archives relocated to its basement. S. Lawrence Whipple, the archivist, greeted me on the first of countless visits and highlighted Ellen Stone's life, noting that the library in East Lexington is called the Stone Building, the result of her gifting it to the town in 1888. Then came the best part; boxes of Robbins-Stone family papers—journals, ledgers, letters, wills and deeds, memorabilia, all in long flat, gray boxes that would have each housed a bulky winter overcoat with ease.

Yes, Ellen was remarkable for her era: European traveler, supporter of schools for freed slaves in the South, law school graduate/philanthropist. Yet I had found something that intrigued me even more—a journal kept by her aunt, Julia Robbins, and letters, wonderful letters. There were letters to Julia from abolitionists Samuel May and Parker Pillsbury; letters from her friends Mary Plumer and Elizy Gerry, the former concentrating on the social scene, the latter on the political scene; letters to her family in East Lexington during her five years of work in Lowell designing carpets for the Lowell Company; and letters home from her sister Ellen Robbins Stone living in St. Louis with her husband Abner, who was venturing in real estate, and their young daughter, Ellen.

Each letter was a piece in the puzzle of Julia's life; some provided names of friends and descriptions of activities while others only raised more questions. Genealogies and newspaper clippings, school certificates and local histories helped sketch the broad outlines of her life. But, who was Julia? Privileged as few young women of her age were, Julia was the daughter of a prominent local businessman, Eli Robbins. She spent two years at Adams Female Academy in Derry, New Hampshire, following in the footsteps of two of her older sisters, Abigail and Ellen.

An independent-minded soul, Julia had an innate sense of what was fair and right, perhaps due to being Eli's daughter. It was Eli who had built a hall (later the branch library) across from his home on Main Street, so abolitionists and others would have a place to speak. This was the time when abolitionist William Lloyd Garrison was stoned, the abolitionist hall in Philadelphia torched, and Professor Charles Follen's contract at Harvard College to teach German not renewed because of his abolitionist views. So, Julia's work in circulating a petition on behalf of Washington Goode, a black seaman charged with the murder of another black man over a woman's affections, surely created a stir. It was Julia who arranged for some of the speakers in her father's hall and who lent time and talent to the 1850 Anti-Slavery Fair in Boston.

At times it seemed as if there were two Julias—one a serious young woman who attended Emerson's lectures and considered joining the Transcendentalist community at Brook Farm, the other a fun-loving, even frivolous, young lady who loved social events and followed the latest fashions. Julia, who had started drawing using her Aunt Caira's pastels, reveled in color. There seemed to be no limit to her bonnets, new or retrimmed. When she could not afford a new dress, she altered one she owned, even turning one into a "Bloomer" outfit.

After attending the Boston School of Design, she practiced her craft for five years at the Lowell Company, leaving that position to assume family responsibilities in East Lexington in 1857; she was then thirty-five years old and single. The Panic of 1837 had ruined her father and his death in 1854 left Julia and Ellen responsible for the welfare of their mother and deaf older sister, Hannah Maria. Lawyers, disputes over legal fees and property rights, and rentals of the property filled her days and sapped her energy, leaving her exasperated. Julia had several suitors, but the enigmatic Harvard graduate she favored married the widow of a mutual friend. Julia, hurt and angry, was dissuaded from suing for breach of promise only by the admonishment of her friend Mary Plumer.

In 1860 Julia married John Barrett, a Concord farmer seven years her junior, noted for good deeds and conviviality. With Julia's help—she picked strawberries and other berries in season, earning up to $100 in a summer—he paid off the farm's debts and expanded their holdings. Julia, still thirsty for ideas, attended Bronson Alcott's School of Philosophy, dragging along with her a reluctant husband. With a battle being waged for women's municipal suffrage, Julia circulated the petition from Concord to the state legislature, collecting sixty-two signatures.

For three decades, Julia was mistress of the Barrett farm on the River Road to Carlisle, taking an active role in some town affairs. A few years after her husband's death in 1890, Julia sold the farm to William Brewster, a noted ornithologist who had already purchased their woodlot on nearby Ball's Hill. Brewster's photographs of the area, preserved by the

Audubon Society with the assistance of the current owners of the Barrett farm, renamed "October Farm" by Brewster, show the land as Julia knew it—with lady slippers and partridges both in abundance.

Julia died in 1900, the end of the century. She had a role in its major aspects—industrialization, abolition, and women's suffrage. As the water-powered factories of Lowell resounded with the clanking and clattering of machinery, Julia was there, one of the few women who designed carpets. Standing with the reviled minority against slavery, Julia did not let the expectations of others determine her course of action. Undeterred when the prevailing sentiment in Concord was against women's suffrage, she canvassed neighbors for their signature on a petition for this, her last and perhaps most resounding campaign. Educated and committed, Julia had lived the century in the company of family and friends, working for its causes and dabbling in its fads. To this historian who has come to know and to admire her, Julia was steadfast in her beliefs, courageous in her actions, and thoughtful in her daily activities.

Here is Julia's story, told in a larger context to provide the reader with a clear understanding of the historical events that impacted her. It is a tale told with fidelity to the Robbins-Stone family papers—diaries, documents, and over 150 letters. Throughout *In Haste, Julia*, thoughts and feelings of individuals are sometimes inferred from the factual evidence found in the primary sources and in the historical record. Historians have called this practice "inferred probability" or "reach of inference." For example, there is no written record that Eli Robbins took his daughters to the 1824 Fourth of July celebration, but one may logically infer that was what a public-spirited patriarch would do. Similarly, nowhere does Julia record her retreat to the outdoors to mourn the passing of Grandfather Robbins, but abundant evidence of her love of both her grandfather and the natural world exists. Extensive endnotes detail the sources for the material presented. For ease in following the story, quotations from letters and diaries appear in italics.

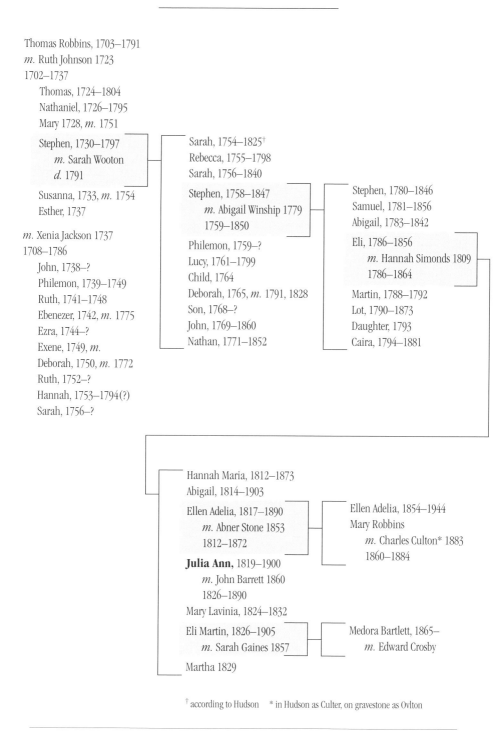

Thomas Robbins, 1703–1791
m. Ruth Johnson 1723
1702–1737
 Thomas, 1724–1804
 Nathaniel, 1726–1795
 Mary 1728, *m.* 1751
 Stephen, 1730–1797
  m. Sarah Wooton
  d. 1791
 Susanna, 1733, *m.* 1754
 Esther, 1737

m. Xenia Jackson 1737
1708–1786
 John, 1738–?
 Philemon, 1739–1749
 Ruth, 1741–1748
 Ebenezer, 1742, *m.* 1775
 Ezra, 1744–?
 Exene, 1749, *m.*
 Deborah, 1750, *m.* 1772
 Ruth, 1752–?
 Hannah, 1753–1794(?)
 Sarah, 1756–?

Sarah, 1754–1825†
Rebecca, 1755–1798
Sarah, 1756–1840
Stephen, 1758–1847
 m. Abigail Winship 1779
 1759–1850
Philemon, 1759–?
Lucy, 1761–1799
Child, 1764
Deborah, 1765, *m.* 1791, 1828
Son, 1768–?
John, 1769–1860
Nathan, 1771–1852

Stephen, 1780–1846
Samuel, 1781–1856
Abigail, 1783–1842
Eli, 1786–1856
 m. Hannah Simonds 1809
 1786–1864
Martin, 1788–1792
Lot, 1790–1873
Daughter, 1793
Caira, 1794–1881

Hannah Maria, 1812–1873
Abigail, 1814–1903
Ellen Adelia, 1817–1890
 m. Abner Stone 1853
 1812–1872
Julia Ann, 1819–1900
 m. John Barrett 1860
 1826–1890
Mary Lavinia, 1824–1832
Eli Martin, 1826–1905
 m. Sarah Gaines 1857
Martha 1829

Ellen Adelia, 1854–1944
Mary Robbins
 m. Charles Culton* 1883
 1860–1884

Medora Bartlett, 1865–
 m. Edward Crosby

† according to Hudson   * in Hudson as Culter, on gravestone as Ovlton

CHAPTER I

JULY 4, 1824: Both the Robbins and East Lexington flourish and remember
LATE SUMMER 1832–SPRING 1833: Growing up in East Lexington and Montpelier
AUGUST 1835: Julia—a student at Adams Female Academy
JUNE 1836: Julia surveys her belongings—books and a bonnet

Both the Robbins and East Lexington flourish and remember
JULY 4, 1824

The house now existing only in the fine gray lines on the yellowing paper of an old book was new then. Its broad front with a prominent central doorway and five generous double-sash upstairs windows bespoke the care of the builder who had studied the latest architectural pattern books. The extensive fields and hillsides were all of a piece, unmarked by the street signs that would later denote Independence Avenue, Bridle Path, and Robbins Road. The green of mid-summer was everywhere—the first crop of hay had been cut, the August dry spells were weeks away. The area is not quieter or noisier now—the calls of drivers and the rumble of their wagons have been replaced by equally noisy twenty-first century traffic. The yard sloping down to the street was neater than its neighbors, but then again, what would one expect from East Lexington's most prominent citizen who was always planting trees and otherwise working to beautify the neighborhood.

Inside, in the front chamber, Hannah Simonds Robbins cradled her fifth daughter, Mary Lavinia. The three-month-old had awakened, crying, as the new East Village cannon was fired for the Fourth of July. Hannah's other daughters had gone with their father Eli and grandfather Stephen Robbins to the celebration. Some visitors to the festivities may have surmised that Stephen had dressed in the old style for the occasion, wearing a ruffled shirt, knee breeches, and a low-crowned broad-brimmed hat. Any East Villager could have told them that this was his everyday outfit, whether he was selling wood or plowing his fields.

Hannah sighed. Eli loved such events and generously funded civic improvements in East Lexington Village, using revenues from his real estate ventures and varied businesses—fur mills with 100 or so workers making caps, boots, and collars; a spice and grain mill; a calico printing mill; and an established East Lexington industry—peat-cutting from the meadow. Hannah's husband even experimented with manufacturing rubber coats. Not to be deterred from operating a tavern near the center of Lexington—since the teams from New Hampshire and Vermont with four to eight horses each, Boston-bound with their loads of produce, provided a steady source of customers for the public houses—Eli had hired a lawyer to successfully reverse the town's decision against licensing yet another tavern. As was his inclination, Eli had sought out the best and was represented by Daniel Webster, then fresh from his success in defending the charter of Dartmouth College against the proposed state takeover of the college. And yet, Hannah mused that her husband still found time to play his violin and give dancing lessons.

The Robbins' homestead was on the west side of Pleasant Street near the intersection of today's Massachusetts Avenue. Eli's summer house on Mt. Independence is seen above the residence.

In Haste, Julia

How different was her day, thought Hannah. No longer was she the privileged youngest daughter of a local squire. Married at twenty-three, she spent her time in the confines of her home, caring for husband and family, cooking, cleaning, washing and ironing, her work seemed never ending. There was an endless pile of mending, to say nothing of the sewing needed for a growing family with five girls. Her daughters were of an age to be of some assistance. Hannah Maria, the oldest at twelve, was deaf; she was willing enough to follow another's example and completed many of the small chores of the household. The bursts of anger born of her frustration of living in a silent world were understandable. Abigail and Ellen, ages ten and seven, could be entrusted with simple errands and minding the baby, Mary Lavinia. Even five-year-old Julia helped out, setting the table at meal times and fetching vegetables from the root cellar. The older girls were expected to mend their everyday clothing. Julia was willing enough to learn some basic stitches, provided it did not interfere with her frequent visits to her father at work in the fur mill or with her solitary rambles on the hillside. A strong-willed child, Julia sometimes managed to evade her mother's entreaties while anticipating her father's wishes. Hannah could not always suppress her annoyance with such behavior while recognizing some of herself in her fourth daughter. Both had expectations of the best life had to offer. As an artist, Hannah was delighted when itinerant painter Rufus Porter had painted watercolor portraits of both her husband and herself just four years ago. In hers, a side view presents a fashionably attired and coifed woman, young-looking and slim at the age of thirty-four.

True, she did have some help with the never-ending tasks, but visits to nearby and sometimes distant family and friends were prized. And they, in turn, relished Hannah's pies when they returned the visit. Her nieces helped from time to time, as did her unmarried sister Lucy, but Hannah tried to spare Lucy heavy tasks as her declining health was of constant concern to the family. Eli's sister, Abigail, known as Nabby, had married a Vermonter, James Langdon, providing an excuse to travel to Montpelier. This was a welcome change for the girls who loved visiting their five Langdon cousins and for Hannah herself who loved the freedom from everyday chores.

Hannah's thoughts turned to her daughters and the Fourth of July celebration. Hannah Maria would enjoy seeing friends and neighbors,

Julia's parents, Eli (1786–1856) and Hannah (1786–1864), were married in 1809. The itinerant artist Rufus Porter painted their portraits in 1820.

many of whom were relatives, as would Abigail and Ellen. Julia would come home wide-eyed, asking to hear again the story of her maternal grandfather, more important, in her mind, than George Washington. To Julia, every civic celebration was for Grandfather Simonds. The watercolor mourning picture Hannah had painted in his memory was a constant reminder of his death almost two decades earlier and an ever-present prompt to Julia's request for the story of his heroism.

Joshua Simonds was in charge of the ammunition, or as it was called then, the powder, stored at the Lexington meetinghouse located on the Green. On April 19, 1775, the British marched through Lexington enroute to their destination—Concord—where they knew the recalcitrant, soon to be rebellious, colonists had stores of powder. The British were surprised by Captain Parker's Company assembled on the Green. In the early morning light, Lexington militia and British regulars faced each other. Then a shot rang out. The ensuing skirmish left eight of Parker's men dead. Grandfather Simonds was in the meeting house when he heard the tramp of British soldiers' boots on the steps. He placed the muzzle of his loaded gun on the open cask of powder, determined to blow up the meeting house and himself rather than surrender the powder to the British. The British commander quickly appraised the situation and gave the order "Halt," quickly followed by "Right about, march." Grandfather Simonds, then thirty-nine and father of five of his eventually eight children, looked out the window, saw the fallen on the Green, and watched as the British departed for Concord. Leaving the meetinghouse, he encountered a British army straggler whom he captured and presented to the Captain of the Lexington Militia, John Parker.

Hannah knew how her older brother William relished the tale of their father's bravery on April 19, convinced that their father had saved both the meetinghouse and the supply of ammunition. As the youngest of Joshua's eight children, Hannah had heard the tale innumerable times from her siblings, especially from William who told it with an enthusiasm now shared by William's own son Eli. Joshua Simonds and his family became further identified with the story of April 19 with his purchase of part ownership of the Parker Farm when Captain John Parker succumbed to tuberculosis five months after the skirmish on the Green. Hannah's ties to that April day strengthened as her older sister Elizabeth married Robert Parker, the son of the Captain of the Lexington Company of Militia. It seemed to Hannah that every story about events in Lexington turned out to be a family story. She and her husband Eli even shared the same great-grandfather, Samuel Winship, a feisty soul who had served as high sheriff of Middlesex County, and who, widowed at seventy, had remarried three years later.

And now the stories continued into the next generation. The Parker-Simonds farm was replete with the lore of April 19. Even the old town belfry from which the alarm had been rung had been moved there for use as a mechanics' workshop where wooden pumps were made. The belfry also served as a gathering place for the elderly men of the town, especially veterans, and for the young boys of the neighborhood. Among the latter was William's son Eli who talked incessantly about the gun his grandfather had recovered from the British soldier he captured; his father had promised Eli he could use the gun to hunt squirrels when he was big enough to hold it. Now this same seven-year-old Eli would be at the festivities, no doubt regaling his younger cousin Julia with the tale of Grandfather Simonds.

Hannah looked up at the commotion at the door as her daughters tumbled in with details of the celebration. There was no doubt that the girls were growing up. Her husband had already broached the topic of their education. His sisters, Caira and Abby, had attended an academy and Eli wanted no less for his daughters; their future should hold more than doing piece work for his fur mill. But what did the future hold for them? Hannah Maria would probably always be part of her parents' household, but what of the others? Hannah quietly surveyed her brood, looking longest at Julia Ann who seemed to have inherited the determination and force of will of her Grandfather Simonds. It seemed this strong-willed little girl had the character to take risks and hold independent, even unpopular, positions. With her interest in Eli's books and newspapers, she would have a bent for learning. Or perhaps she would resemble her paternal grandmother, Abigail Winship Robbins, who was noted for her sense of style and color. Maybe Julia's model would be her unmarried and lively aunt, Caira Robbins, whose name reflected the spirit of the French Revolution and who was so interested in little Julia, finding time from drawing and traveling to spend hours with her. With the blood of colonial town officers, extensive landholders, astute businessmen, and public-spirited citizens in her veins, Hannah knew that Julia would be more than able; her opportunities would be another matter.

Growing up in East Lexington and Montpelier
LATE SUMMER 1832–SPRING 1833

In 1828, there was another revolution—this time in politics as Andrew Jackson, proclaiming his status as a common man, was elected president. His political maneuvering was outside Julia's realm as was the intensifying debate over the nature of the Union; was national unity or state sovereignty the priority? Jackson was elected to a second term in 1832 when Julia at thirteen showed interest in the wider world. Her childhood, replicated in small towns through the northeast, was a life regulated by the seasons. She reveled in long summer days spent outdoors and learned to sew as she edged closer to the fireplace in winter. Proficient at most household chores, Julia frequently chafed at her mother's demands. How she preferred to spend time with her father. Eli, a personable and successful man of many businesses—mills, a tavern, a store—was considerate of Julia's feelings and alert to her wishes. The end of the work day was his favorite time.

The fur mill was quiet in the early evening light. The men and boys had finished for the day, the horses that had powered the machines of the fur mill had been turned out to pasture, brushed, watered, and fed. The smell of hides pervaded the air. There were boxes of finished goods, especially fur caps. On such a pleasant summer day it was hard to think how these would be appreciated in less than six months. The thousands and thousands of fur caps were the most produced item, but the hundreds of pairs of fur gloves, the many muffs and capes, fur trimmings, and fur-lined overshoes crafted in the mills of Eli Robbins and his competitors, notably Ambrose Morell, made theirs the largest business in town while making Lexington one of the busiest manufacturing towns in the Boston area.

Eli Robbins tucked his account book under his arm and pulled the door shut. Tonight he would tally the recent expenditures, which included the cost for the most recent shipments of furs as well as the

In 1820, Eli Robbins built this store, the first brick building in Lexington. Today it is still in commercial use at the same location on Massachusetts Avenue in East Lexington.

wages paid to local young women who took piece work to sew in their own homes for pin money. When the business was his father's, the supply of furs for the caps and capes was local. Now he was dealing with men who brought furs from the backwoods of New Hampshire, Vermont, and eastern Canada. When his son and namesake was born six years ago, Eli thought there would be a third generation to inherit the business. The rapid changes in the country made him wonder about that plan.

Eli needed to review the accounts for his other ventures as well. Four years ago he had built his store, the first brick building in Lexington, housing not only his grocery and dry goods business, but the post office as well. This building, with its graceful design of five large windows spanning the front of the second floor, reminded the villagers of Eli's delight in good design. He was counting on a profit so that he could build his hall, a place where men could speak out on any issue.

The next day, on the way to check on the operations of his calico printing mill in Burlington, he would stop at Lexington Center to see if there were any problems at his tavern there, situated west of the Green. Taverns seemed to run in his family. His father's, at the east end of the village, was known as Cutler's Tavern for the man who ran it more successfully than Stephen Robbins ever could. Perhaps Stephen was too kind-hearted to run a tavern; his generosity to poor families and widows was legendary.

As Eli walked past his father's yard, he saw his father stretched out on his chair beside the front door and the wood pile, his broad-brimmed hat covering his face, his blue and white work stockings beginning where his breeches ended. Sitting on the ground next to Stephen's chair, engaged in serious conversation with their grandfather, were two of Eli's daughters, thirteen-year-old Julia, and eight-year-old Mary Lavinia, who was Julia's shadow. Aunt Caira, his younger sister and their favorite aunt, stood in the doorway conversing with the small group.

A single lady, Caira had more time for her nieces, unlike his wife Hannah's two surviving sisters who, now in their sixties, had fifteen children between them. Only eighteen years older than Eli and Hannah's oldest daughter, at thirty-eight Aunt Caira seemed more like a caring sister than an advising aunt. The Robbins girls loved to call on her, to talk about the latest neighborhood news and, a favorite topic, fashion. Always admired was Caira's dress with the label, "The Dress I made to walk down Broadway in." This creation was of white muslin "with two embroidered ruffles with insertions of lace, and cape to match. . . . White chip hat, faced with blue and edged with netted lace, completed the costume." Another favorite dress was a salmon pink gown with a hat of sea green silk; this was worn with a salmon pink shawl, white silk stockings and mitts, and salmon pink kid slippers.

Caira was never too busy for her nieces—not even when she was drawing, her box of English pastels open on the table beside her. Julia loved rearranging the short stubs of color in the patterned box whose twenty-four sections provided opportunity for myriads of combinations of color. Often, while Caira drew and Julia dabbled in the color box, Julia's aunt regaled her niece with tales of her academy days and travels to New York City, Niagara Falls, and Montreal. Aunt Caira's many trips provided endless material for the stories Julia loved. Her current favorite was that of a trip on the recently-opened Erie Canal; some described it as "the Grand Canal," but Aunt Caira thought it was appropriately called a ditch.

RESIDENCE OF STEPHEN ROBBINS,
Erected about 1720.

This picture of the home of Julia's grandparents Stephen and Abigail Winship Robbins is attributed to their daughter Caira. In 1948, the house was moved from the intersection of Pleasant Street and Massachusetts Avenue to its present location at #1295 Massachusetts Avenue.

As Eli approached the tableau, he noticed that somewhere Julia had found a copy of the town report (probably his copy) and it was this that the four were considering. As Eli slowed his steps and joined the three generations of his family, Julia waved the single-sheet report at him, pleading with him to take her side in the discussion. The "Account of the Expenditures of the Overseers of the Poor" actually listed the names of the unfortunate souls who needed town assistance for shoes, clothing, and funeral expenses. Julia argued, shouldn't they be spared this indignity? Was it their fault they had a run of bad luck—an accident that left the farmer crippled, a fire that could have happened anywhere in town, a death in childbirth that bewildered a young husband and devastated a family with toddlers? Holding family and friends to a strict code of behavior, Eli's daughter was always ready to defend the less fortunate. Eli laughed, scooped up Mary Lavinia, and with Julia at his side, took leave of his father and sister and headed across the street toward home.

Sensing her father's good mood, Julia reminded her father of his promise to take her to Boston with him on his next trip to the city, starting her on a journey to his older sister Nabby's home in Vermont. Marrying at twenty-six and "well," as the New Englanders expressed it, Nabby enjoyed entertaining her family. Caira, in her late teens, had spent the better part of a year with her older sister Nabby, who had been educated by the English actress and author Mrs. Susanna Rowson at her well-known school near Boston; here, "sound intellectual training" was matched by "instruction in the social usages and polite accomplishments of the time." A gracious hostess, Nabby made everyone feel comfortable in her home. Not only had Julia been pleading to visit her Langdon cousins, but Eli and Hannah had been concerned about Julia's fainting turns and felt that the country air at Nabby's would do her some good. With her parents' blessing but unaware of their concern for her health, Julia packed some clothes into the family valise and left for Montpelier.

Summer cooled into autumn, and Julia stayed in Vermont. Now accepted as part of the Langdon household, she did her chores and played with her cousins. Soon, however, everything changed. In mid-November, Aunt Nabby received a letter from her niece and namesake, Julia's eighteen-year-old sister Abby who wrote:

I address myself to you thinking that Julia would be better able to bear what I [am] about to communicate than if addressed to her, as she was subject to fainting turns and fearing she might have one of them.

My dear sister Mary is no more—she died on Wednesday—she was taken sick about 2 o'clock Tuesday morning & lived about 36 hours. . . . We do not know what the matter was with her—The Dr. did not appear to know he called her disease the malignant fever.

Julia was devastated by the news; how could this happen to her little sister? The world now seemed a hostile place where nothing was guaranteed. Privately, Aunt Nabby and the other adults whispered their question—cholera?—as they parsed Abby's grammar—*"The Dr. did not appear to know."* Just the previous winter, Boston had joined other Atlantic ports in quarantining passengers and goods from the Baltic, Russia, and the British Isles where cholera had broken out. It wasn't far-fetched to think that members of the Robbins family, who frequently went to the city on business, could be carriers of the disease from Boston to Lexington. Hadn't Boston appropriated the sizeable amount of $50,000 to clean up the rotting rubbish and cesspools in the city and even set up a Relief Association? But cholera did not have to come from the city. Rural areas throughout New England all seemed to have "festering manure and other nuisances capable of attracting the disease." Death, like Mary's, came suddenly for its victims, often within twenty-four hours of the first symptoms of "[d]iarrhea, acute spasmodic vomiting, and painful cramps."

Most likely, Mary's attending physician was Stillman Spaulding who lived nearer to East Lexington than did the town's other doctor, Joseph Fiske. Then forty-four years old, Spaulding was no country apprentice doctor but a Harvard graduate with a medical degree from Middlebury College. Though a member of the Massachusetts Medical Society, maybe he truly did not know what was the matter with Mary Robbins. He did know that a diagnosis or even a suggestion of cholera would certainly panic the neighborhood, particularly if they realized, as Abby had also written, that the rest of the family was also very sick at the same time.

Aunt Nabby remembered when she was ten years old; then a new little sister did not live long enough to even have a name of her own. With memories of that difficult time, Nabby was especially kind to thirteen-year-old Julia; the Langdon cousins, notably Cousin Caira, were solicitous. They watched silently as Julia, at a loss for words or feeling, stoically sewed the black ribbon her mother had sent onto her bonnet. Mary had been gone more than a week before Julia had heard the news. How could she not have known for so long? With Abby and Ellen away at school in Derry, New Hampshire, and with their oldest sister Hannah in a world of silence, eight-year-old Mary had been Julia's special charge and constant companion. Julia was heartsore.

As she grappled with the news of her sister's death, Julia waited for letters from home. The first one to arrive was written by Abby on December 7, a month after Mary Lavinia's death.

> *As Mother is going to send a small bundle to Aunt Nabby, I thought I could improve the opportunity in writing a few lines to you. I suppose you have received the bundle we sent, but you have not wrote and informed us. Julia, you ought to write once in a while, I suppose you think you cannot, but you need not be afraid to write to me, I will excuse all inaccuracies. I want to know how you pass your time—whether you go to School or not— if you go to School, I should like to have you attend to your Latin. If you have not your books I will send them up. I want you should write & tell me what you wish for—Stocking, gowns, or anything. I suppose you have concluded to pass the winter. I want you should write & tell me how you like [it], and if you are not afraid you shall be homesick before Spring.*
>
> *I did not know but you would want to come home when you heard how sick we were and the death of your little sister Mary: but you will never see her again. I hope you will reflect upon it, read your Bible, and be a good girl, for you know not how soon you may be called upon to die, and in as sudden a manner as she was perhaps. We had not been at home from Derry but 4 days before she was taken sick. I had hardly seen her.*
>
> *You must not let anyone see this, for I have taken no pains & did not write it thinking any one was to see it but you.*
>
> *Your affectionate sister, Abby Robbins*

Julia read and re-read Abby's letter, in turn solicitous and stern. She did not need anyone to remind her of Mary's death or the time away from her family. Should Aunt Nabby have sent her niece home straightaway on hearing the news? Were her dual concerns of an inconsolable thirteen-year-old making the long journey alone and of illness in the East Lexington household sufficient to assume Julia should stay in Vermont? Abby's letter ignored Julia's feelings, instead reprimanding her for not writing and admonishing her to be good. Julia, feeling guilty that she had not been at home when her sister died, was unsure of her place in the family, vacant these many months. She was certain that her mother's attention would pivot on her youngest surviving child, seven-year-old Eli. When Eli was born, Julia was too young to help care for him, instead devoting her attention to a little sister, alive now only in memory. With the season of winter storms making travel treacherous, it seemed that staying with the Langdons was Julia's only option.

Julia's spirits rose with a letter from her sister Ellen, only two years older, but already in another sphere as an academy student. In enthusiastic bursts, and, as was her style, without punctuation, Ellen explained:

> *Having a few leisure moments I thought I would improve them in writing you a little news It is now after eight O'Clock and mother has retired and I am sitting in the middle kitchen writing this scrawl In the first place I will give you a short account of what Mr Davis said of you He arrived hear [sic] about ten days ago he said he had seen you and that he did not hardly know you he said he thought it agreed with you to live in the country.*

Ellen recounted the news of neighbors and friends; Mary Morell's plans to attend school in Natick, and Mr. David Penn's sudden burial of his wife, his little children taken in and cared for by a friend for the winter. This elicited a sympathetic cry from Ellen—*"What will become of them in the Spring?"* Ellen had been to the fur mill, informing Julia that *"We have got a young Sweden [sic] here cutting caps he cannot speak our language hardly any."* Recently returned from Adams Female Academy in Derry with her sister Abigail, Ellen passed on two pieces of school-related news: she had had eight visits from the doctor for throat distemper while at school and Abby had received a diploma from Adams Female Academy, a singular distinction for a young woman of this time. Few pupils stayed at an academy long enough to earn a diploma.

Mirroring her sister Abby's command to keep the letter private, Ellen twice cautioned Julia not to let anyone see her letter. For Abby and Ellen, academy-educated young women, any letters of theirs that passed from hand to hand for perusal and inspection, as was the custom, had to reflect their status. They were proud of their ability to present themselves well. In a world pre-dating the telephone, letters assumed great importance with the post office the hub of village news. Even in Montpelier, Vermont's capital city, a letter addressed to the visiting "Miss Julia A. Robbins" needed only the city and state to be delivered. On the folded page that became the envelope there was no need to add "care of Langdon." Everyone's business was everybody's news.

Julia spent the winter with her Langdon cousins. A month into spring, on Thursday, April 18, she left Montpelier with two traveling companions, identified only as Edwards and Charlotte, for the three-day trip home. She arrived in Boston on Saturday, April 20, where she met her father and sister Abby. Abby, who had gone to Boston that day with her father, had planned to spend the night in the city, but, as Julia expressed without enthusiasm, *"finally concluded to ride home with me."*

In a letter written the next day—a Sunday—to comply with Cousin Caira's request to write *"as soon as I arrived in Lexington,"* Julia chronicled her *"very pleasant journey from Montpelier."* Julia had traveled through Barre and *"found it very muddy,"* through Williamstown, Chelsea, Tunbridge, and Norwich, and then crossed the Connecticut River to Hanover, New Hampshire, where she spent the night.

> We had very good accommodations indeed there. We slept in the second best room they had as I suspect, as the number on the door was two. . . .

With her traveling companions, she left Hanover in a barouche, a carriage with a collapsible top with seats for four inside and an outside box seat for the driver. Julia informed Caira that she had left Hanover about three in the morning:

> . . . through Lebanon and Enfield to Springfield. The driver gave us a description of the Shakers at Enfield which we found very interesting indeed. We might have rode in the stage with the rest of the passengers if we wished but we preferred the barouche.

The trip continued to New London where a little girl, about nine years old, traveling alone to Nashua, boarded the stage. Julia sympathized, *"Poor little girl[,] she was sick in the stage and had to get out and ride on the outside."* Next came Sutton, Warner, Hopkinton, Weare, Goffstown, Bedford, Merrimack; they crossed the Massachusetts border to Dracut and spent the second night in Lowell. Julia recounted, *"They gave us a room where the plastering smelt as if it was not dry."* At eight the next morning, they left by stagecoach, riding through Tewksbury, Wilmington, Woburn, Medford, and Charlestown, finally reaching Boston.

Although her letter to Caira was lengthy with neighborhood news, including plans for a Unitarian meeting house and surprise at Lexington's warmer weather with mayflowers in bloom, Julia wrote very little of her family and nothing of her reception in East Lexington, relying on a single emphasized word to express her feelings:

> *I thought I would write a few lines and send them up to the post office this afternoon when* **they** *went up to meeting.*

Instead, she chattered away about her neighbor Mary Morell, who had paid an evening call, trying to convince Julia to join her at Woodworth's Academy. Mary, a year Julia's junior, had attended two balls this past winter. Of a recent hire in the fur mill, the *"young Sweden"* of whom Ellen had written, Julia noted: *"I have not got so I can understand all that he says yet. He is very smiling indeed."*

Away from home for more than half the year, Julia was back in East Lexington where it seemed her family had become strangers. The daily routine remained as it had always been, etched for posterity in Ellen's diary:

> *Wash Monday Iron Tuesday Wednesday sweep the house from top to bottom Thursday clean the silver, make cake.*
> *Fryday [sic] clean chambers Saturday Clean brass, sweep carpets.*

But there was a seismic shift in the household.

Eli Robbins, pre-occupied with the construction of his hall for speakers, was engaged in constant discussions with master builder Issac Melvin, an admirer of the influential architect Asher Benjamin. Eli's Grecian style hall with four Doric columns, pilasters, fanlight and sidelight windows was, indeed, influenced by Benjamin's 1833 work *The Practice of Architecture*. Not only was the hall architecturally pleasing, it set the standard for dwellings in "the prosperous and progressive community of successful small businesses" where many of the houses still standing almost two centuries later display a center entrance with five windows on the second floor.

Eli Robbins, a strong believer in freedom of speech and thought, built this hall in 1833. Decades later, his granddaughter Ellen Stone gave the building to the town for a library.

Without her little sister, Julia's place in the family had shifted—no longer was she one of the young ones with Mary. Julia had missed Mary's birthday on March 23 and wondered if Mary was even mentioned on her special day. Or, had she joined the silence surrounding another sister, Martha, who would have been four had she not died a few days after her birth?

Julia was identified in town as one of the Robbins daughters, joining Hannah Maria, twenty-one, Abigail, nineteen, and Ellen, whose sixteenth birthday was only a month away. In her diary, Ellen now referred to her sisters as *"J.A.H."*—Julia, Abigail and Hannah—in recording such events as *"J.A.H. got their gowns all greast [sic] getting out of the Caryall [sic]."* That was not the end of Julia's woes that day as Ellen added to her diary entry that *"Julia fell her length."* In two weeks Julia would turn fourteen.

Julia—a student at Adams Female Academy

The last two years had seemed interminable to Julia. Her sister Abby, only five years older than Julia, had completed Adams Female Academy. When Ellen returned to finish her program at the New Hampshire school, Julia was forlorn; friends could not compensate for the loss of companionship of her sister. Finally, it was Julia's turn to head north to the same school.

Her summer cotton petticoats had seemed light enough when Julia stepped into them in the early morning. Now, hours and hours later, they seemed as heavy as her pieced winter quilt lined with an old blanket. The heat seemed to come from all sides—from the earth and the sky and the buildings along the road. Compounded by the dust of the August day, the heat settled over the coach like a hot, prickly cloak. True, it was a bit less humid once the coach had crossed the Merrimac River; in the low hills of southern New Hampshire it was cooler than Lexington, but Julia was hot and hungry, anxious to reach her destination. Throughout the journey she thought of what she had heard from her sisters Abigail and Ellen about Adams Female Academy.

Julia knew of the Academy's proud history and its visit from General Lafayette of Revolutionary War fame in June of 1825. She knew that two of preacher Lyman Beecher's nieces had attended Adams, even though the girls' aunt, Catherine Beecher, had established a seminary for young women at Hartford, Connecticut. Adams Female Academy's "firsts" had been repeated so frequently that Julia could cite them chapter and verse: one of the first academies "endowed exclusively for girls" with a $4000 bequest from Jacob Adams in 1823, the first academy for women in New Hampshire, and the first female academy to issue diplomas, with Julia's sister Abby one of the few students to qualify for this distinction.

Now that the sign "East Derry" was in view, Julia felt a surge of what—excitement, nervousness? Her family was concerned about her possible homesickness but Julia had brushed away their concerns. The winter in Vermont after Mary Lavinia's death had eradicated any such feelings of homesickness she might have once held. At sixteen, she would at last have some independence! True, she would be under the watchful eye of Mrs. Gale, the principal's wife, at whose home Julia was boarding. She knew of the school regulation stating, "All pupils are required to attend church regularly on the Sabbath" and had heard the rumors about the uninspired sermons of Reverend Edward Parker, the local minister who was also a trustee of the Academy. But she was no longer under her family's roof!

A few days after Julia had settled in, a letter from her sister Ellen in East Lexington expressed the family's surprise that Julia was "*so well-contented*" so quickly. Julia raised an eyebrow at their surprise—why wouldn't she be content? True, she had a bedfellow, Miss Amelia Scott, but privacy was not the same as independence. Julia, who had frequently walked to the top of Mt. Independence behind her house in East Lexington to survey the panorama extending to Boston Harbor, had a new landscape to provide her with a much-needed sense of distance and perspective—the view of Mount Monadnock from the school grounds. Sometimes it was an impression on the hazy horizon, sometimes it was etched clear against a late summer sky. But she once again had a place to look to, to escape the nearness of the every day.

Julia surveys her belongings—books and a bonnet
June 1836

It had been almost a year since Julia had enrolled at Adams Female Academy. In that time she thought of little but her academic world—her classes, teachers, assignments, and friends. Andrew Jackson was finishing his second term as president, there was news of a battle at a place called the Alamo, and hints of a looming national financial crisis were unheeded. Julia and her school mates were ensconced in their own world.

Julia opened her hand-sewn notebook with its marble paper cover to record her purchase—"*Bonnet $7.50.*" It looked so stark on the page, only the second entry; Julia turned to the previous page listing earlier expenses for the year. This confirmed it; the bonnet was her most expensive purchase this year. A bonnet purchased in January had cost $2, but this new bonnet, as lovely as a midsummer garden, was a costly item, even for the daughter of East Lexington's most prominent citizen.

Turning to her assignment, Julia began the draft of a required composition, due once a fortnight. What would she write? In one of her essays last year, she had addressed the evils of whispering, which she called "*a parent of many vices.*" She cited disturbance, bad example, and time wasted as evidence. Zilpah Grant, the first principal of the academy, who had left when the trustees added music and dancing to the curriculum, had worked to terminate whispering by meeting with girls individually and having them pledge to stop, but whispering was never eradicated. Julia looked out the window—the light of the late June afternoon beckoned her outdoors. First, however, there was this composition. This year, her senior year, required a more serious subject than the oft-discussed whispering. She was determined to excel so all who compared her with her older sisters would be forced to notice that she equaled or surpassed their scholarship. Not content with only being one of the four Robbins daughters, Julia was determined to stand out from the others—with her writing and report card grades as well as with her new bonnet. Of the four, Julia was the one who had inherited the Robbins' flair for color and fashion, passed on from her grandmother and Aunt Caira. Julia felt that Abby had earned a diploma to please her parents; Ellen had done well as a bright, engaged student. Julia herself loved playing with ideas and delighted in understanding a topic sufficiently to clearly express herself. When others raised their eyebrows at her contributions to conversations, at first she was pleased. However, Julia had difficulty suppressing her irritation when anyone questioned the value of education for young women, who, according to some, had no business expressing opinions on worldly subjects, but should confine themselves to matters of home and hearth. She had no intention of remaining quiet when interesting issues were being discussed. Julia was sure she could earn better grades than Ellen, and was glad that Adams was one of the few academies which issued reports on student progress. How she looked forward to those reports—tangible proof of her accomplishments.

The Adams Academy schedule and its monitorial system suited her. Following the organizing principles of Miss Grant and one of her former teachers, Mary Lyon, who had since left to establish Mt. Holyoke Seminary, Adams Academy had instituted the practice of student concentration in just a few subjects each term, as well as the monitorial system.

Under this system, a small number of students, trained as leaders for a specific lesson, led small groups through the topics with discussions or recitations. Understanding, not rote memory, was rewarded with good grades and approving looks. The school catalog referred to the course of study as "thorough, comprehensive and systematic." The total list of classes was dizzying. It included elocution, orthography, grammar, arithmetic, geography, history, algebra, philosophy, natural theology, American economy, geometry, astronomy, chemistry, botany, rhetoric, logic, composition, and three languages for an additional charge—French, Latin, and Italian. Adams Female Academy was one of the more rigorous schools for young ladies; indeed, it bordered on radical. Only in the previous decade had Yale College in New Haven officially adopted French in the curriculum, ignoring concerns of morality associated with things French. Julia loved seeing the surprise on people's faces when she told them that she was studying French as some believed that French was not a proper study for young ladies, fearing that "Where the French language went, depravity, frivolity, and indolence were sure to follow."

Pushing aside her French dictionary, an old math exercise book with its problems on market price corn and blistered steel, the penmanship guide with the imposing title of *Scholar's Guide to Chirography, Containing Writing-Book, Copies, Rules, and General Direction to the Art*, and Upham's *Intellectual Philosophy*, Julia's eye fell on her Bible, inscribed to her from Mrs. Gale and dated Feb. 12, 1836. Julia started her composition.

If we wish to improve our minds, it is essential that we devote a portion of our time to reading and also highly important, that we be exceedingly careful in our selection of books; since there are many in circulation, which are not useful, which only imbue the mind with wrong ideas, and tend to vitiate the taste. Our attention should be particularly directed to those books which teach morality, since our happiness depends upon the right performance of our duties, to God, to mankind, and to ourselves. Upon this subject there are a great number of books, written by wise men of past ages, and also by those of the present, which are to be highly valued; but these are exceeded by the bible, that book, which of all others should be the most preferred [sic]; its instructions are universally applicable; there is no one that cannot here find, if he reads with care and attention, lessons that seem especially intended for himself, and by which he can be profited.

Warming to her topic, Julia's pencil fairly flew across the page, her ideas racing ahead of her writing.

History is next in importance; in this, we are are [sic] presented with a view of those, who have performed their part part [sic] on the stage before our existence; we see them in almost every variety of situations in different states of civilizations and under different governments; we see them worshipping the idol, and embracing the christian religion; we see them in the tumult of war, nation enraged against nation, and in the quiet lap of peace. From this valuable lesson it may be inculcated; we find that those, who were in a state of ignorance vice and wickedness were wretched and miserable, while those, who were more improved, virtuous and good were prosperous and happy.

In her concluding paragraph, Julia turned to the sciences.

Those sciences from which we derive a knowledge of surrounding objects, ought not to be neglected; by an acquaintance with them, we shall find them a source of much truee [sic] pleasure; whenever we walk abroad in the open fields, whatever we behold will fill us with admiration and wonder; we shall be induced to notice the large trees of the forest and the beasts which they shelter, the little plant beneath our feet and the still smaller insect, which it nourishes, and by examination, we shall find them all equally provided for and protected by an allwise [sic] and benevolent Creator.

There, it was finished. Julia was pleased with her essay. Putting it aside to copy in ink later, Julia went in search of her friend, Mary Plumer, to put into practice the same idea she had just expressed in her composition; there was still time for a walk before sunset.

Passing younger girls in the hall, Julia thought of the day last October, at the end of the twelve-week summer term, when she received her certificate making her a member of the senior class of 1836. She had committed the phrasing to memory:

Agreeably to a standing Ordinance of the Board of Trustees, these presents witness, that Julia A. Robbins for correctness of moral conduct while a member of the Seminary and for honorable improvement in her various studies, is entitled to this Testimonial of their Approbation and Introduction to the senior Class of 1836.

Julia loved being a member of the Senior Class and reveled in her friendships. She had counted almost 150 student names in the school catalog: Susans and Lucys, Catherines, Carolines, and Clarissas, as well as Persis, Phebe, Sophronia, and Serena. There were more young ladies her age here in this one academy than there were in the entire town of Lexington; the last town census had enumerated ninety-three white females between the ages of fifteen and twenty. Julia studied the columns of names in the catalog, marking the seventy-one she knew, including the sixteen she designated with a plus mark. Included in this select list was Mary Plumer, whose hometown was fifteen miles north as the crow flies, in Epping, New Hampshire. Mary's father was a United States senator, her grandfather, a former governor of the state. Julia felt sure that she had made some life-long friends.

There were other students from notable families and from families whose first distinguishing mark was their daughters' attendance at Adams Female Academy. A few students were older than Julia, including young women who had already taught in country schools. Some students stayed a year for three terms; some stayed for a shorter time. Each term averaged twelve weeks in length with tuition at $5 a term. Board, which included "washing, fuel and light" ranged from $21 to $30 a term. This was a fair sum of money; back in Lexington, Doctor Spaulding received $25 for attending to the poor of the town for an entire year. Language instruction had an additional fee while the "Use of Books recited and stationery" ranged from 50 cents to $1. Additional boarding funds were charged for those who did not return home for the three to four week vacation between terms. For many of Julia's peers—most of whom were from New Hampshire, but some of whose addresses ranged from Farmington, Maine, to New York City and Baltimore, Maryland—the cost of traveling expenses loomed. Each student was additionally required to fund the cost of apparel as her finances allowed.

Coming from a town that valued education sufficiently to appropriate fifteen percent of the town budget, or $1000, for a year's school expenses in 1835, Julia came from a family that valued education even more. As unusual as it was to be the third daughter in a single family to be sent to an academy, it was even more amazing that Julia also had two academy-educated aunts. Julia, with stagecoach fare to Lexington and the sundries a young lady at school sought, as well as her sense of fashion to satisfy, spent a considerable sum above tuition and board while at Adams Female Academy; in 1836 this amount totaled $54.19. For the same amount of money, the town of Lexington paid its most costly female teacher, Miss Mary Wellington, the sum of $45.50 for teaching the school in the East Village for thirteen weeks at $3.50 a week; John Underwood $5.50 for leveling the South schoolhouse yard; Jacob Robinson $1.75 for whitewashing the Southeast school house; and William Clapp 55 cents for two brooms, and still had almost a dollar's worth of change! While the Lexington Overseers of the Poor were buying cotton flannel at 12.5 cents a yard, or 75 cents for the total amount of six yards, Julia was satisfying her fashion sense with a purchase of six yards of Alipine fabric at $1.42 a yard, for a total bill of $8.52—more than two weeks of a teacher's salary! Julia's father was proud of his daughter's academic success and her ability to express herself and so willingly paid for her expenses.

What did her mother, Hannah, have to say about such frivolities as this bonnet? Did Eli similarly indulge his wife and other daughters who may have looked askance at Julia's extravagant purchase? Julia would be certain to rationalize its cost as the need to put one's best foot forward—be it a matter of compositions or clothes. Julia reveled in her summer bonnet. She tied the ribbons under her chin as she left the building and crossed the lawn to where Mary Plumer was waiting by the roadside.

1836 Julia A. Robbins.

1836		$ c
Jan 4	7 Sheets letter paper	06¼ / 12½
9	12 " letter "	04
"	1 " marble "	04
	Candy	03
12	1 Ounce French chalk	07½
18	Nuts, candy	07
	Mending Shoe	03
	1 yd ribbon	08
	Candy	25
	2 yds Cloth	22
	Bill at post office	20 / 2 00
	Lavender	
	Bonnet	
	Stage fare	
Mar 5	2½ yds Flannel	
"	Comb	
12	Letter Postage	
	For Mr Taylor	
21	11 yds Shirting a 18 cts	
"	1 Skein Sewing Silk	
"	Comb, needles, cotton	
29	Frida	
"	Belt	
"	4 yd Silk	
"	Perforated Cards	
May 9	Shoes	
	Tape	
	Soap	
	Belt	
	10½ yds Calico a 25	
	Sent to Hopkinton	
	Paid Miss Winship	
June 13	Shoes	

1836 Julia A. Robbins

		$ c
June	Swing	
	Bonnet	12¼
	Lining a bonnet, finding lining	7 50
	Cake	66
	3¼ yds Ribbon	06
	1 pr Stockings	62
	Paid for altering and lining a bonnet	58
Aug 15	Writing Book	6 2½
19	1 yd checked Muslin	10
	1 comb	69
	4½ yds Cam Trim 20	08
27	1½ yds Ribbon	90
Sep 13	Letter Postage	19
	1 pr Gloves	
	1¼ yds Ribbon	15
Oct 22	3½ yd Cam Muslin	38
	6 yds Alipine a 1.42	8 52
	Belt	50
27	1 pr V L Shoes	10
28	7/8 Bro Linen	1 50
29	2 Sk Silk	80
Nov 9	5½ yds Merino a 1.12	6 18
	7/8 Bro Linen	
22	2 Skeins Silk	90
	1 pr Hose	10
	2 yd S Jean a 56	70
	House keeping	1 12½
Dec	Sundries	25
	Hose	10
	Muslin	87

Julia kept this record of her expenses as a student at Adams Female Academy.

CHAPTER 2

FEBRUARY 1839: Financial ruin for the family and a new interest for Julia

MARCH 25, 1844: Local happenings fail to satisfy Julia's restless spirit

MAY 11, 1845: Julia takes a serious look at a utopian community

OCTOBER 12, 1847: Loss, legal matters, and—perhaps—love

SEPTEMBER 10, 1849: A cause and a petition keep Julia occupied

Financial ruin for the family and a new interest for Julia
FEBRUARY 1839

Julia had returned from Adams Academy a young woman bursting with energy and idealism. She whirled through her chores, hurried to social gatherings and lectures, and engaged in a myriad of activities. Foreshadowings of a financial downturn appeared across the nation, but Julia was occupied with thoughts of friends with whom she maintained a lively correspondence. It seemed every post either took a letter from Julia or had one for her; letters that carried the news of marriages, children, and, in a few cases, early death. What was Julia writing to her friends? Who was mentioned in her letters? Whom would she marry? The men in her life included her cousin and best friend, George Simonds, who had lived with the Robbins family for years. There were the young men like Quincy Dow whom she met when she visited her friend Mary in Epping, New Hampshire; friends of Mary's brother William; and neighbors of the Plumers. Of course, there were the local lads as well. Of these, only Theodore Parker, nine years her senior, whose later preaching she would follow with enthusiasm, seemed to be worth her mentioning in her diary and letters.

Then it struck—the Panic of 1837—and life at the Robbins was forever changed. Eli, whose splendid hall was now a reality, had fallen from the ranks of entrepreneur to debtor. To Julia, this was incomprehensible, as she had grown up with the boom that began in 1825 with the opening of the Erie Canal; she knew of the waterway from Aunt Caira's tales. A high tariff policy fueled the nation's prosperity as the supply of paper money tripled between 1830 and 1837. However, when President Andrew Jackson ordered all obligations to the federal government to be paid in hard coin, or "specie" as it was called, overseas creditors made the same demands. The simultaneous failure of the nation's wheat crop, coupled with falling cotton prices and declining foreign investment, led to rising unemployment. This, in turn, resulted in an increasing number of bank and business failures. The downward economic spiral accelerated. By May of 1837 all Boston banks had suspended payments. The final tally for broken and depreciated banks in Boston alone was twenty-three broken and seven depreciated.

Eli Robbins' businesses were among those that failed. Unable to collect the money owed him, Eli could not meet his financial obligations. Hence, the Robbins' homestead with its approximately twenty-five acres of land fell into the hands of one James Russell with the mortgage held by Mr. C. Cutler. Russell conveyed his ownership to Eli's daughters Ellen and Abigail, skipping over eldest daughter Hannah who was deaf. With Abigail's wedding to Reverend Stillman Lothrop likely to occur before the year's end, Julia's name would soon join Ellen's on the property papers. Julia and Ellen, who had already witnessed their father's deeding some of his remaining land to Grandfather Robbins, now bore full responsibility for meeting all of the terms of the mortgage.

There seemed no end to the difficulties resulting from the complexities of legal and financial matters. With her twentieth birthday only months away, Julia entered the labyrinth of property and bankruptcy law. Over the next two decades an increasingly wearied Julia would be forced to deal with lawyers, loans, and leases due to the complexities of her father's contracts and the resulting indebtedness. No longer were Julia and Ellen such eligible daughters of a local businessman; their prospects declined with their family's economic standing. The only bright spot Julia noted that spring was her marvelous bonnet from Derry; it would encore very nicely this year.

Just as Julia needed a diversion, a visiting preacher captured her attention. Ralph Waldo Emerson seemed to speak to Julia directly, addressing her sense of self with his demand "that we act according to how the moral law of our being directs us." Julia felt that Emerson understood her as he emphasized that one's thoughts and actions must be in accord with one's

Ralph Waldo Emerson (1803–1882) visited
East Lexington as a minister to the East Village
congregation from 1835 to 1838 and later as
a lecturer in Eli Robbins' hall.

beliefs. On one February afternoon in 1839, Julia perched on the broad
sill of the front window in the lecture hall as the thirty-six-year-old
speaker gave another of his lectures on human life.

Julia's mind spun as it always did when she heard Ralph Waldo Emerson speak. She occasionally had heard him preach when she was home
from Adams Academy as he was the minister to the East Village congregation from May 1835 until last year. When Emerson resigned that post
for the lecture circuit, Eli scheduled him to appear at his hall. Eli, who
shared Emerson's views on the necessity for men to speak freely, welcomed
lyceum speakers, individuals who were part of a loosely-organized educational movement that both informed and entertained townspeople and
city dwellers from the Atlantic Ocean to the Mississippi River.

Julia attended every Emerson lecture that she could. She had not
missed a single one in his "Human Life" series this winter. Some folks
who attended said Emerson looked like a "perpendicular coffin," standing six feet tall and weighing only 130 pounds. When speaking, Emerson gestured with one hand; to emphasize a point he would stand on his
toes. It was not only the ideas he presented that created a near-hypnotic
effect on his audience but also the manner of presentation with splendid
diction and pauses between passages in his manuscript, some pages of
which occasionally fluttered onto the first row.

Julia had read Emerson's book *Nature,* which validated to her aspects of her own behavior such as her walks on the mountain and in the meadow. As Emerson had predicted for the tradesman and the attorney, Julia was restored by "the sky and the woods." Delighting in "the charm . . . of a January sunset" as did Emerson, she agreed when Emerson observed "the graces of the winter scenery and believe[d] that we are as much touched by it as by the general influences of summer." Those city dwellers who believed that the country was pleasant only half the year were wrong, Julia concurred. This was her world—all twelve months of it—and she intended to follow Emerson's energizing advice: "Build, therefore, your own world." Emerson preached what Julia wanted to hear—that one must rely on oneself, that the most important religious experience was one's "inner spiritual experience." Emerson gave Julia permission to be herself.

In a letter to her friend Mary Plumer, Julia wrote:

I have been attending a course of lectures on 'human life' by R. W. Emerson with which I have been very much interested. His first lecture was upon home, the next upon school, love, genius, & soon taking up the different periods of man's life at each successive lecture. He is indeed a great scholar and a very original character writer. I believe you heard him deliver a lecture in Cambridge last summer. Did you not like him? He has published a book called Nature. *Have you ever read it?*

Now, as she unconsciously shifted her position on the window sill, today's lecture reminded Julia exactly why she so admired Emerson. As she wondered how to best navigate her daily life, a life increasingly constricted by her father's business failures, Emerson provided a guide. She must be herself, trust herself; she must draw on her inner resources to achieve right conduct. Unlike some adults who use the expectations of others to guide their thoughts and actions, Julia followed Emerson's advice to select a course of action according to her own deepest beliefs.

When the lecture concluded, slowly Julia slid forward on the window seat and stood, turning to look out the window that framed her house in the winter landscape. It pleased her to see the lengthening day. The full moon at month's end would add more light to the scene. Julia turned her focus back to her surroundings in the upstairs room of her father's hall; the fireplaces, on the east and the west side of the room, held only embers.

She crossed the room and descended the staircase, pausing on the landing to look for Aunt Caira. Seeing her aunt in the doorway, Julia moved quickly to take her arm. Julia loved to listen to Aunt Caira's pithy comments after a lecture. What would she have to say about today's lecture from Emerson? Caira's view of a sermon on "Giving thanks for all things unto God" by the town's John Fessenden was family legend: "He spoke better than I apprehended."

Together Julia and her aunt left the multi-columned building and headed east toward Grandfather's house and Caira's collection of books. Julia wasn't sure what she would choose to read. From among the hundreds of volumes that Caira owned, titles ranged from *Captain Cook's Three Voyages to the Pacific Ocean* to Goldsmith's *The Vicar of Wakefield*. Julia looked forward to making her selection. Such a private library was unusual given the time and the town, but Julia gave it no thought. Aunt Caira, well-educated and well-traveled, still single at forty-five, was an unusual woman. Julia, a young woman as interested in Emerson's lectures as in fashion and social events, might also be considered unusual by some of the townspeople.

Local happenings fail to satisfy Julia's restless spirit
March 25, 1844

The nation slowly recovered from the Panic of 1837 and a new decade—the 1840s—began. The times and the young woman were well suited to one another. Both were caught up in excitement and invention, energy and exuberance, causes and fads. A spirit, fueled by the adventurous, swept the county; cautious souls found themselves caught in its wake. The Lyceum Movement gained momentum; speakers and writers like Emerson and Tocqueville redefined what it meant to be an American. It was high tide for the Utopian communities in Massachusetts at Brook Farm, in New York at Oneida, and in Indiana at New Harmony, capturing the feeling of unlimited possibilities. Temperance and abolition movements gained ground as young women like Julia attended meetings, circulated petitions, and advocated for a cause. In the 1840s, both the young woman and the young country came of age.

By 1844, Julia had been home in East Lexington for seven years. When she had first returned from Adams Female Academy, she had been part of a large group of young women in the town; gatherings, parties, and town events filled the time left after household duties and the lectures she considered captivating. Even as this group saw its numbers diminish with marriages and moves to others parts of New England and the country, Julia's social circle expanded to include members of the Harvard Class of 1845, specifically William Plumer and his friends. William was the carefree younger brother of Julia's school friend Mary Plumer. Despite his history of trouble-making—he had been expelled from Phillips Exeter Academy—Julia's mother doted on the young man and hoped for a marriage with her fourth, and entirely too independent-minded daughter.

As the seasons slipped away, Julia became increasingly restive. The young Harvard students of her acquaintance had so many opportunities to study, to travel, to express their opinions. As intelligent and capable as these young men were, Julia, more interested in learning than some of them, knew that as a woman her role in society was restricted. She also knew that she had no wish to live her life under such constraints. How delighted she would be when the railroad finally came to Lexington. No longer would she be dependent on Grandfather's good will and the loan of his horse to escape from town. There would be a way—besides walking— to get to Charlestown and Boston for visiting, shopping, and lectures.

This afternoon, March 25, Julia was visiting across the street at Grandmother's. Aunt Caira cleared away the tea cups before bringing out the most recent letter from her niece and namesake, Caira Langdon. Julia suppressed a spurt of jealousy toward her Vermont cousin. Why did Caira have all the opportunities to travel while Julia was stuck at home? It wasn't fair; it was Caira who had been invited to travel to England for an abolition convention and Caira who now wrote from Washington, D.C. Julia tried to dismiss her feelings, excusing them with her weariness. Today was Monday—another laundry day—an event always accompanied by commotion in the household. Just stringing the clothesline had seemed a chore this morning. The line had to be re-hung each laundry day, otherwise it would get dusty and moldy, staining the clothes. The stirring of the clothes in the wooden tub, the rubbing of soiled ones on the washboard, the hanging of heavy garments to dry had sapped Julia's

Caira Robbins (1794–1881), the sister of Eli Robbins and the beloved aunt of two generations of Robbins and Stone families, also had her portrait done in watercolor by Rufus Porter.

energy. The hired girl could never be depended on to be careful with Julia's dresses. And all good housewives knew to take in the clothes as soon as they were dry so the brisk March winds wouldn't wear them out; an hour's whipping by the wind took the same toll as a month's wearing.

Julia turned her attention to her aunt who began to read from Caira's letter:

> *Since I last wrote you at Mobile I have been at New Orleans, and from there cross all the Gulf of Mexico in the Steam ship* Alabama *to Havana, Cuba, where we spent a delightful month. . . . arrived in this place on Tuesday last and have filled up our time in visiting the Capitol, and paying our respects to the President Tyler, who by the way is very agreeable and social in private conversation, but not very decided. He seems very much depressed since the accident on the* Princeton *and well he might for I am told that Mr. Upshur was his particular friend. And Mr. Gardner was father to the Miss Gardner whom report says the President is to be married. Although she is almost as young as his youngest daughter. The White House is still hung with crape and looks like some deserted castle. . . .*

Meeting a president was not unusual for the Robbins; Eli and Hannah had met Andrew Jackson when he stopped in Lexington on his northern tour in 1833. But Julia was dumbfounded—a visit to the White House! How did Caira manage to live this charmed life? The papers had been filled with the news of the explosion on the warship *Princeton*; the most notable victim was the Secretary of State, Abel P. Upshur. Mr. Gardner's passing, also a result of the explosion, was duly reported with some interest by the press as his daughter was to marry the widowed president. Tongues had wagged over the difference in their ages.

Julia was stuck in Lexington. By her own admission, it was now *"a barren place indeed"* devoid of any parties. Even the temperance meetings Julia attended, held in private homes with a list of the attending women like a roster of local worthies with the names of Munroe, Wellington, Sanderson, Smith, Tuttle, Harrington, Milliken, and Locke among them, couldn't match her cousin's travel. Julia's name was also on the list of those active in this reform. Here is how she reported on one such gathering:

> *We had a temperance lecture last week and there now seems to be a prospect of doing something for the cause in L. You know it has hitherto been very backward. We are in hopes to have one if not two Temperance Hotels in the East Village. Are you not surprised! We also know there is need enough of it.*

Participating in temperance activities was a safe and timely outlet for the energies of active young women. How could anyone protest their involvement in a cause that defended home and hearth? At this time, a married woman's property was held in her husband's name, subject to his actions, according to his virtues—or his vices. But Julia's activities and interest did not end there. More daring than most of her gender, Julia also dabbled in the fads of the era. She attended lectures on mesmerism, *"a truly mysterious subject,"* which was equated with hypnotism; one speaker compared it to electricity. Phrenology, the study of the size and shape of one's head to determine an individual's characteristics, also caught her attention. Despite Julia's vehement protest, some New Englanders would also relegate Emerson's philosophy and Parker's theology to this category of passing attractions.

Julia considered her recent busyness. While Caira was visiting Havana and New Orleans, Julia was visiting her neighbors, the Phinneys, who lived on the southern edge of town. She tried to console the recently widowed Charlotte Phinney Swett, left with an infant daughter. Charlotte, herself ill at the time of her husband's death, *"did not even know of his danger until afterwards."* Eli would sometimes join Julia on these visits so he could confer with the prominent Elias Phinney, father to Charlotte and her nine siblings. Phinney was the Middlesex County Clerk of the Courts as well as a trustee of the State Agricultural Society. It was his knowledge of cultivation and application of scientific principles to animal breeding that drew Eli to visit his farm, fruit trees, and livestock. Julia considered that even visits to the Alcotts in Concord or to the Plumers in Epping could not hold a candle to a month's stay in Havana. Aunt Caira, who herself loved to travel and had reveled in a visit to New York City, sensed Julia's dismay; Caira Robbins loved all her nieces but had a special interest in Julia and Ellen whom she saw so frequently, with whom she discussed books they had shared and lectures they had attended. Caira folded the letter from her namesake niece and slipped it into her pocket, out of sight. Then she addressed Julia directly, reminding her that even though she might feel stuck in East Lexington that she was making her presence known, not only in temperance matters, but in church affairs.

The church was a major force in the life of East Lexington. For years, the people here wanted their own church; traveling the two miles to the center of town was difficult in heavy winter snows and in spring mud. The congregation of the existing church in Lexington opposed a new church in the village as funds from the town's ministerial lands would then have to be shared. In 1833, as one-quarter of the town taxes were from East Village with its 300 inhabitants and fifty-three dwellings, the East Villagers were convinced of the rectitude of their request. When subsequent town meetings vetoed any distribution of money from the Ministerial Fund to residents at the eastern end of town, the issue reached a standstill. Then Charles Follen, a former German professor at Harvard College, arrived in town.

Julia was fascinated by the thirty-seven-year-old newcomer—minister, scholar, teacher, German immigrant—who was not afraid to speak his mind. Because he had expressed views favoring the abolition of slavery, Follen's contract with Harvard had not been renewed. As her father subscribed to the *Liberator*, the anti-slavery newspaper, Julia was well versed in the opening salvos of the anti-slavery debate in Boston. The paper's editor, William Lloyd Garrison, was someone she admired; she saw the validity of Garrison's and Follen's position. In East Lexington, the villagers approved of Follen's views of free speech, even if all did not yet agree with his stand against slavery. Noting their failure to gain funds for a separate church from the town, Follen urged that funds be raised through subscription, an idea seized upon by East Villagers. On April 5, 1835, Reverend Follen preached the first sermon to the new religious society, which met in Eli Robbins' hall. That fall, at the Lexington town meeting, approval was granted for the Ministerial Funds to be shared with the new congregation, which had called Charles Follen to be its minister.

As much as Julia admired Charles Follen, she saved her highest regard for his wife, Eliza Lee Cabot Follen, of the illustrious Cabot family of Newton. The arrival of Charles Follen and his *"beautiful wife"* had made an indelible impression on the Robbins sisters. The Follen marriage seemed different from those Julia had observed. A friend of Julia and her sister Ellen, herself the mother of a large family, had warned against marriage as a *"state of slavery."* Julia saw none of that in the marriage of Charles to Eliza, seven years her husband's senior. A published author prior to her marriage, Eliza continued writing for adults and children. Here was an alternative model for marriage, with intellectual activity given its rightful place.

To Julia's dismay, the Follens stayed only six months in Lexington; Charles Follen had been recruited to parent and teach three boys whose father was recently deceased. The East Lexington congregation, however, found a replacement—Ralph Waldo Emerson. So Julia had known him as a minister before she delighted in his lectures. When Emerson left the active ministry in 1838, another Harvard Divinity School graduate, John Sullivan Dwight, took his place. Follen reappeared when he was once again relieved of a position for speaking out against slavery, this time at a pastorate in New York. He now assisted the East Lexington villagers to realize their goal of a Christian Association. Chosen as pastor, Follen designed a distinctive octagonal meetinghouse to be erected on the Robbins' land to the west of Eli's hall.

The dedication of the new meetinghouse was set for Wednesday, January 15, 1840. Follen, who had been lecturing in New York, boarded the steamboat *Lexington* on Monday, January 13, planning to arrive in plenty of time for this momentous event. On Monday evening, the *Lexington*, with its seventy-six passengers, crew of thirty-five, and a large cargo of cotton was in Long Island Sound when a fire broke out aboard the ship. Attempts to use the lifeboats were futile; "one [lifeboat] was lost over-

Doctor Charles Follen (1796–1840) and his wife Eliza Lee Cabot Follen (1787–1860) were active in East Lexington church and community activities.

board, and the other three were swamped by the waves as soon as they were released." Follen was lost at sea. His congregation, as yet unaware of Follen's fate, proceeded as planned with the dedication of the meeting house for the Christian Association.

The town learned the news of Follen's death the morning after the disaster; the parishioners were devastated. The only good news was Mrs. Follen's survival as she was ill and unable to accompany her husband on the return journey.

Without their beloved pastor, the question arose if the church should be a Free Christian church or a Unitarian church. Julia, along with most of the women, favored a Free Christian church, which would invite to the pulpit speakers favoring reforms, especially abolition and temperance. By church policy, the women, despite their fund-raising teas and a fair on Mt. Independence, were denied a vote in this matter. Julia was furious.

In righteous indignation over the quarrel between the Free Christian and the Unitarian camps, Julia penned a manifesto that read in part:

Two women established a Sabbath school—the first permanent effort made for religious instruction in East Lexington. It was the women. When a sufficient interest was produced . . . for preaching and Unitarians of Cambridge refused to come to them, who placed their position before Dr. Follen and

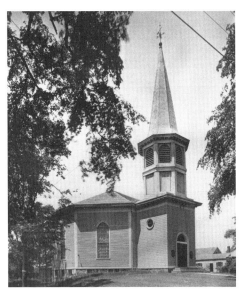

Follen Church, an octagonal structure designed by its first minister, Charles Follen, was later named for him. It is still a place of worship.

induced him to come. It was a woman. When it became necessary to build a church, whose arguments brought Dr. Follen back after a short absence. It was woman's. Was it not a woman who solicited the largest donations from people of different faiths, as well a very many small, without which they could not have built their little church, setting aside 11 hundred dollars that was procured by tea parties and hard work at a fair . . . Finally, was it not a woman who consented to give up all party and sectarian ties to establish a truly free Christian church. It would seem so, for as soon as the Lords of East Lexington—priests of Unitarianism—step forward and take control . . . Anti-slavery and temperance are actually pushed out, not even a notice can be read. . . . an effort is made to purge the Library. It is a woman who comes forward to oppose it. . . . [The books were] selected by Dr. Follen, R. W. Emerson and other liberal minds.

The controversy ended with the Unitarians and the men prevailing. When pews became available for purchase, not only did Grandfather Robbins purchase one, but so did Julia with her sister Hannah Maria. Their pew was Number 35, purchased on the day of dedication, January 15. Where Julia and Hannah Maria found the considerable sum of $75—a pew cost the same as the chandelier—is a mystery as is Ellen's failure to join her unmarried sisters in this venture. Their mother Hannah was a church supporter, even loaning the family Bible for use at services.

As Julia continued her conversation with Aunt Caira, it is most likely that some of these salient points in the church's history were mentioned. Julia was exasperated at how the women had been treated. After all of their work, the women had no voice in the church's future. Aunt Caira considered Julia's experience with the church as Julia's first encounter—she was sure there would be others—with the controlling male society. Julia, liturgically voiceless, continued her rant. Even her position as a proprietor of a church pew did not gain her entry into church decision-making. Yet, at the utopian community in West Roxbury, Brook Farm, women had the right to vote on community matters!

Julia takes a serious look at a utopian community
May 11, 1845

By 1845 some of the optimism of the early years of the decade had faded—both for the country and for Julia. Federal troops were ordered to Texas to secure that recently annexed republic. Cries of manifest destiny—the obvious future of the United States to take over the entire continent—collided with fears that the Mexican War was a ruse to drag in another slave state. There were clashes as well in the Robbins household as Julia scrambled for her independence. It is not surprising that Brook Farm, a place where a woman's views were given credence, intrigued Julia as she pondered her future. In conversations with friends and family, particularly with her brother-in-law—Abby's husband—Reverend Stillman Lothrop, this cooperative utopian community located on 200 acres of land in West Roxbury was a frequent topic. It had been established four years earlier by a group called the Transcendentalists, reformers who extolled the spirit of the individual. Julia applauded the high thinking that had been such an important part of the early community. For a long time she had wondered about it, thought about it, asked about it. Her mentors Emerson and Parker spoke of it; some forward-thinking individuals were consumed with its ideals. Of importance to Julia was that women here had the same voting rights and property rights as did the men. Despite his role as spokesman for the Transcendentalists, Emerson had not joined.

Neither had Reverend Theodore Parker whose Spring Street Church was also in West Roxbury and whose congregation usually included associates from Brook Farm. Why was this, Julia wondered. Julia turned a critical eye to her surroundings on this day, her second visit to Brook Farm.

Besides being hot, Julia was annoyed at how the day was turning out. Along with some friends, she had left Lexington hear Reverend Theodore Parker preach at his Spring Street Church. After losing their way and riding endlessly, they arrived at Brook Farm in late afternoon.

Now, at half past five, while the others took tea at the former farmhouse rechristened the Hive, Julia set off on her own, not able to bear the thought of sitting indoors on a hard pine bench. She needed to put some time and space—be it brief—between herself and her traveling companions whose tempers also had frayed, what with the day's heat and missed roadways. With the world outside exploding in spring greens and clouds of blossoms, Julia had no wish to stay inside in a colorless world of white painted benches and long pine tables covered with white linen cloths. She didn't begrudge spending the cent, the customary offering for a cup of tea. With thousands of visitors a year, it was reasonable for this cash-strapped community, which practiced every frugality, to charge its visitors for meals, typically twenty-five cents for dinner and twelve cents for supper. Meals for visitors were very different from those consumed by the associates, as members of the Brook Farm community where known. Under a food "retrenchment" policy established the previous December, the associates had removed meat, tea, butter, and sugar from their diets, unless these foods were needed for health reasons. Julia thought a potato/turnip/squash pudding menu a dull choice for daily fare.

The overarching elm that would soon shade the Hive, the center of community activity, was just coming into leaf as Julia began her walk. Her first stop was at a square, gray-painted wooden building given the unlikely name of the Eyrie. An ornamented top cornice and low French windows were the only appealing features as she regarded the building with an eye schooled by her father's buildings in East Lexington. Its sturdy cellar, built on a ledge of local stone, gave no hint of the flimsy construction of the upper floors, so described by its occupants.

Here in their rooms on the second floor, Julia called on Mr. and Mrs. Ripley—George and Sophia—the community's founders. They remembered Julia from her visit nine days earlier when she had been accompanied by her brother-in-law, Stillman Lothrop. At that time the bespectacled Ripley had expounded on the history of the community with its balance of work—manual and intellectual. He had explained the ideas of the French utopian socialist Charles Fourier, ideas that were the basis for changing the Brook Farm Institute of Agriculture and Education to the Brook Farm Phalanx, newly incorporated by the Massachusetts legislature on the first day of this very month. Believing that a rearrangement of economic relationships would result in "perfect order," Ripley and the other associates set out to transform Brook Farm into a phalanstery, the name Fourier gave a planned community. It seemed to Julia that the community's financial and organizational problems were compounded by adapting Fourier's plan, which changed the focus from the individual to the group. With new principles, laws, and harmonies to consider, "Universal Unity" was the watch phrase among the people of the community. Three departments of labor were established—agriculture, domestic industry, and the mechanical arts. Julia much preferred the original plan—to put democratic ideals into social practice.

Even a casual visitor would realize that education was the community's most notable product: the Ripleys made this so, as they were both outstanding teachers. George Ripley had graduated first in the class of 1823 at Harvard before earning a degree from Harvard Divinity School. His private library was reputed to be the finest collection of foreign literature in the city of Boston. His wife, Sophia, whose grandfathers were respectively the president of Harvard College and the chief justice of the Commonwealth, had been privately tutored. Her assignment was to teach history and modern languages to the young male students, many sent by Harvard to prepare for entry to that institution. Julia glanced at Sophia Ripley's reddened and chapped hands, which rested against the folds of her checked domestic cotton dress. This tall and imposing—some said regal—woman also managed the Brook Farm laundry room. Here were washed all the clothes of everyone in the community, from the babies who spent many hours in the communal nursery to the young students who did a turn in the fields, to the associates themselves and even to the boarders at Brook Farm. Julia knew from her own Monday laundry days that the pounding, wringing, and hanging of the wet clothes tested one's physical endurance.

And Sophia, at age forty-two, with a minimal number of helpers, did it for the entire community! It didn't seem right to Julia that this educated woman spent hours ironing undergarments and nightcaps. Surely this wasn't the best use of her talents. If Sophia, a gifted teacher in the community was also in charge of the laundry, what did the other women do?

As Julia stood to take her leave, Reverend Ripley offered to send for his sister, Miss Marianne Ripley, Julia's guide on her previous visit. Julia, who declined his offer, felt that the formal and hardworking Miss Ripley, nicknamed "Her Perpendicular Majesty" by her primary school students, had shown her around Brook Farm on her earlier visit only in answer to a request, most likely from Reverend Ripley. Another associate, Mrs. Ryckman, had been delegated the task of dealing with women visitors. Julia, feeling as if she had received special treatment, wondered if she was being recruited to join the associates of Brook Farm.

Once again outdoors, Julia looked around for the other Marianne—the twenty-nine-year-old sister of John Dwight who had served as Emerson's replacement as minister to the small congregation in East Lexington. Miss Dwight had come to Brook Farm with her parents and siblings Fanny, who assisted at music lessons, and John. In their long conversation on Julia's previous visit, Julia had found her to be a kindred soul, a single woman three years older than herself and similarly interested in social reforms, women's rights, and abolition. Marianne had spoken with enthusiasm of walking the four miles to nearby Dedham or the eight miles to Boston for Anti-Slavery Society meetings. The two young women also shared a knowledge of and inclination for the French language.

As Julia looked about for Marianne Dwight, she remembered what had been explained to her. Brook Farm had a standard of 300 work days a year for everyone in the community, with an eight-hour day in winter and a ten-hour day in summer. When Julia had questioned Marianne about her work, Marianne had shut her eyes, recapturing the sight of her first assignment; nursery duty for four hours each morning. In a single fortnight the previous September, three babies were born into the Brook Farm family. Marianne had told Julia that she grew to enjoy this and later graduated to managing the school. Perhaps Julia would wish to teach? Julia had no interest in teaching, she assured Marianne. Several classmates at Adams had urged this course for her, but Julia turned them away. Even the enticement of a tuition-free Normal School in Lexington could not change her mind. To which group might the community assign her, Julia wondered. The mending group, perhaps? Even the long hours at a task at home suddenly seemed lighter as Julia thought of her continued choices that leavened the more odious tasks, of her ability to escape to the mountain behind her house when she felt the need for solitude, of her freedom to complete a task without someone constantly checking that the task was completed and recording the time spent in working.

Julia might choose to be in the "fancy group" as well, painting pictures, lampshades, and fans or making caps, capes, and collars. These items were sold locally at Mr. Houghton's shop or in the city at the Holmes and Hutchinson store.

On Julia's last visit, Marianne had told her that even serving as a nurse the previous spring when scarlet fever swept the community was acceptable to her for the good of the community. After being indoors for several weeks at the make-shift hospital, she had been rewarded with seeing the beauty of spring, especially the flowering columbine. It was not surprising that Marianne's flower paintings with botanically accurate renditions of leaf and stem, bud and blossom, line and color sold for fifty cents apiece. One group of sixty paintings earned an amazing thirty dollars for Brook Farm. Several young women passed Julia, but Marianne was not among them. Perhaps she was with John Orvis, whom she had described as her true friend. The rumor seemed true, that Brook Farm was a good destination for a single man looking for an intelligent woman not afraid of hard work. Julia considered the women's outfits, a sort of knickers under a short skirt of the same material, and conceded their practicality but she looked with reservation on the custom of young women letting their hair fall loose to their shoulders. Although her family might disagree, Julia felt she was a conventional young woman. Maybe she did have some unconventional ideas about women in society, but she was more than willing to follow the fashions of the times.

Marianne's descriptions of the reading groups, the tableaux vivants, and the picnics were charming, but Julia realized they were only a small part of life here. There were problems in plain sight. Some were man-made, such as the questionable construction; some were givens, like the paucity of fertile soil. The peas were up in the field and the potatoes had been planted, but the sandy soil would dampen expectations for any crop. The blueberry and raspberry bushes now in blossom would yield their fruit, but Julia knew the associates of Brook Farm would not be the ones to enjoy it. Sale of berries was too good a source of income to allow that!

Continuing her walk through the orchard and over the terraced embankments, Julia arrived at the so-called unitary building then under construction: the Phalanstery. This was a wooden structure an unbelievable 175 feet in length; Julia did the arithmetic and realized it was over three percent of the distance of a mile! All the public rooms for Brook Farm were to be on the first floor; seven private suites, each with a parlor and three bedrooms comprised the second floor, leaving the third floor for single rooms. She could never live in such a huge structure with so many people around her. Then she remembered what her friend Emerson had said when asked why he had decided not to join Brook Farm:

> Whilst I see that it may hold many inducements for others, it has little to offer me, which, with resolution, I cannot procure for myself.

Theodore Parker supported Brook Farm with his friendship but not his membership. Boston's most radical woman, Margaret Fuller, had said she had no wish to peel potatoes for the community. Julia agreed with their sentiments.

Realizing she had been gone about an hour, she regretted there was not enough time to see the greenhouse. She returned to the Hive and her waiting friends for the trip home to Lexington. For all the annoyances and the tensions in her family, it was home. Although, at times, her sister Hannah Maria may be cross and her mother demanding, they were kin. Julia's family understood the contradictions of her character; a social Julia who reveled in fashionable frocks and frolics and a serious Julia who alternately climbed Mt. Independence for solitude and attended crowded lecture halls to hear the latest ideas for bettering society. Who but family would allow her to be herself?

Loss, legal matters, and—perhaps—love
October 12, 1847

It had been two years since Julia had visited Brook Farm. In that time the United States had declared war on Mexico and trained its sights on California as further spoils of the war. Last month's news that the United States had captured Mexico City and that Marines now guarded the halls of Montezuma brought no joy to Julia. Like many of her Northern neighbors, she was troubled by the spread of slavery. But all of that dimmed with word that Grandfather had died.

Julia, as was her inclination, sought refuge outdoors—in the orchard, the meadow, or on the mountain behind her home. Twenty-first century residents call it a hill, but to Julia it was always a mountain and its size seemed to reflect her concerns over her grandfather's death. Grandfather's death was expected, but still she was taken aback by the news. Her footsteps crunched on the gravel walk between the stone walls in the spots where weeds had not sprung up. The long trellis for the Isabella grapevines, once a showpiece over 200 yards long, had fallen into disrepair, a few grapes still on the vine. Julia remembered when they were newly planted and the three-story observatory just built. That was when her father was a prosperous businessman and visitors drove here to admire the distant view of Boston Harbor. In the best of times, her father would take on the added responsibility of the demands of Grandfather's property, working through any mortgages and leases as his former business partner. Since Eli's financial ruin in the Panic of 1837, however, property registered in his name would be subject to seizure for unpaid debts. The property kept by the Robbins after the Panic was legally held by Julia and her sister Ellen, who were personally responsible for leases and loans; it is no wonder they were always in arrears.

Now Julia came here to find solace in her memories. The rest of the family was planning her grandfather's burial in the family cemetery with its low stonewalls just east of Grandfather's house on Main Street. It seemed to her and Ellen that *"Aunt Ca[ira] seems to want to have the whole ordering of everything."* Julia wanted to remember Grandfather so fiercely that she would never forget his kindness, as when he slipped her and cousin Caira a few coins when they were young; his joking and storytelling; his willingness to let her take his horse when she wanted or needed to go someplace. Now the man who was always ready to listen to her and laugh with her was gone; all she could do was remember. She smiled despite her sadness as she recalled how Grandfather was always one to think young. When a neighbor had the temerity to call him old, Stephen Robbins replied that he wouldn't be old until he was ninety. He won that one—dying young—at the age of eighty-nine years, eight months, and seven days.

Poor Grandmother! She had been married for sixty-eight years and had borne five sons and three daughters, but few of them seemed to have inherited their parents' propensity for longevity. Julia took a mental inventory: Uncle Stephen had died last year; Uncle Samuel was dying; Aunt Nabby, who had sheltered Julia when she heard the shattering news of Mary Lavinia's death, had died five years ago. Next in the birth order was her father Eli who was still alive, then Martin who had died young, as did an unnamed daughter. Uncle Lot, in his late fifties, was a life-long resident at McLean's Sanitarium in Charlestown. That left Aunt Caira, in her early fifties, to care for her mother, Abigail Winship Robbins.

Julia worried about her father and his shrinking world. Stephen and Eli had been more than father and son, they had been business partners and friends. It would be a difficult day when Grandfather's business properties were auctioned; her father couldn't afford a single one, not even the land Eli had deeded to Stephen in 1837, the year of the Panic. Eli's homestead and its acreage had fallen to James Russell with Cutler holding the mortgage. Russell, in turn, had conveyed it to Ellen and Julia who were listed in the Lexington tax records as the owners of:

> 1 dwelling house, valued at $1620
> another dwelling $450
> 1 barn $225
> 2 shops $655
> 2 store buildings $60
> 29 acres of till and meadow land $4350
> 93 acres of pasture $1040
> 38 unimproved acres $297.

With a real estate tax assessment of $58.94 and Eli's name nowhere on any deed or tax bill, it was Ellen's and Julia's responsibility to pay the taxes as well as to pay off the mortgage. These payments were made from rentals of both buildings and farm land. One can only wonder how Eli felt knowing that the responsibility for supporting himself, his wife, and Hannah Maria fell to two of his daughters. And what of Julia, whose excursions now included not only lectures and shopping but visits to lawyers and lenders to discuss the tangled property problems? The care of her mother and sister would be hers for life. Now twenty-eight, Julia was years past the age when most of the Robbinses had married; her grandparents Stephen and Abigail were nineteen and twenty respectively when they married. Both her parents, Eli and Hannah, were twenty-three. Julia's sister Abby, married at twenty-five, had two sons. Ellen, at thirty, was still single, and Hannah Maria, now thirty-five, would probably never be anyone's wife. Life continued with its routines and rituals, with death a frequent caller for the Robbins family.

Julia's marriage prospects, or as she referred to them in correspondence with Cousin Caira, her *"particular attractions,"* included Henry Goodrich, from William Plumer's circle of friends, who had written her from Columbus, South Carolina:

> *May morn '45*
> *Oh! Thou adorable ever beautiful one—May kind angels Watch and guard over you through all trials. Thou knowest that I consider you one of the beautiful of the earth. Wilt thou accept my proffered Love. Tis all I have to give. But thou shalt have it from as true a heart as ever beat. If you will only accept [it] my future life shall be devoted to your service. Please address a line to No 6 Cedar St. and you will please one whose whole life will be to serve you.*
>
> *Write immediately if you would not agonize one who truly loves.*
> *—Henry*

Henry had then moved to Belfast, Maine, where he had *"taken a contract of a lumber speculative,"* trying to deal in timber in a declining market. Knowing Julia's interest in Emerson's poetry, he proudly claimed that Mr. Young, a fellow boarder and ministry student, *"has learned from me to like many of them [Emerson's poems]."* After writing of his wish to attend

Young's graduation *"next Divinity Class day"* with Julia come summer, Henry couldn't resist adding *"there are some very pretty girls here, but I remain unscathed as yet."* After asking that Julia remember him to his Lexington acquaintances, particularly Harriet Monroe and Elizabeth Whitcomb, he ended his letter:

> *Thanksgiving is here of little moment, they let it pass like any other day; I would give V dollars to be with you, on that day, but it's no use.*

Even though he had taken Julia on an excursion to nearby Lincoln before he left for Maine, Henry corresponded with two Robbins sisters, Julia and Ellen. Sisterly camaraderie was replaced with tension; Ellen noted in her diary:

> *A letter from Goodrich and Billet Doux from him to me. Julia read it before I did. Not right but mean. [She] claimed the right. [She had] sent one.*

Which sister was he really courting? Ellen seemed to think she had won, noting with glee that this suitor had written her father, although the contents of this letter were unknown, even to Ellen.

Another part of Julia's landscape was her friend Davison with all the complications that he brought. Across the years, he remains an enigma. Julia referred to him in her diary and letters only as Davison. He had often spoken to Julia of wanting to use his birth name, William Henry Davison. However, less than two months after his birth on October 24, 1824, his brother, Benjamin Rice Davison, died at age two, and William was hence called by his deceased sibling's name, not an uncommon practice in those days. Even the Order of Exercises of Commencement Day at Harvard College, held August 27, 1845, listed the sixteenth of the thirty-three speakers as B. R. Davison. Julia wondered countless times about the real Davison. Davison had links to the Plumer as well as to the Robbins family. His roommate at Harvard College was William Plumer, Mary's brother, while his blind, widowed father found shelter with the Robbins. Ever since Davison had told Julia of losing his mother when he was six, he had Julia's sympathy. Davison wrote to Julia:

> *From my sixth year to about my tenth I was tossed about the world by fortune, now here, now there, learning nothing except what would have been better unlearned.*

Encouraged by a teacher, Davison won admission to Phillips Exeter Academy in New Hampshire and then a place in the class of 1845 at Harvard. Plagued with health problems including an eye affliction, Davison was the first to admit that health was more important than honors to him, conscious of the talk that he could have been a better scholar.

On many long evenings, enlivened only by conversation, some reading material, and perhaps a card game, Davison's intelligence and wit added a sparkle to the Robbins' gatherings. His poem about one of the Robbins' goldfish, written when Ellen and Julia were at a temperance lecture, delighted the entire household.

Epitaph on a Goldfish
Here lies poor Goldey [sic] in his earthly bed.
(A modest fish)
Having no airs, while but on air he fed,
Leaving no heirs, begrudging ere he sped,
His room is the dish.
He had no wish
(A pious fish)
To longer live, for he never thought to die.
He was a traveler bold, his joy to ply
Around the Globe continually.
A temperance move.
Although over
Fond of lipping his glass in sport or
Spite he'd pledge to drink cold water—
Yet while his virtues slusing
No fault enumerating
His crime must bear relating.
He was a miser ever prone to plod
Over his riches, and if not caprice
Filled his cold heart, he'd surely been an odd
Fish for some time told.
His crowning guilt, was an enormous vice
O horrid and unheard of avarice!
Lost soul alack!

He crossed the piscatory Lethe, with his gold
All on his back.

But there was a darker side to Davison, a deficit in awareness of other's feelings. As he wrote to the 1845 Harvard Class secretary,

I have not been very communicative and am not naturally disposed to search for though I can grasp the hand, which is extended to me, with warm affection, and show a heart, which will love its object of attachment in every condition, through all times.

Julia remembered how hurt she had been when Davison had escorted her to a lecture by the abolitionist Parker Pillsbury in West Cambridge but walked home with another young woman. But Julia's hurt feelings over Davison's behavior never lingered, whether he ignored her and read all afternoon, or, as Mary Plumer referenced in a letter to Julia, did something that warranted Mary's thoughts that *"he ought to be talked to."* Julia always excused Davison's behavior—he suffered poor health, he had the burdensome worry of his father, he was unhappy with his first position as superintendent of a school in Watertown, he was frustrated directing recalcitrant farm boys while nursing the ambition of returning to Harvard for an engineering degree. Like Julia's friend Quincy Dow, Davison had a desire to leave his mark on the growing country with a railroad, a bridge, or a tunnel. Julia certainly understood his wish for action and need to move about the world.

Then Davison received a letter from his sister Nancy, who was married and living in Illinois. In this letter, which he shared with Julia, Nancy wrote that their brother Andrew, four years his senior

. . . expects to leave for the East the first of September. . . . Our beloved brother is but poorly calculated to grapple with the cold, unfeeling world: he, of all others most needs kindness & sympathy. . . . Our dear brother has a good heart, is kind and affectionate, and generous to a fault . . .On you, now my dear brother, devolve in a measure, the business of making Andrew happy & useful; think not you are to have a burden, it must be a pleasure. . . . You are younger than he . . . you have many advantages over your brother . . . make him feel at home among your friends . . . Never if you can avoid it tell him he looks or appears like his father; for the reason that

he has been told that he looks and acts like him, and that he will one day be crazy like him.

Was history repeating itself? In 1834 their father, also named Andrew, had been committed without a hearing to the State Lunatic Hospital at Worcester and from hence "clandestinely conveyed to the McLean Asylum in Charlestown" before being transferred to Boston's Leverett Street Jail and then back to Worcester. His petition to the General Court in an attempt to regain his property was discharged, leaving Andrew C. Davison without recourse, dependent on the Robbins for a home. Nowhere in the Robbins-Stone Papers is there a clue as to how the Robbins knew the senior Davison and why they opened their home to him.

Even without Davison's health and family issues, another concern nagged at Julia. Last summer Davison and Henry Goodrich—the same Henry who had written the "May morn" missive to Julia—walked from the Robbins homestead in East Lexington to the home of the Langdon cousins in Montpelier, Vermont. Recounting the adventures of the *"two pedestrians"* in great detail, Davison sent the letter not to Julia, but to Ellen. In that letter he also delighted in teasing *"Elin"* about her spelling, asking *"How long does it usually take you to learn how to spell names, one, two, or three years?"* making it clear that Ellen had corresponded with him. Did he take delight in hurting Julia? Were all of Julia's suitors to be shared with her sister?

A chill came over Julia. The sun was setting before five thirty now, earlier each day, a distinct difference each week. Noticing the settling dusk for the first time, Julia rose and slowly made her way back to Grandmother's. Neighbors would be calling, the same neighbors to whom Stephen Robbins always extended a helping hand would now come to honor his generous spirit. The congregation of the East Lexington church, built on land given by Grandfather, realized their debt to him. Julia slipped her hands through the slits in her skirt to the pockets on her petticoat as she made her way down the hill. Seeing the lights in what now would be known as Grandmother's house, although to her it would always be Grandfather's house, she half expected that Grandfather would be reading in his old memorandum book, rousing himself to stir the turf ashes for a good fire. With a pang, she realized all she had of Grandfather now were memories.

A cause and a petition keep Julia occupied

When Julia thought about life and her place in it, she recognized the contradictions she presented. Yes, she loved finery, but the reality of finances thwarted her wishes; she hoped for a serious suitor but delighted in her independence and ability to attend lectures; she chafed at the constraints of the Robbins household but had no means to reside elsewhere. Her lodestar was Emerson's advice to act according to one's conscience. Like Emerson, Julia had thoughts about slavery. Emerson had invited the most radical abolitionist of the Unitarian ministers, William Lloyd Garrison, to speak from his pulpit over two decades earlier. By the late 1840s, those who spoke out against slavery were considered to be more than trouble-making liberals, they were thought of as rabble-rousers intent on social upheaval. They were people like the radical abolitionist Parker Pillsbury, a hulk of a man in patched clothes who faced opposition both with his speech and his stature. Of all the reformers—women's rights advocates, temperance fighters, utopian socialists, education reformers, and abolitionists—the latter were considered the most dangerous to the existing order.

Julia, though constrained by her gender, could still make a difference. In complete agreement with her father's views on freedom of speech and the abolition of slavery, Julia was glad to act as his secretary, corresponding with speakers for his hall. Among these speakers was Samuel May, a Unitarian clergyman and abolitionist speaker who had been dubbed "the Lord's chore boy" by his brother-in-law Bronson Alcott. A note from May to Julia, dated only *"Sunday noon,"* postponed a meeting scheduled for that very evening, due to the weather and his health—*"I have taken some cold."*

Last spring one of the abolitionists, J. G. Dodge, commended Julia for subscribing to the principle of *"universal brotherhood & the equality of man"* and for her *"Anti-Slavery devotedness and zeal."* At least that is what she deciphered from his rapid writing, punctuated by dashes, to read. Careful to keep his correspondence to two pieces of paper, Dodge, on completing a page, would simply reverse it, continuing his message in the narrow spaces thus gained. At first his letters came to Miss Julia A. Robbins, care of Mr. Eli Robbins, but increasingly, they were addressed solely

Samuel May (1797–1871), the brother of
Mrs. Bronson Alcott, was tireless in his work
for the abolition of slavery.

to "Miss Julia A. Robbins." In correspondence with Dodge and others,
Julia arranged dates and times for speakers in East Lexington, events then
announced in Garrison's anti-slavery newspaper, the *Liberator*.

From her reading of the *Liberator*, Julia was conversant with names of
various individuals working for the cause of abolition. When Dodge
wrote to Julia asking her to bring some Lexington friends to an anti-slavery meeting in West Cambridge to hear Brown and the Crafts, she was
already familiar with these names and knew of their actions. William
"Box" Brown had acquired his nickname as he audaciously, with the help
of some friends, mailed himself north. Mrs. Ellen Craft was a former
favored house slave, who, with her husband William, had escaped from
slavery last year. Ellen, with her lighter skin, disguised herself as a spec-
tacled young man, bandaged sufficiently to disguise her hair and to pre-
clude any request for her to sign a hotel register. William, of darker hue,
served as the manservant on the trip north.

When Reverend Dodge asked for Julia's help in circulating petitions
to rescue Washington Goode, a black sailor convicted of murder, from
Boston's gallows, she was ready to act. From reading the article "Shall He
Be Hung" in the *Liberator*'s March 30, 1849 edition, Julia knew that
Washington Goode was a black sailor accused of murdering another black

seaman named Thomas Harding. The article noted that the verdict rested on circumstantial evidence of the most flimsy character. It was questionable whether Goode, who claimed to be innocent, was the murderer; he was supposedly identified at midnight on a dark and rainy night by persons on the other side of the street. Goode had been indicted by a grand jury for beating Harding on the head and stabbing him on the left side. Goode was living with a woman named Mary Ann Williams, with whom Harding had also lived, in a section of the city known as the Black Sea. Supposedly, Goode's jealousy was aroused when Harding, home from sea, gave presents to Williams. Dodge appealed to Julia and her family to exert themselves to prevent what he called a crime so infamous on the part of the state that it would be judicial murder.

Women in the previous decade, the 1830s, had circulated petitions as prayerful requests to Congress or the state legislature. At mid-decade, in 1836, the unlikely abolitionist Angelina Grimke, daughter of a Charleston slave-owner, had cited petitions as an especially suitable means of political expression for women in her pamphlet, *Appeal to the Christian Women of the Southern States.* That same year the Boston Female Anti-Slavery Society urged women to petition Congress for abolition of slavery in the nation's capital. This was countered by the growing number of women who considered petitioning to be an activity outside their proper sphere. Their refusal to sign petitions was influenced by the stance of some church associations that denounced public activity by females as irreligious. Petitioning had become "a political activity akin to advocating women's suffrage." At the end of the decade, in 1839, the Philadelphia Anti-Slavery Convention had identified petitions as the only recourse for women who could not vote or hold office, enact or enforce laws. When women stormed Congress with petitions, they were confronted with the gag rule that prohibited the printing, discussing, or even mentioning of the contents of anti-slavery petitions in the national legislature. The gag rule lasted until 1844.

Five years later, in 1849, Julia engaged in this radical activity and circulated petitions for the commutation of Goode's sentence. It did not make the work less difficult that most petitions were on local issues and submitted to local authorities. Julia was pitted against those who believed that justice had been well-served by the verdict condemning Goode to the gallows and those who believed that too many black men had been given clemency after committing crimes. Men as well as women circulated the Goode petitions; in neighboring Concord, Henry David Thoreau may have been the one who collected the 398 signatures in that town—119 men, 279 women—for the cause. All over the Commonwealth, a large number of citizens both male and female, 23,607 in all, signed petitions on Goode's behalf. It is unknown how many signatures Julia garnered at a time when it was not unusual for an abolitionist to place a brick in his tall hat before walking through the streets of Boston, the better to protect his head from the missiles hurled at him. There was no room in Julia's bonnet for a protecting brick. Although women were jeered at and subject to mob violence when they were part of an assembly, they were not individual targets. Julia looked like the respectable young woman that she was, of sturdy patriot lineage, dressed as fashionably as her purse permitted, most eager to circulate the Washington Goode petition.

Because of the petitions on Goode's behalf, the Executive Council reheard the case with Wendell Phillips, considered abolition's most effective spokesman, pleading for Goode. Reviewing the conditions of the dark and foggy night, Goode's poverty and ignorance, Harding's provocation, as well as wavering witnesses, Phillips concluded that both men were intoxicated. Further, Goode was a victim of society. Urging that Goode's punishment should be shared with those who had provided the poison, in this case, liquor, Phillips, in a single sentence, made temperance, as well as society's treatment of blacks, an issue. The result? The committee studying the case found no reason to commute the sentence. Goode was hanged.

Julia was dismayed by Goode's execution but undaunted. Of the twenty-three million people in the United States, over three million were slaves. That was reason enough to move her forward in her work. When Julia wasn't working for abolition in the public sphere she was prevailing upon her friends to support freedom for those enslaved. One such friend was Quincy Dow.

On this September day, Julia stood by the window in the front parlor looking at the men and the wagons in the crossroads and across to Aunt Caira's house, a letter in hand. The shortening days of September gave credence to what she knew but did not want to recognize—summer was over. Julia reread the letter from Quincy Dow, an engineer working in Portsmouth, New Hampshire.

> *I hope you will forgive me for not noticing in a suitable manner your many welcome mementos of happy days agone [sic]. My inattention is only seeming. I have many kind friends whom I am conscious of treating in the same ungenerous manner.*

After commenting on their missing the *"pleasure parties"* still held by their friends, the Plumers, in Epping, New Hampshire, Quincy again expressed his appreciation to Julia for *"Those addresses in the* Liberator *which are worth volumes of* Congressional Proceedings.*"* Julia frequently quoted from the *Liberator* in her letters and enclosed clippings in letters to friends, doing her part to spread abolitionist doctrine. She recognized Quincy's teasing when he wrote:

> *I want to see the operation of the "Peculiar Institution"—perhaps I shall become a convert to pro-slavery. I think not. I hope our newspaper correspondence may not be broken off. I will do better in the future.*

Then Quincy dropped his bombshell—he was moving to Florida, for work on the Pensacola Navy Yard dry dock. Florida! So far away, it had been a state for only four years. Quincy hadn't visited Lexington when he was just across the state line in New Hampshire or even when he was in and around Boston working on the Old Colony Railroad two summers ago. What chance would there be of her ever seeing him again? Yes, he wrote of staying in New Hampshire until summer, but in her experience, temporary work often merged into a condition of permanency. Clearly, Quincy was in love with his work, with the progress of the country. Was Julia in love with Quincy? She was surprised by the dismay she felt at his plans to leave New England. Had she, indeed, sent him the valentine he had teased her about? Was she realizing her love for Davison was not returned and had she placed some hopes on Quincy? Davison shadowed her friendship with Quincy. Even though the two men had never met, Julia solicited Quincy's advice for Davison who had left teaching to study engineering. Quincy generously replied that if Davison could not *"get a situation with as good a man"* as his boss, he would *"endeavor to assist him"* in finding employment at Portsmouth. Quincy had written Julia, *"Shall*

I hear from you often?" Yes, concluded Julia, their correspondence would continue if she had anything to say about it.

The distribution of clippings from the *Liberator* accomplished two purposes. Not only did it advance a cause close to Julia's heart, it also gave her an opportunity to write to young men, suitors perhaps, more frequently than convention warranted, or without waiting for a reply from a previous letter. Now she wondered if her letters would reach their destination. She had heard that Southern mobs had forcibly entered some post offices in that part of the country, bent on destroying antislavery literature. There was so much to be set to rights in this country!

Julia loved the sense of being in the center of things. Helping her father arrange speakers, corresponding with abolitionists, attending lectures—all these activities imparted a sense of belonging to something larger than herself. Thirty years old, single, particular about her appearance, and weighing only 108 pounds, Julia certainly didn't resemble anyone's idea of an abolitionist rabble rouser. In the sixteen years since her father had built his hall she had heard Emerson, Follen, Parker, Phillips, Pierpont, and Pillsbury. She had attended lectures in Boston, West Cambridge, and neighboring towns; she pored over the *Liberator* and any other newspaper that came her way. A century and a half after their work, it would be written of women petitioners like Julia that they shared a "new political consciousness of their responsibilities as female citizens of the American republic." Julia would have said they were just doing what needed to be done.

CHAPTER 3

AUTUMN 1850: Julia, alone amidst family, is disappointed with Davison

DECEMBER 30, 1850: Julia volunteers in the army of abolition

FEBRUARY 1851: Shirts, a toothache, and an uncertain future

DECEMBER 1851: Finally, Julia sets her own course

SEPTEMBER 5, 1852: Early days in Lowell

AUGUST 1854: Julia receives letters from a dangerous man

MARCH 17, 1855: Letters from a life-long friend and from a disconcerting cousin

JUNE 3, 1856: An attack on Senator Sumner shocks his supporters

APRIL 24, 1857: A loss in Lexington; letters and visitors to Lowell

MARCH 30, 1860: Julia feels alone against the world

Julia, alone amidst family, is disappointed with Davison
AUTUMN 1850

The sun shone as brilliantly as it had in the prior years, but the country's mood was darker. Massachusetts Senator Daniel Webster, in an attempt to save the Union itself, endorsed the Fugitive Slave Law under which runaway slaves were to be returned to their owners. As the country, already divided over the war with Mexico, slipped toward civil war, Julia pondered her fate. There were always things to do at home: varnish the furniture, whitewash closets, put up curtains, clean the chambers, wash the chandeliers, and shake the carpets, all in addition to the daily cooking, washing, and ironing—the list was endless. But, for Julia, more frequently there were days of *"sick headaches"* and days when nothing seemed to go right.

Some darkness had crept into Julia's world—shadows of doubt about Davison, somber thoughts about slavery, the overshadowing of plans by family demands. Julia's thoughts and her days were chronicled in her diary—a small book not much larger than a three by five index card—which was found among the letters, school books, and saved memorabilia of the daughters of Eli and Hannah Robbins. Covered in red leather and written in Julia's characteristic cramped handwriting, the diary provides a lens into how she spent her days, days filled more with endurance than

This is the first page of Julia's diary, a small red-covered book measuring 3⅜ by 5½ inches, which she kept from October 25, 1850 to November 21, 1851.

delight. Her sighs are audible as she considers that the past is often prologue. Were these days a template for the days stretching across the future years?

Julia had listened to Emerson's lectures as he cautioned lyceum audiences that relying on oneself and on one's convictions would result in a sense of loneliness and alienation. In the first entry for her diary, in October 1850, Julia wrote of being lonely.

*This day I will take for the **birthday** of a Journal. I find that I am quite forgetful of dates &c. &c. and, of course, regret that I had nothing to refer to, to refresh my memory. I intend it for no eye but my own & should be very sorry if it falls under the inspection of another. The last summer has been one continued scene of disappointment to me. I have spent a great part of it **entirely** alone, strange as it may seem when we have had so large a family. I hope the coming season will afford more pleasing remembrances. . . .*

Subsequent entries for the month were filled with news of William Plumer, the brother of her friend Mary. Having completed the course at the Law School at Cambridge, what is today Harvard Law School, William passed the bar in 1848. His current project was moving his law practice to Lexington. As William needed a place to stay prior to his October 2nd marriage to Miss Emily Lord, the Robbins had welcomed him as a boarder. When Charles Flagg, the census enumerator, tallied the Robbins' household on August 21, he listed the occupants as Eli, Hannah, Hannah M., Elen [*sic*] A., Julia A., George W. Simonds, Gentleman, William Plumer, Lawyer, and Thomas Burk, Labourer. All were Massachusetts born, except Plumer, of New Hampshire, and Burk, born in Ireland.

Now thirty-one years old, Julia had known William for almost half of her life. Julia's mother, Hannah, was very fond of William, cooking his favorite dinners even when she had a large household to tend to. Had Hannah's approval of this educated and politically-connected young man meant that Julia, so often at odds with her mother, would reject him? Hannah fretted that Julia had given her heart to William's friend, Davison, which did not please her. Would Julia's Davison turn out like his father and elder brother? Didn't that sort of peculiarity run in families? Hannah worried about her marriageable daughters; if Julia didn't marry William, who was there with a good name, family means, and excellent prospects for the future? Julia had gone to parties with William and corresponded with him, but seemed content to let the nineteen-year-old Miss Lord rule his affections. Hannah had determined that Julia was much more suitable to be William's wife, despite being four years his senior. Julia insisted that she and William were just friends.

With her love of color and flair for design, Julia was the logical choice to accompany William to select the wedding flowers on the day before his wedding. But when the wedding day arrived on Wednesday, October 2, Julia buried herself with property matters, not seeing the wedding couple until an evening reception at the Lords. Julia recorded her activities for that day in her diary:

> . . . *started with Father for Charlestown. Went to Cobb's office on business. Saw Dana, his partner. Some conversation. I consider him an impudent, impertinent, ungentlemanly person. Went back second time to see Cobb. I was over to Boston. Called to see Mary Marsh. Went over to Lothrops to spend night. Go to Levee at Mrs. Lords. Rather a pleasant time. Saw many of my old friends. The bride looked very handsome, William very dignified & Very cool. They appeared disappointed that I did not come earlier to the wedding. Apologies &c. Emily had many elegant presents.*

How could party-loving Julia miss this wedding? Was business in Charlestown too urgent to postpone or did Eli provide a convenient excuse for his daughter? Did Quincy Dow's role as best man make a difference to her? Julia felt alone in a swirl of festivities.

The following days seemed similarly unsettled. Julia's October did not provide the *"pleasing remembrances"* she desired when she began her diary. Family obligations and expectations constrained her actions and clouded her mood as the entry for Wednesday, October 23, indicates:

I made Grape Jelly. Varnished furniture. This day the great Convention in Worcester to discuss Woman's rights. Was greatly crossed not [to] be able to go. Had planned & looked forward all summer to this affect [sic]. But, as I said, this seems my lot the last few months. Mary Plumer seems to delay her visit.

The sense of gloom was palpable two days later when Julia noted in her diary:

. . . I am very low spirited and everything in [the] future looks & seems anything but agreeable. W. Plumer here to dine; settled with Mother for board. Received a letter from Davison, the first since he left. Quite a coincidence, I think. I wonder what gets my lost letters.

Even a letter from Davison did not cheer her. Julia began her reply with displeasure at the three month wait for his letter, three months that had been filled with disappointments, a missed convention in Worcester, and someone else's wedding plans.

I had given you up long before as at least a very negligent correspondent, if not three months is a long time. You speak as if you had written previously, if so I cannot imagine what has become of your communications. It certainly would have given me great pleasure to have heard from you before this late period. & think you must have known that I should have answered if you requested it. I am sorry that it has so happened and hope that we may not be subject to like accidents in the future.

Without reference to Davison's whereabouts, she expressed her continued concern for his health.

But [I] must own I feel a bit anxious for safety with regard to your health &c. I suppose in that region much exposure would be likely to give you a fever & ague that you might never recover from or perhaps not without shattering your constitution for life. I beg you will be very careful. I hope you have flannels & warm clothes to protect you from getting chilled & making yourself sick. Your stories about snakes . . . [are] alarming. I should be afraid that they would crawl into the . . . apartment & bite in the night.

Then Julia's practical side emerged.

> *A person ought to have pretty good pay for living in such a wilderness and subjecting themselves to so many deprivations. It must be hard work to scramble over such hills. . . . If you stay[,] your salary ought to be increased.*

After airing her concerns for the time lapse between letters, his health and his financial status, Julia proceeded with the news of William and Emily's marriage, which *"came off not withstanding your prophecy to the contrary."* William had gifted his bride with a gold watch; Julia had *"saved some of the cake to give you a taste when you get back."* Was a piece of the stale wedding cake Julia's magic potion to steer Davison's thoughts toward marriage? Julia hoped that news of Ellen's fortnight trip with Abner Stone to Montreal and Quebec or of the visit of Cousin Caira with her Greek husband, baby, and nurse to Lexington that past summer would make it clear to Davison that others were moving on with their lives.

Julia was as aware that time was passing as Davison seemed oblivious to all but his professional goals. She had her list of hints—William's wedding, Ellen's trip, Caira's husband and baby. Then Julia played her trump card, news that an eligible engineer, one of the Plumers' New Hampshire neighbors, would be visiting Lexington. This was the only recorded bright spot in a dreary existence, as she wrote to Davison:

> *Quincy Dow visited us this summer. He is really very interesting. . . . We danced & had a gay time. I enjoyed his visit very much. Wish you had been here. I want you to make his acquaintance. . . . He even mentioned trying to hunt you up if he went back through Cincinnati.*

Under the guise of neighborhood news, Julia informed Davison that a boarding school now occupied her father's hall, which Eli had sold a few years earlier. Optimistic plans were for a large establishment with additional buildings necessitating a sizeable staff. Then, linking her future with Davison's, Julia explained:

> *Each member pays two hundred dollars and shares in the profits of the institution. In case of extremity here will be a chance for you & I. It strikes me it will be right pleasant if they succeed.*

Surely, she had not forgotten how Davison disliked teaching school! Julia subtly reminded Davison that she knew him and his conservative views very well. Commenting on various conventions held in the area this autumn to consider important issues, Julia noted that there were some *"brilliant speeches"* but she decided not to write the details which *"may not be agreeable"* to him. To strike a lighter tone, Julia reported on Jenny Lind, the Swedish songstress who had *"bewitched"* Bostonians at her concerts. Ticket prices topped at $6.25 but Lind gave $6,000 to charity when she left the city. Julia slipped in that she was anticipating a visit from Mary Plumer; they would both consider how William and Emily *"appear in married life."*

Davison knew the Robbins homestead and environs very well from his many previous visits—some to see his father, for whom the Robbins provided a home, and some with other young people for social gatherings. He was acquainted with the arbor and the orchards, so it was not unusual that Julia would describe the harvest. There was an abundance of fruit this autumn, but a hundred or more bushels of the grapes did not ripen. Eli, ever ingenious, pressed them for vinegar while Julia *"made Jelly to my heart's content."* This section of her letter concludes with the request that if Davison finds anything he likes *"in the cooking line,"* he should *"write of the rule if you can get hold of it for me."* She would be happy to cook the dishes that pleased him.

Not until the last paragraph of her letter to Davison did Julia express her feelings outright. Even so, in her draft copy she has crossed out the line *"I shall most gladly do anything that I can to promote your happiness,"* instead leaving the following:

> *I want you [to] come home in the course of the winter. If you have a chance you must improve it. I should like to have your business in old New England but I suppose you know best what is most for your interest. It is not wise any way to give up health for money. If I can be of any service to you in any way, you have promised to inform me. I wish you to write me very soon & pray it may never be so long again that I do not hear from you. I suspect it has been quite a wonder among the good folks why you did not write me before. No questions asked however. I keep my own counsile [sic]. Please accept my best love.*
>
> *—Yours very affectionately J. A. R.*

Did Julia sense that Davison—who had moved so far geographically—was slipping away emotionally as well? It seemed that nothing was going right in her life. Even Mary Plumer's visit to Lexington at month's end seemed unsatisfactory. Perhaps this was partly due to the declared purpose of the visit: Mary and Julia were to help settle the newlyweds in their temporary quarters. On November 3, the day before Mary took her departure, Julia wrote in her diary:

> *Sunday Mary & I rode up in town to see Wm. Went over [to] his new house, walked around the ground. Spent an hour or so at their boarding place. Home to dinner. . . . Mary wrote letters first part [of the] eve. retired rather early. I wish I knew how Mary enjoyed the visit. I have been so unwell & she too, things seemed to go wrong. We had some private confabs in bed. No very particular developments. . . .*

For the remainder of the autumn, Julia busied herself with a blend of household and anti-slavery activities, some days, as on November 15, combining the two.

> *Started for Boston with apples. Left some in to Cambridge. Bought wagon bow. Called at Cobbs. Got stove in Boston, Calico dress &c. Went to Mrs. Yerringtons. They went with me to welcome George Thompson [a noted British abolitionist] in a disgraceful mob pushing and crowding. Cheers for Webster & such like. My first experience of the kind. Mrs. Y [and] I got out and walked home alone which I looked upon as quite a feat. . .*

Other days were spent quilting, preserving tomatoes, lining a bonnet, sewing a green petticoat, doctoring herself with rhubarb for a bad cough, or traveling to Charlestown to straighten out property matters. Cooking and other chores were omnipresent. Washing day, always hard work, had *"the usual preliminaries and commotion."*

A sense of lightheartedness had escaped from Julia's personality with family restrictions and responsibilities and with the passage of time. In parallel, her interest in ideas, awakened at Adams Female Academy and reinforced by Emerson and other speakers, developed to fill the void in her life. Julia concluded that the spiritual knockings, heard in the séances that once interested her *"seemed rather faddish business after all."* She devoted more attention to serious lectures. On Sunday, November 17, her *"first*

Sunday in B[oston] for many a day," she heard three lectures. In the morning Theodore Parker preached on "Our Ideal & Our Idol"; Fernald's afternoon topic was on divine and spiritual law, *"a regular argumentative affair, more so than I had anticipated"*; in the evening she heard Channing lecture on the divine and spiritual relations of woman. Some snippets of these lectures survive in her diary, such as Channing's view that

> *Woman [is] Superior to man naturally, but both [are] invited to make a perfect whole. [Woman has] intuitive perception, quick to see, man more deliberate, &c.*

In her diary Julia also captured the words of her long-time friend, Theodore Parker, preaching at the Meionaon, a large hall on Boston's Tremont Street. He reflected on the affections and the secondary role of the intellect, with woman being *"better adapted to affections"* than was man.

Increasingly, Julia commented on the anti-slavery cause, sometimes with a quotation from the anti-slavery newspaper, the *Liberator*, copied into her diary for safe-keeping. The resolution passed by the black community in reaction to the Fugitive Slave Law was one of these.

> *God willed us free; Man willed us Slaves. We will as God wills. God's will be done.*

In the waning days of autumn, with winter soon to settle in, Julia and Ellen discussed the Boston Anti-Slavery Fair, a leading event in the city. Yes, it would be long, exhausting, and controversial work, but Julia never shied away from that, especially for a cause dear to her heart. An added incentive to working at the bazaar was the invitation to stay with friends in the city for the duration of the event. After missing the Woman's Convention in Worcester in the fall, Julia felt she had earned this time away from home. She was determined to grasp this opportunity for some breathing space.

Julia volunteers in the army of abolition

DECEMBER 30, 1850

The Anti-Slavery Bazaar, held in Boston each December, was a momentous event for supporters of this cause. Beside serving as a fundraiser for the American Anti-Slavery Society, the annual bazaar, of which this was the seventeenth, was a highlight of Boston's social season. All three aspects of the American Anti-Slavery Society's work were important: support for the society's newspaper, the *National Anti-Slavery Standard*; printing and circulating tracts and documents on all aspects of slavery; and—her favorite—sustaining agents who preached truth to a guilty nation. Without these fairs and bazaars, the struggling and impoverished anti-slavery movement might well collapse. And, of course, they served to rally supporters and to raise new recruits to the cause. This year, Julia had been a dedicated volunteer for the duration of the fair, assisting in setting up the festivities as well as working at the glassware booth. Her two-week adventure had begun when she and Ellen helped decorate Faneuil Hall with spruce, running pine, rhododendron, and other evergreens as was the custom. Author and abolitionist Lydia Child had designed the gothic arches for the hall, which Julia described as *"beautifully trimmed."* After working on the hall the entire day Ellen and Julia parted company, with Ellen returning to Lexington while Julia remained in the city for the bazaar.

Together with a Mrs. Ober, Julia was assigned to the glassware table; the two women noted with satisfaction that the opening day crowds purchased a considerable amount of their wares. The glass was Bohemian Glass, carefully selected at Frankfort, Germany, by the Abolitionists' Committee in Europe and sent to Boston expressly for the bazaar. An article in the *Liberator* thanked Messrs. Ober, Smith, and Morey for a well-furnished table of glass and Britannia ware, making it clear that Mrs. Ober was the one in charge. With $110 from the glass table, the bazaar raised a total of $3400, a surprising thousand dollars more than anticipated.

Because Boston was split on the issue of slavery by the position taken by its former senator Daniel Webster, this year's bazaar was not expected to be as successful as previous bazaars. Webster's supporters boycotted the bazaar with their cries "The Union is in danger; the anti-slavery agitation must be stopped; we will not go to the Faneuil Hall Bazaar." Webster, once again serving as Secretary of State, this time for President Fillmore, had ignited the argument with his speech last March 7 on the floor of the U.S. Senate. There he had spoken "not as a Massachusetts man, nor as a Northern man, but as an American, and a member of the Senate of the United States" arguing "for the preservation of the Union."

Julia felt that Senator Webster *"lived in the past"* and that he was *"governed by commerce."* She was not surprised when Webster had aligned himself with the supporters of the Compromise of 1850, four separate pieces of legislation: California was to be admitted to the Union as a free state; states were to be created from the New Mexico and Utah territories and would be admitted as slave or free by the vote of the people there, a concept known as popular sovereignty; the slave trade would be abolished in the District of Columbia; and runaway slaves would be returned by mandate. This last provision inflamed public sentiment in Boston, long a center for abolitionist activity. It was in Boston, on January 1, 1831, that the abolition movement began with the initial issue of William Lloyd Garrison's newspaper, the *Liberator*. With support from men in all walks of life—including Eli Robbins—the *Liberator* had been expounding its doctrine for almost two decades. In 1843, the Massachusetts General Court, as the state legislature was called, passed the Personal Liberty Act, of which the abolitionists in the Commonwealth were especially proud. This law not only denied the use of state buildings as holding places for fugitives slaves, it also prohibited state officers from assisting in the capture of runaway slaves.

For his championing of the Compromise, Webster was condemned by the abolitionists. Orator Wendell Phillips "consigned his senator to the lowest circle of hell" and poet John Greenleaf Whittier, in his poem *Ichabod*, condemned Webster as one "who might have lighted up and led his age," but instead, one from whom "The soul has fled." Julia, well-versed in the arguments on each side, agreed with her hero, *"the divine Emerson,"* who won rave reviews for his condemnation of both slavery and Webster. Of the United States senator from Massachusetts, Emerson had written:

Why did all manly gifts in Webster fail?
He wrote on Nature's grandest brow, For Sale.

Once an admirer of Webster, as Julia had been, Emerson noted "The fame of Webster ends in this nasty law." Julia had committed some of Emerson's lines to memory as well as to her diary: *"The air is full of infamy. . . . The very sunlight seems different. . . . An immoral law is void in itself."*

By working at the bazaar, Julia was able to put her principles into practice. Well-schooled in abolitionist doctrine, not only was she an assiduous reader of her father's copies of the *Liberator*, but she frequented anti-slavery lectures. She had heard the British abolitionist George Thompson when he was welcomed to Boston, as well as Edward Everett and Wendell Phillips. Mrs. Alcott's brother, ardent abolitionist Samuel May, frequently spoke in Eli's hall and socialized with the family.

With a commitment to working at the bazaar, Julia cast her lot with a group of radical women who supported Garrison's stand for immediate and unconditional emancipation. One historian has noted that "Garrisonians championed women's rights, grew antagonistic to orthodox Christianity; and endorsed an anarchistic doctrine called *nonresistance*, which condemned all human government as resting immorally on force." Julia delighted in this dangerous company. In addition to following Garrison, Julia had another tie to these women. Many of the feminist-abolitionists, like Julia, not only listened with great interest to the sermons of Lexington-born Theodore Parker, but counted him as friend. Parker "exercised a strong personal influence" over many of these women as he "personified the religious beliefs of the group." Hadn't her much-admired neighbor Eliza Follen called abolition women's work?

Julia had a high regard for the woman who was the prime force behind the bazaar—tall, slender, blonde Maria Weston Chapman, Garrison's chief lieutenant in the war against slavery. The editor of *The Liberty Bell*, the prized anti-slavery annual, Chapman joined her sisters in organizing the Boston anti-slavery fairs. It had been Chapman who thirteen years earlier, in a dispute known as the Boston Controversy, denounced the clergy for hindering abolitionist efforts. At the time, the General Association of Massachusetts (Congregational) Churches issued a pastoral letter entitled "Appeal of Clerical Abolitionists on Anti-Slavery Measures." This letter was critical of women speaking in public and thus neglecting the duties of their traditional, "biblical" role. Closer to the truth was the fear that the women who were speaking up on issues of moral reform presented a threat to the clergy's leadership. According to Chapman and her sisters, there were two warring parties in the Boston Female Anti-Slavery Society: the "peelers" whose "layers of commitment" peeled off "just like an onion" and the "thorough going abolitionists" who remained loyal to Garrison's ideals. Julia was definitely not a "peeler."

In common with many of the feminist-abolitionists, Julia was a New Englander with a Puritan-Yankee heritage. Hadn't her maternal grandfather Joshua Simonds confronted the British on April 19, 1775? As did many of these women, Julia enjoyed a comfortable class position; even after the Panic of 1837, Eli Robbins was a force to be reckoned with in East Lexington affairs. Like many of the other fathers of female abolitionists, he was sympathetic to then-radical social reform; he had sent three of his daughters to a private academy. As did many of the feminist-abolitionists, Julia sought knowledge of herself and of the world, expressed eclectic religious beliefs, and exuded optimism and confidence. The bazaar allowed Julia the chance to support a cause about which she was passionate, expressing her view both as an abolitionist and as a woman.

One day while working at the fair, when heavy rains kept attendance low, Julia left the glassware display to walk around the hall, from table to table, noting items from distant places: Swiss wood carvings as well as hand-crafted articles from international friends. Boxes of goods to sell had come from Dublin, Leeds, and Paris. There were shawls from Glasgow, knitted and netted work from Perth and Edinburgh, embroidery from Cork, papier mache items from Manchester, and valuable autographs. Those of British novelist Sir Walter Scott sold for $5 each—a princely sum for such an item when coffee was 12 cents a pound and molasses 27 cents a gallon. The pupils from the Bristol Blind Asylum contributed both the necessary materials and the needed labor for baskets they sent, all of which sold at a good price. A quarrel in the anti-slavery ranks in Scotland yielded fewer Scottish goods, but the women of the New England countryside had answered pleas in the *Liberator* for stockings and mittens. Abolitionist friends in the rural areas beyond Boston sent provisions for the food table. Unsold items were never a problem, as they were sent to local anti-slavery fairs.

Going by the book table Julia unconsciously touched her copy of *The Liberty Bell* safe in her pocket, ready for her perusal in the quiet hours in the hall. All volunteers received a copy in its familiar 4¾ by 7-inch format with an engraving of the Philadelphia Liberty Bell on the cover. Forward-dated as was the custom, this was the 1851 edition, 304 pages in length. Included in its thirty-eight selections of poems, essays, and short stories were poems by James Russell Lowell, Ralph Waldo Emerson, and Theodore Parker. The latter wrote of Daniel Webster, "Stained and dishonored lies that ample brow. . . ." Abolitionist lawyer Wendell Phillips, who had defended Washington Goode, wrote in praise of Mrs. Eliza Garnaut, Matron of the Home for orphan and destitute children on Albany Street in the city, who recently died of cholera contracted from infants in her care. Reverend Samuel May had two entries: "The Root of Slavery," and "The Gospel of Freedom," while William Lloyd Garrison titled his essay, critical of Daniel Webster, "The Great Apostate." Harriet Martineau, commentator on American life, Maria Weston Chapman, *The Liberty Bell* editor now in Paris, and Caroline Healey Dall, a popular short story writer, were among those contributors who not only defended the abolitionists but explained the cruelty of slavery and romanticized the black man. A number of the bazaar's attendees purchased this year's edition of *The Liberty Bell*; some would put it on a shelf with treasured volumes from past years. For others, it would be the only piece of abolitionist literature they would ever own. Many of those who came to the bazaar would ignore the publication; for them this was a place to shop, not a place to collect ideas in support of a radical ideology.

Some Bostonians did their Christmas shopping here; December 24 was a good selling day as items advertised for taste, beauty, utility, variety, and value made excellent presents. The bazaar was quiet on Christmas Day. On Friday, the 27th, Julia was pleased to see her mother, who visited the bazaar with a few friends. By this time Julia had experienced two snowstorms, days of hard work, some exasperating moments, a lost veil on the omnibus, and a toothache, but she was determined to continue to the end and was pleased to hear comments about the good delegation from Lexington. Mrs. Alcott and her daughters stopped in, as did many others, the famous and the ordinary, to browse, to buy, and to hear the popular evening speakers—Channing, Thompson, Phillips, and Garrison. Now it was over, the crowds, the quiet times, the articles for sale, the lectures. And on this last Monday of the year, Julia was on her way home to East Lexington.

It was so cold that her fingers came near to freezing. Yesterday's storm had filled the sidewalks with snow; just getting to the train depot in

Charlestown was a challenge. Then, Julia had missed the train she had planned to take to Lexington and had to wait for a later one. True, she could have headed home after the bazaar ended on Saturday, but she had stayed in the city to hear Theodore Parker preach. When, she wondered, would she have this opportunity again? As always, she was energized to have heard Parker. Presently ensconced in the car of the Lexington & West Cambridge Railroad, she tucked her chin further into her cloak. She was worn out; she had been in Boston for the last thirteen days, staying with the Yerringtons, her anti-slavery friends, while she volunteered at the Anti-Slavery Bazaar.

Julia rested her feet on her valise. Inside was her precious copy of *The Liberty Bell*. She was proud of her efforts at the bazaar to raise funds for the American Anti-Slavery Society. The train slowed as the conductor called out "Cutler's," the first of the two East Lexington railroad stations. Julia was home.

Shirts, a toothache, and an uncertain future
FEBRUARY 1851

Since her exhilarating time working at the Anti-Slavery Fair, Julia had spent most of her days at home, neither the winter weather nor family plans conducive to venturing forth. When the new year—1851—began, the sun didn't rise until 7:30 in the morning and set only nine hours later. But, by the end of February, an hour of daylight had been added to the day. Julia hoped the diminishing darkness would parallel a diminishing number of *"sick headaches"* that had been plaguing her, headaches that increased in proportion to the number of days spent at home.

Julia tucked her sewing into the folds of her skirt and scooted her chair closer to the window, to catch the early afternoon light. The aromas of spices and apples lingered in the air, a remnant of the morning's pie making. Now the last of the apples stored in the root cellar were gone, an indication to Julia that the worst of winter was over. The baking had been a welcome respite from the endless days of sewing, especially sewing shirts for her only brother, Eli, still unmarried at age twenty-five. Other household tasks—whitewashing closets, varnishing the furniture, washing the chandeliers—would have to wait their turn, their season. This was the season for sewing.

Julia's sisters Hannah Maria and Ellen burst into the room. Ellen, energetic and opinionated, was always good for a commotion. Hannah Maria was looking for the scissors, which had mysteriously disappeared, moving her fingers to imitate cutting. Julia smiled warmly at her deaf sister for she did not blame Hannah Marie for being terribly cross at times. Julia could not imagine a world without sound, the strains of her father's violin, the laughter of her friends, the words of Emerson and Parker.

Julia looked around her—there were no aunts here today and no Grandmother Robbins. Abigail Winship Robbins had died last month, her bright personality mourned by the entire Robbins clan. Everyone remarked how Julia seemed to have inherited her grandmother's flair for fashion; not everyone's grandmother had a dress of plum-colored silk with matching embroidered plum-colored kidskin mitts, white silk stockings initialed A for Abigail, and a red wool hooded riding cape. Julia had loved helping her on those special occasions when Grandmother took out her best china, the Wedgewood.

The dinner table cleared, the food put away, and instructions to the hired girl given, Julia's mother, Hannah Simonds Robbins, joined her daughters, her sewing in hand. Julia looked at her mother; aging, but not easily, she would never live to be ninety as Grandmother Robbins had. After an illness a few years earlier, Hannah had endured the blows of losing her sisters Elizabeth and Martha within weeks of each other. Her world of female companionship was diminishing, seeming to diminish her in the process. Living in her mother's constricting world left Julia struggling for air. Her adventure at last December's Anti-Slavery Bazaar left her envious of the women she had met there; although some were not as educated as she, they were doing something with their lives beside the humdrum day-to-day existence. Her family was more than content to let things fall to Julia, knowing what Ellen called Julia's *"bump of order,"* her talent for organizing the household, would put things to rights.

Julia thought of the days she had escaped. One day she and her father had taken the sleigh to town to collect the railroad shares they were purchasing. One wonders how they cobbled together the funds needed—was it money slowly saved or a sudden windfall for work done? To her father's disappointment, the shares were not ready to be picked up. She had called at Aunt Caira's, as was her custom, but that didn't really count as she was family. A visit to the Phinneys no longer held allure; the last time Julia had visited, only twenty-five-year-old Alice was at home. Julia had hoped to find Mary or Jane, closer to her in age and still unmarried, unlike their sisters Susan, Catherine, Elizabeth, and the widowed Charlotte.

The time was broken up with occasional trips to Boston—too few Julia always thought. Though there was a shopping trip for buttons and belts not available in Lexington, it was an eagerly-awaited excursion to an abolitionists' gathering that Julia noted with pleasure in her diary:

> *A most splendid time. Words will hardly describe it. The time was completely filled with wit & music. . . . All in high spirits. . . . We all rode home together in wagon. Got to L. about 3 o'clock in morn.*

Julia admitted to herself that she had heard some excellent lectures, like Starr King's presentation on Socrates, described as *"an eternal questioner [who] lived for the sake of reform."* But some lectures were simply tireless collections of facts. Even noted British abolitionist George Thompson, whose speeches usually won plaudits, disappointed her. An anti-slavery meeting got a split verdict: Wendell Phillips was very interesting in the afternoon session, a welcome relief from the morning session monopolized by Mr. Davis from Lynn.

Almost every day for the past two months Julia had sewed. She had begun work on the shirt fronts the day after New Year's and here it was the end of February. Her fingers ached from the thousands upon thousands of stitches. How she longed for one of those wonderful new inventions—a sewing machine. Then she could make shirts for all the young men in East Village. The advertisements promised a shirt sewed on a machine took only seventy-six minutes; sewing by hand averaged fourteen hours and twenty-six minutes for a single shirt. That would be eleven shirts for a single hand-sewn one!

Hannah brought Julia's attention back to the present as she asked about Abigail's whereabouts. Julia frowned. Her sister Abigail, the wife of Reverend Stillman Lothrop, was busy with her two young sons, although the family's residence in the dwelling attached to Eli's hall made her a welcome presence, to her mother at least. Julia felt that Abigail depended too much on her mother's generosity and kindnesses made possible by Julia's hard work on the farm. Hannah caught Julia's unhappy look. What was to be done with Julia and her sister Ellen? Now at thirty-two and thirty-four years old, they were long past marrying age. Hannah reflected that by the time she was thirty-four she had been married for eleven years and had borne four daughters.

Hannah set her sewing aside and studied her daughters. Ellen and Julia were such independent young women! Julia, always busy with her father and his causes, seemed to chafe at a life under her parents' roof. Had Eli been wise to involve Julia so directly in his work against slavery? As a mother, she would have preferred that Julia spend that time on her art, something Hannah herself understood with her own work evident on the wall. Aunt Caira also encouraged this talent, letting Julia use her colored chalks. Young ladies were expected to dabble in art. Who would want a wife who collected signatures on a petition for clemency for a murderous black man? How could writing letters to arrange speakers for Eli's hall compare with the domestic skills Hannah had brought to her marriage? True, Julia was competent in household tasks and she did make wonderful jelly, but Hannah, who had nursed hopes for Julia and William Plumer, was out of patience with her daughter. Her daughter's head seemed filled with thoughts of "her Emerson" and "her Parker."

Hannah had known Theodore Parker all his life, as he had grown up on the Parker-Simonds farm and shared adventures with her nephew Eli. Even as a youth, Theodore was known for his passion for learning. Unable to afford Harvard's tuition, he studied the texts for Harvard's classes, took the exams, and completed the course of study as allowed by college policy. It wasn't until he had graduated from the Theological School at Cambridge in 1840 that his accomplishments were noted with an honorary master of arts degree. But all his learning and studying didn't make him welcome in Boston's churches, Hannah thought ruefully. Parker believed that one's own intuition mattered. For denying "the miraculous authority of the Bible and of Jesus," he was "generally ostracized by his Unitarian colleagues." When pulpits were closed to him for his radical views, the clergy cheered, but only temporarily, as Parker's supporters, determined that his voice for social justice be heard in Boston, formed a new—and sizeable—congregation in the city. Julia, for one, would sit in church

Theodore Parker (1810–1860), a towering nineteenth-century preacher and abolitionist, encouraged Julia's independent thinking.

all day to hear Parker. Ellen, too, was taken with Parker; she had called him *"a perfect specimen of progress."*

Hannah considered how out-of-sorts Julia was when her plan to go to Boston for a lecture was not realized, as the weather would not permit traveling. What was the magnet that drew Julia to lectures in the city? Her mother half suspected it was the movement of the place, the flow of city life where something was always happening, as much as the content of the lectures that attracted Julia. Of a decidedly practical bend by necessity, Hannah could not imagine the delight her daughter took in ideas. To Hannah, facts were what mattered—the length of cloth needed for a new cloak, the amount of vegetables left in the root cellar, the size of the woodpile. In the city, even for a day, Julia was able to be independent, making the decisions of where and when. How her youngest surviving daughter longed for this freedom! Hannah remembered Julia's delight as she left for Adams Female Academy years ago. Once there, there was no spell of homesickness as had beset her sisters. On another occasion Julia had sulked when relegated to stay home and keep house when her mother and Ellen went to the city. What and—more importantly—who would make Julia happy?

Julia's diary chronicled the days streaming by. To Hannah they seemed busy, filled with tasks to keep a household running. To Julia they seemed repetitious and boring. Consider how she recorded some of these days:

Jan. 4: About house as usual in Morn. Sewed some in afternoon. Cooked supper as usual. Read some & discussed matters, matrimony &c in eve.

Jan. 10: Talk about old note. Mother, Father & Ellen set out for Concord to see Hoar. Called to see W. Plumer and returned. I worked about house all morn. . . . Dreamed of D[avison].

Jan. 12: Beautiful day again. I should like to hear Beecher in Boston. Today traveling will not admit . . . Went to hear Pierpont all day. Old sermons I thought. . . .

Jan. 15: Started with Father, Mother early for Concord. Called on Wm. Plumer. Emily very pleasant. Rode up to Mr. Hoar's with Wm. . . . Found Mr. Hoar at home. [He] was asked about Mother's note. [This was an] equity case, he thought, no doubt [about it]. [We] must petition in third person's name. . . . Got home little after dinner. I wanted very much to go to Thompson's lecture in eve. Horse to[o] tired . . . spent eve over to Mr. Williams. Played cards. . . .

Jan. 28: Washed, ironed, sewed on scarf. Tremendous toothache most all night.

Feb. 2: Snow storm. Read today History of Audubon the Naturalist. *Also [read] in [the]* Liberator *an account of [the] festival. Quimby up in afternoon. [He] walked from Boston. Adolph in eve.*

Feb. 7: About house in morn. Cut out another shirt. Sewed in eve. Very cold.

Feb. 10: Rained all day. Sewed steady. Mr. & Mrs. Williams [and] daughter in. Play'd whist.

Feb. 19: Ellen went to B[oston] for Mother. Called into Aunt Ca's. I kept house. Sewed. . . . I dreamed last week of seeing Davison who said he would come home in July. I put this down for a reason.

Feb. 22: Rec'd letter from Davison. Read &c. Quimby came in eve, brought present of Gloves—just returned from Washington.

Julia remembered two beautiful mild, sunny days in January and rainy, blustering ones in February. Regardless of the weather, the usual household

Julia's diary page shown here details her experiences at the Anti-Slavery Bazaar from December 20 through December 28, 1850.

chores always needed doing—washing, ironing, cooking, and cleaning. Other tasks varied with the seasons, but work was omnipresent. There were days of conversation and days of quiet. There were nights her sleep seemed dreamless and nights she dreamed of Davison.

Julia put aside her sewing, the afternoon spent. Would she always be sewing shirts for a brother, never for a husband? The shadows of late afternoon fell across the yard, a yard that two months ago was in darkness by this time of day. Maybe this year spring would not be a tease. She still remembered the spring a decade ago when newly home from Adams Academy and yearning for warm weather, her hopes were dashed by a foot and a half snowfall in April. Nature was as capricious as man. Julia turned from the window. It was time to start supper.

Finally, Julia sets her own course
DECEMBER 1851

A year's end is a time for summing up accomplishments, tallying accounts, and reminiscing. If someone asked Julia to list the most important events of 1851 for the city of Boston, for the village of East Lexington, and for herself, she would have three different answers. Yet, she was involved in each of them. For the city of Boston, the most important event of 1851 would have been the capture of Sims, a fugitive slave, and his subsequent return to his Southern owner. This galvanized public opinion against the Fugitive Slave Law. For days the city buzzed over the event with the subsequent volley of speeches as leading abolitionists garnered more supporters for their cause. Julia joined the throngs at Tremont Temple and later at the State House, castigating this version of "Massachusetts Liberty." Her star, Theodore Parker, preached a "Fast Day" sermon, an attempt to have Bostonians do penance for the shame brought on the city. Spurred to action, Julia distributed notices for a meeting in Lexington Center to discuss the hated law.

East Lexington's most important moment in the sunlight would have been Theodore Parker's speech at the dedication of the South School House. The school was located on land to the west of Eli Robbins's homestead on Main Street, known in the twenty-first century as Massachusetts Avenue, where the parking lot for Follen Church is presently located. From Julia's diary, one learns that Parker spoke on the history of education since 1760, enlivening his address with anecdotes of how his father, then he, had learned to cipher. It was Parker's conviction that *the district school should teach morals as well as intellect, learn[ing] then piety and goodness.* It was his decided opinion that *only the preachers [should] learn sectarianism and such fixing.* Parker's presence reflected the town's pride in a native son. Finally, for Julia, the event of the year was not her summer trip to Vermont. There, one afternoon while fishing with her cousin George Langdon, she had caught fifteen trout; that was *hot and tedious.* It was not her attendance at the Middlesex Anti-Slavery Annual Meeting in Concord in April or even the Anti-Slavery Convention in Boston a month later. Without question, Julia would have said that her decision to attend the Boston School of Design was the most significant one of the year for her. Her determination had been realized to find a way to break the endless cycle of, to her, mindless work and gain some independence. She had heeded Emerson's advice to follow one's conscience. Tending to the constant stream of visitors and the endless tasks—whitewash closets, paper the dining room, wash curtains, clean the chambers, preserve peaches, and on and on—would be someone else's lot. For Julia, being busy did not equate with happiness.

Julia's unhappiness with the state of affairs at home was sometimes palpable as expressed in these diary entries throughout the year:

May 30: . . . I don't know after all but it is best after all to go your own way without regard to others. You might stay at home all your life. No one [will] think any better of you.

June 1: A beautiful day. Wish I could be in B[oston] today to hear Mr. May. Tis unnecessary for me to be here. I might go once in a while as well as not go, but whenever I want to go there are always objections. I don't know why I should tie myself.

September 18: Mother, Ellen, [and] Hannah went up to Wm. Bowers' funeral [and] left me to do the work. [I] did not like it very well. 3 great Irishmen to wait upon. [I] worked hard all day.

October 15: Mother scolds at us because she works so hard waiting upon [the] Lothrops. Ab[igail] took [the] wagon and [a] load [of produce]. [I] gave her a piece of my mind. She would be glad to have us work to support her children. She will never get me to do it. Mother & father may scold as much as they please. She has had three loads of our produce within four weeks. Sometimes I think I will let the old property go. It don't pay for me to spend the best part of my life trying to keep it as I see no thanks for it neither.

*October 20: Washed. Nothing especial. Eli came home, talk about domestic affairs. Ellen & I have to take the brunt of **all** the battles. It don't pay.*

So, when Julia heard that a Miss Ednah Littlehale had started a School of Design for women in Boston, she was intrigued. Julia may have already crossed paths with Miss Littlehale as they shared both an abolitionist stance and friendships with Ralph Waldo Emerson and Theodore Parker. Miss Littlehale's goal for the school—to widen women's opportunity for paying work—meshed with Julia's aspirations. And hadn't many people remarked on her talent for color and design?

On Tuesday, October 28, when the design school had been open for just three weeks, Julia went to Boston with Ellen for a visit. After a conversation with Miss Littlehale, Julia *"Decided to join."* On subsequent days, she confided her qualms to her diary: *"In a great quandary about my future plans."* This step would lead to her goal of independence, but at what cost? She certainly would not be considering this step had she married Davison, or Quincy Dow who would have given $5 to be with her on one Thanksgiving, or Henry of the May morn letter.

At week's end, on Saturday, November 1, Julia traveled to Boston to purchase a season railroad ticket at a cost of $7.34. That Sunday, Julia wrote to Mary Plumer, declining her invitation to visit her in New Hampshire. School began for Julia on Monday, November 3. On this day, she wrote in her diary:

*Up bright & early & off to Boston to join the **School** of **design**. Six young ladies came in the same day. A very pleasant set so it seems. . .*

By Tuesday, November 4, the pattern for her days was set—*"Down & took lesson as usual. Got home tired & hungry."* The following weekend, Julia worked about the house, *"copied in drawing book,"* attended a lecture, and *"engaged in drawing some &c."* For Monday, November 10, a rainy day, her entry noted that the school moved to a new location on Summer Street, making it *"Rather late when things were in order to take our lesson."* In the more spacious quarters, the routine was soon re-established. *"Morn as usual. Home at ½ 3. Engaged in drawing."* Julia's focus was now on her classes. What would have caught her attention earlier—news of Davison from a mutual friend, trimming a bonnet, visitors—received short shrift as she explained in her diary.

I find I have but little time except to draw. I suppose it is best for me to devote my time to this now I am in for it.

The operation of the design school was the responsibility of Mr. Whittaker, a graduate of the Kensington, England, School of Design. Whittaker, whose dissent from the established church closed employment to him in his home country, came to the United States with letters of introduction to some Unitarian clergy, among others. With his training, he seemed an excellent choice to run the school. One afternoon during the second week of classes, Julia noted with approval the *"very pleasant"* party Mr. Whittaker hosted in the schoolroom. He introduced his wife to his students, provided refreshments, and displayed drawings. Whittaker's sudden departure the following week took the students by surprise. Julia's diary entry for Thursday, November 20, reads:

To Boston. Mr. Whit[t]aker in trouble. I was thunderstruck to hear he had sent in his resignation. He gave his reasons therefore. We all felt bad enough. Not a few tears shed on the occasion. . . . I was fairly sick.

Neither Julia in her diary or Miss Littlehale, known as Mrs. Cheney after her marriage in 1853, specified the problem. Years later Mrs. Cheney wrote that Mr. Whittaker left as he was unsuitable to administer the school. Julia's reaction to Whittaker's departure was predictable. The next day she was *"sick in bed with [a] headache."* By Saturday she was *"able to draw some & to work about [the] house."*

Despite Mr. Whittaker's departure, Julia persevered at the school. A Miss Jane M. Clark arrived from New Hampshire to serve as an assistant teacher; Mr. Andrews taught wood engraving; Miss Parsons and Mr. John L. Russell taught classes in botany. Although the minimum stay was two quarters, with tuition set at ten dollars a quarter, Julia stayed for three quarters. Where did she find the thirty dollars for tuition? The only hint is in a mid-November diary entry. *"C[ousin] Ca[ira] was at [our] house this week. Very generous."*

In addition to money from tuition, the school was supported by local manufacturers, but they became disappointed with the school's results. In hindsight decades later, Mrs. Cheney noted the mistake of having only women in the school; boys were used to the idea that learning involved time, attention, and practice of the skills taught, and she concluded that boys would have been a good influence in the school. In her description of the school for an 1886 article in *The Woman's Journal*, Mrs. Cheney admitted:

> . . . the school did not produce the industrial results desired. Few of the pupils found employment. One went to Dover and one to Lawrence to work in factories, but they had not sufficient training and skill to compete with the foreign designers employed, and the positions were soon relinquished. . . .

Mrs. Cheney may have thought her account of the school complete, but after an unknown correspondent contacted her, she wrote this letter to the editor of *The Woman's Journal*. It began:

> I am reminded that I neglected to mention in my account of "The School of Design," that Miss Julia Robbins, a very accomplished Pupil, was engaged for five year's [*sic*] as a designer in a carpet-factory there.

When Julia finished her courses at the School of Design, she was thirty-two years old, on her way to becoming an independent woman with gainful employment as a carpet designer at the Lowell Company. Julia had followed Emerson's advice to follow her own course and now, in her words, she was *"in for it."*

Early days in Lowell
<small>SEPTEMBER 5, 1852</small>

As the crow flies, Lowell is only fourteen miles northwest of Lexington. By the mid-nineteenth century, this stellar example of an early American industrial city run on waterpower had lost its uniqueness and become a crowded place, teeming with looms and immigrant laborers. Despite its proximity, Lowell was worlds away from Lexington. It was a mill city covering less geographic area than Lexington, but once the mills began to roar, its population of New Englanders, then waves of immigrants, climbed dramatically. It was like another country for Julia who reached it by train and at some cost. Expense accounts for her years in Lowell itemize the cost of railroad tickets for her weekend and occasional trips home. In January 1857, she spent $30 for railroad tickets and, a few months later, in April, another $40, for more tickets. These were considerable sums when her average monthly salary was $30.

Soon after arriving in Lowell with her friend, a Miss Stoddard, Julia's pen fairly flew across the page in a letter to her sister Ellen.

> *"We are looked upon as* **wonders** *here. It* **never** *dawned upon the good folks that* **women** *could design."*

Four days later, on September 5, she wrote again, to recount her adventures in the city. Armed with her education at the Boston School of Design, Julia arrived at the famed Lowell Manufacturing Company, the "largest and best-known producer of American carpetings." Her timing was perfect, coinciding with the explosion of the company's business in ingrain carpets. This was due to Erastus Bigelow's invention of the world's first power carpet loom, "an invention so wonderful that it seems to be almost endowed with intellect." To feed the looms at the Lowell Company, eighteen tons of wool from South America and the Middle East were used each week. This massive amount arrived the same way the finished product was

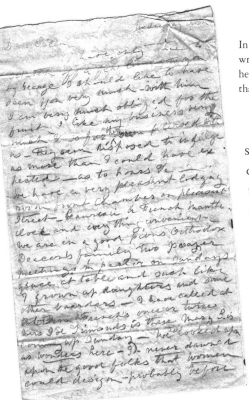

In her first letter home from Lowell, Julia wrote, "We are looked upon as **wonders** here. It **never** dawned upon the good folks that **women** could design."

sent out—on a railroad spur directly into the mill yard, along the south bank of the Lowell Canal. Each day, four-fifths of an acre of carpet was produced by the company's work force, which numbered almost a thousand people, then half the population of the entire town of Lexington.

As Julia and her companion searched for accommodations in this crowded city of 33,000 inhabitants, Julia studied the faces of the mill workers they met on the streets as they hurried home to lunch or back to the factory for another six hours of work. The wave of bright, eager New England farm girls who had flocked to Lowell when the mills were first opened in the 1820s had receded. Since then conditions had deteriorated, wages had decreased, and the prestige associated with mill work had disappeared as immigrant operatives increased in number. The city's days of glory were over. Twenty years earlier when Congressman Davy Crockett visited Lowell, 2,500 mill girls, marching two by two, had taken half an hour to pass the reviewing stand. The *Lowell Offering*, the often-praised and much quoted magazine written by the mill girls themselves, had ended its four-year run almost a decade earlier. Still, Julia was optimistic. As a carpet designer she would earn about seven dollars a week, more than double that of the average female worker's wages. To Julia, even more important than the money was the independence. She knew she was unique among her kind to hold a paying job that wasn't teaching school. The reigning philosophy governing women's lives rested on four pillars of rectitude—piety, purity, domesticity, and submissiveness. Julia had her own definition of piety while purity was not a matter for discussion. Domesticity and submissiveness were other matters entirely. Julia favored Theodore Parker's view of women that it was "a monstrous waste of the most precious material that God ever made" to "consume all their energies in the functions of Housekeeper, wife and mother."

Julia was pleased she would have a carpeted, spacious office in which to work. On her tour of the Lowell Company, she found that her very bones shook with the tremendous racket of the machinery, a noise that made thinking almost impossible. Julia looked around the enormous single-story room, the size of an acre, where all the looms were housed. She counted eighty, with room for more. Julia was shown every department of the carpet mill and introduced to all the people with whom she and Miss Stoddard would work; at first impression, Julia noted that all seemed very pleasant. Tomorrow morning, September 6, Julia and her friend would begin drawing and painting designs at seven o'clock. They would be under the supervision of Mr. Fontarire whose office was nearby; his advice to them was simple—be original and artistic. They were also admonished to study and follow the rules posted in the design room, which read:

1st. When patterns are ordered into the Loom, the samples of carpeting if there are such at the mill, are to be ticketed and placed in the finishing room, so that the Weaver may at all times have access to them, and fully understand what colorings have been adopted.

2nd. The shading papers are to be made out as soon as practicable after orders are received, and are to be placed in a box on the desk in the finishing room. The design is at the same time to be placed in a draw [sic] in the finishing room, where it can be seen by the Overseer. and no carpet will be considered as ordered into the Loom until this shall have been done.

3rd. In case the colorist is to be away from the mill exceeding one half day, he is to notify the Overseer of the Carpet Weaving Room, who will take charge of the Card Cutting department in his absence.

Signed Saml. Fay Supt.

The two novices were also advised to study the work of the other Lowell Company designers, which included Peter Lawson's "great blossoms with sweeping foliage asymmetrically arranged" as well as Elmer Ney's symmetrical patterns of the requisite foliage with flowers and fruits. The designs of one Mr. Allen were not a good model, as they were reported to "have made every body at Lowell melancholly [*sic*]." As the newest designers, the Misses Robbins and Stoddard were instructed to address both technical and aesthetic problems in the design, to plan carefully "to eliminate any large spaces unoccupied by pattern, since such space made 'pockets' between the plies which were not good for wearing purposes." The public's taste for "the large, floriated scroll designs" fit the plans "because the many serrations in the leaf and flower motifs, requiring an interchange of colors, held the two layers of woven web firmly together."

Julia and Miss Stoddard had found accommodations with the Wetherbee family at Number 19 Kirk Street, a short walk from the Lowell Company. Crossing Market Street, they walked by the City Hall on Shattuck Street, another cobblestoned stretch of road. Serving as a marker on their walk was the gray stone structure of St. Anne's Episcopal Church on Merrimack Street, clearly in view as they made their way north.

The church was erected in 1824, when the Merrimack Company directors voted to build a church and the company's treasurer, Kirk Boott, designed one in the Gothic style. Named for his wife, this was an Episcopal church, even though few of the New England farm girls working in Lowell in its first decade were of that faith. The mill operatives were mandated to support the church with a contribution of 37 and ½ cents each month. Julia had been surprised when she had first heard of this requirement. The way her church in East Lexington was funded, by willing contributors and a summer fair, was preferable to her. But at least this church was named for a woman, unlike many of the other buildings and streets in Lowell such as her street, Kirk Street, named in homage to a powerful company official.

Around the corner from the church rectory was Julia's Lowell neighborhood. Number 19 Kirk Street mirrored its neighbors. It was a Federal style building, red brick construction, with generous windows, granite steps, and brick dentils decorating the roofline. Across the street, on the west side, was the city's high school.

During the few days that Julia and Miss Stoddard had to themselves to look about the town and get settled, they found themselves not altogether pleased with the situation of things at Number 19. There was plenty to eat and drink; their front room, complete with a French mantle clock on the bureau, was pleasant enough. However, life in a pious orthodox deacon's family was not Julia's inclination. She preferred Emerson's and Parker's approaches, neither of which was favored by conservative churchgoers. How she would have loved to have the deacon's seven daughters meet Parker. How shocked they would be at his pronouncement that women not only had the same political rights as men, but that they were capable of venturing into public life to lecture, work as journalists, practice medicine, and even serve in the ministry. With his seven adult daughters, all living at home, as well as other boarders, Deacon Weatherbee was assured of a small congregation for the two prayer meetings that he held every Sunday in the parlor with everyone expected to attend.

Designing carpets and finding new accommodations were not the only things on Julia's mind. Since arriving in Lowell, she had visited Mr. Abbott, a lawyer the family had consulted about property issues in East Lexington. The Robbinses were known to be a litigious lot. Eli's property had been both mortgaged and rented after his bankruptcy. Ensuing claims and counter-claims resulted with lessees and renters as well as the mort-gage holders. Julia and her sister Ellen found themselves in the middle of the tangle, as they were legally responsible for the care of their mother and their oldest sister, Hannah Maria. Abbott told Julia that she had the law on her side, but it would cost two to three hundred dollars to prove that she and Ellen were owed additional money by the lessees. If the decision turned against her, she and Ellen would lose even more money. To Julia's dismay, when the court decision was made, it did come in against them. When Abbott presented Julia with his bill for services, she wrote Ellen what ensued.

> *I told him I thought his bill rather large. He said he put it very low for the amount of time, attention & expense it had been to him, said he should have charged a man nearly twice that amount. After considerable talk he said that knowing something of our situation and as we had lost &c he would take 25 Doll[ar]s. off from the bill.*

The amount Abbott agreed to remove from the bill was almost a month's wages for Julia. Along with advice to Ellen to direct her mail *"to the Care of Samuel Fay, Lowell, Mass.,"* Julia concluded her letter with an invitation to Ellen and others to visit her in Lowell:

> *I shall be very happy to see any of my friends if they will call at the count-ing room of the Lowell Manufacturing Company. They will probably find me every day in [the] week except* **Sundays** *& evenings after six o'clock I have to myself I shall be at my boarding house, the locality of which I am not quite decided about now.*

Julia was pleased with herself. She had gone to school, improved a talent, and found a position. Thoughts of Davison, disappointments, and domes-tic disputes faded as Julia took her place as a designer at the Lowell Com-pany. She was on her own at last!

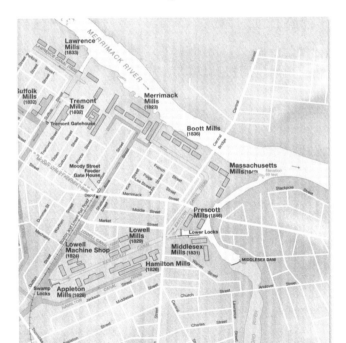

The Lowell Carpet Mills are located in the lower center of this 1850 map of the Lowell Canal System. Kirk Street, where Julia lived when she first arrived in the city, is two blocks to the north.

Julia receives letters from a dangerous man
August 1854

The year 1854 had brought little good news, either for Julia or the country. In January, Senator Stephen A. Douglas of Illinois had introduced a bill in Congress to permit the territories of Kansas and Nebraska—free territories, that is closed to slavery by their position north of the 36° 30' line of the Missouri Compromise—to decide for themselves their status as free states or slave states. The passage of this bill had exacerbated tensions as the Massachusetts (soon to be the New England) Emigrant Aid Society promoted settlement of anti-slavery groups in Kansas. Pro-slavery advocates met this challenge with equal determination that slavery be established in Kansas. The only hopeful news was the establishment of a new political party, the Republican Party, whose platform stated opposition to the extension of slavery into the territories.

Now the August days of heat and humidity were back; known as the dog days, they coincided with the rise of the star Sirius of the constellation Canis Major. Some considered them a time of bad humors while others knew they were just filled with lassitude and laziness. Not only were people affected, but the low water level in rivers and streams frequently led to a shut-down of the mills of Lowell, mills whose looms were powered by water. During her years in Lowell, Julia usually spent those weeks of summer at home in East Lexington or at the homes of friends. It was on such a day that a letter from the abolitionist Parker Pillsbury reached Julia in Lexington. It was not the first letter she had received from him, nor would it be the last.

While serving as her father's secretary as he arranged speakers for his hall, Julia had corresponded with various abolitionists, Joshua Dodge, Samuel May, and Parker Pillsbury among them. Those days ended for Julia with the sale of Eli's hall and her employment in Lowell. Seven years earlier, in 1847, Eli had hosted Pillsbury, a prominent anti-slavery lecturer and the man reputed to be the first to preach abolition in Eli's hall. Pillsbury, known to many as the most radical abolitionist of all, was different from his peers. Pillsbury's contemporaries took his measure. The poet James Russell Lowell described him as "brown, broad-shouldered Pillsbury, Who tears up words like trees by the roots." In his *Journal*, philosopher Ralph Waldo Emerson described him as a gift from New Hampshire . . . a tough oak stick of a man not to be silenced or insulted or intimidated by a mob, because he is more mob than they. . . on whom neither money nor politeness nor hard words nor rotten eggs nor kicks & brickbats make the slightest impression. He . . . is a wit & a bully himself . . . and has nothing new to learn of labor, or poverty or the rough of farming.

His hard head too had gone through in boyhood all the drill of Calvinism with text & mortification so that he stands in the New England Assembly a purer bit of New England than any, & flings his sarcasms right & left, sparing no name, or person, or party, or presence.

Emerson concluded that "Danger is not so dangerous as he." Pillsbury's present-day biographer, Stacey M. Robertson, described him as "a disruptive eccentric who lashed out at authority" as well as "a sensitive visionary." She further noted that Pillsbury

subverted the traditional notions of manly strength and self-control to construct a vision of manhood that rejected male dominance. This central element of his identity strongly influenced his political philosophy and personal relationships. It led him to support women's rights even at the expense of his abolitionist friendships, and it also allowed him to establish affectionate attachments to innumerable progressive women.

Parker Pillsbury (1809–1898) was a radical abolitionist as well as an advocate for women's rights.

Was Julia Robbins one of the progressive women with whom Pillsbury established an "affectionate attachment"?

Sitting now in the middle of the orchard, her back to one of the trees, Julia looked at the recently-arrived letter dated July 30, 1854, from Pillsbury who was writing from Dublin, Ireland. He was on a European trip to work with small groups, especially women's groups, raising funds and lecturing for the American Anti-Slavery Society in Great Britain and Ireland. Having fallen ill, he had spent two months recovering at the home of abolitionist Mary Estlin in Bristol, England. There he had the time on one occasion to write to Julia as well as to his wife, Sarah Sargent Pillsbury. As a bride, Sarah was a partner to her husband, but after the birth of their daughter, Helen, Sarah was forced back into the traditional gender role of domestic submissiveness. To this was added the strain of serving both boarders and traveling anti-slavery speakers despite her poor health. Sarah, thinking her husband had written only to her, sent a note to Julia.

> *My Parker wished me to send you the accompanying note and ask you to read it the first opportunity you should have to the 'dear Wellingtons,' as he was too unwell to write another. Accept with this hasty note, dear Julia, the sincere remembrance & love of your friend, Sarah A. Pillsbury.*

Sarah and daughter Helen had accompanied Parker on some of his trips, visiting at the Robbins's homestead. Sarah was well aware of her husband's "call for civic morality [that] included the championing of women's suffrage, sexual freedom, the right to divorce, and many other feminist issues." This would, of course, bring him in contact with the women who were speaking, petitioning, and working for these causes. With knowledge of her husband's "friendships," she expressed her unhappiness with his fondness "of being noticed particularly by the romantic and visionary soul of women." Accordingly, his correspondence with Julia may not have surprised her; however, the tone would have dismayed her, as would her husband's complaint to activist Maria Weston Chapman of his wife's small-mindedness. When Sarah had written her husband of her suffering when all her upper teeth were extracted, Pillsbury's reply was *"to make the best of it."* Sarah was certainly mindful that, on occasion, her husband's language was not of her choosing. When met with opposition, he had crudely claimed that the mob harassing him had been "vomited out" of the bar rooms. The side Pillsbury showed to Julia was certainly not his public or his husbandly side. To her, he extended "friendship." It seems that for Pillsbury, charity did not always begin at home.

When Pillsbury wrote to Julia in July 1854, he was a forty-five-year-old married man, ten years Julia's senior. Would Pillsbury write this way if she were not a single woman? In a letter to Julia in August of 1853, Pillsbury had written:

> Often my dear Julia, are you in my thoughts—owing something perhaps to the peculiarity of your position. Strangely enough, you have chosen to take your stand heroically with us stern warriors, . . . And God & Nature have endowed you with the gifts & graces to hold an honorable place in the mighty encounter—to be yourself a heroine & host.

He continued:

> But you seem to stand alone a frail, isolated, delicate girl. To me you appear a Lamb among tigers—a dove among ravens & condors—and as such, must you not be devoured! What shall shield you in the hour of trial? God and your own innocence & virtue shall protect you against every assailant, and you shall walk unharmed through dens of Lions and furnaces of Fire.

Julia's reply, like all her letters to Pillsbury, is nowhere to be found among the collections of Pillsbury material; no draft copies, if there were any as there are for letters to other correspondents, have survived. It is known that Julia's reply was courteous and short from Pillsbury's opening of his next letter to Julia, written from Ohio on September 18, 1853.

> Your letter was so short, that, but for its sweetness, it would scarcely deserve an answer. Your reasons for such brevity I accept though it was somewhat a disappointment.

That letter of last September was a four-page missive filled with his views of the West, references to his own *"calamitous"* birth and upbringing, and thoughts on the nature of love and the position of women. Pillsbury wrote:

> Looking over the human family, there is no class that has so wrought upon my sympathies, as the young women, and women out of the marriage state, whether rich or poor, young or old, who are striving to lead a true life.

At the end of this long letter, Pillsbury added:

To love and be loved—these are the permissions granted us all. Let us enjoy the boon. I once thought with "Eloise to Abelard," that 'twas a sin to love. The sin is in not loving. . . . If sin attend any union or attachment, it is not Love. Love between spirits, the highest, the celestial love has nothing of sin, nothing of sensuality in its composition or exercise. Souls meeting and mingling, sympathizing, sorrowing & rejoicing together, in diverse harmony, this is not sin. It is salvation. It is a ray of heaven shining into the darkness of our earthly exile. It is a breeze from the groves of Paradise, fanning our fainting spirits. . . . then Dear Julia, Let us love one another, as long as we live.

Julia had received a subsequent letter from Pillsbury, one he had written on New Year's Day 1854, as he was about to leave on his European journey.

One parting word dear, ever dear Julia. Your image shall go with me wherever I stay. At night, your thoughts of me shall hover about my pillow, little winged spirits; & I will cherish them, until they will love to be with me, as little birds love to play around the hand that feeds & fondles them. And day & night, on land & sea, my hopes, desires & Prayers shall be on your account. And your happiness, now & onward forever, will give joy and gladness to Your Ever Affectionate P.

Was Pillsbury, as Emerson expressed it, a "danger"? Was he a danger to Julia? Or was he a platonic friend who supported her independence, one who acted as he signed himself, as *"your Faithful Friend & brother"* even though he professed his *"esteem and love"* for her? It was with some unease that Julia turned her attention to the letter in hand—the letter written in Ireland several days earlier.

My dear Julia,

I have but a moment, but it belongs, & shall be given to you. The Atlantic rolls between us, but it is no barrier to genuine friendship & true affections. How well I remember the visits made at your house but better yet, the little interviews at Lowell, and the snow storm blockade last winter at Joshua Dodge's. Dear, darling Julia, the pleasant times we had then, have lived in the brightest sunlight of my memory ever since. . . . Somehow, you wrought strongly upon my sympathy when I found you at Lowell. You appeared a beautiful being suddenly let down into a sphere not at all your own, when you were to live, not for yourself, but for others—setting examples and solving problems, by which others rather than yourself were to be benefited and blessed. As for your fate, I pitied you. But for your heroic submission, your fidelity to truth and principle, and your cheerful discharge of the duties of the station, I loved you, loved you very much indeed, and if that be, or were a sin, I must lie under the imputation, nor shall I shrink from the penalty. For it is a sin which will probably lie at my door, as long as I live to love, or you, dear Julia, to be loved.

Pillsbury wrote of his longing for "even a note" from Julia and concluded:

You have a large place in my heart's best affections, nor is it fault or virtue of mine, more than is it the sin of the magnet to be attracted by polar power. The lovely must be loved.

Julia pocketed the letter and meandered among the trees, reluctant to leave both the solitude and the slight breeze that had come up from the east. What would Eli Robbins, who considered Pillsbury a colleague in the fight against slavery, say if she showed him the letters, letters she kept in one of her school notebooks? Eli, now sixty-eight, was still protective of his daughters, especially the two unmarried ones—Hannah Maria and Julia. Long his favorite, Julia, though working in Lowell, came home frequently. Ellen, who had wed Lexington businessman Abner Stone in December 1853, was back at home after spending some time in St. Louis, Missouri, where Abner had business interests. Presently, the household revolved around Ellen as she was preparing for the birth of her first child a few months hence. Eli and Hannah, despite the disruption that a baby would bring to the household, were looking forward to another grandchild—their third. They hoped that Hannah Maria would make a caring aunt, empathizing with Ellen's newborn the inability to articulate one's wishes. Julia would be back in Lowell when the baby arrived so it seemed this event would have little effect on her life. Yet, it would be a further reminder that time was slipping away.

Letters from a life-long friend and from a disconcerting cousin
MARCH 17, 1855

Similarly to most of New England, Lowell had its share of capricious weather. The dog days of last August were long forgotten as winter gripped the region. In February of 1855, on a day dubbed Cold Tuesday, the temperature had dropped to 5.5 degrees below zero by 2:30 in the afternoon. By March 17, the forecast was for snow or freezing rain; New England did not always put on its best face in March. The sunrise of the day before lingered in Julia's memory with its colors of molten gold, rose, and topaz; today the world was a pewter bowl. She pulled her shawl tighter around her shoulders. It was clear that the Godey's fashion writer who counseled wearing a shawl so it was up on one shoulder and down on the other so the wearer would look more interesting never visited here. Fortified with a breakfast of pumpkin mush with cream, liberally buttered toast, and coffee laced with milk and brown sugar, Julia faced the day with a pleasant feeling. She had the afternoon off!

During her hours off, Julia needed to pick up some washing from the laundry woman as well as her shoes, which were being mended at the cobbler's shop. Her family would have been horrified if they knew she had paid the dressmaker, a Miss Stevens, $9 for a silk dress. That was the same amount she paid Miss Maynard for a month's room and board, but the dress would still be a delight long after she had left Miss Maynard's. Her family also needn't know that Miss Stevens was currently making two more dresses for her. They failed to realize that she barely had the time needed to trim her bonnet and sew the needed chemises and petticoats. And, if she made her own clothes, she would first have to pay $1.37½ for a pattern from Godey's. Her sister Hannah Maria might be satisfied with copying last year's style, but she wasn't. How lucky men were to be able to purchase mass-produced ready-made clothing. Fashion—she loved it! She remembered the delight that she and her Vermont cousins had a few summers ago when they each altered one of their dresses into a bloomer costume. Her purple dress was so practical in that much-derided fashion; she wished she had brought it to Lowell to wear at work. That would shock some people here.

Perhaps she would even have time during her afternoon off to write to her good friend, Elizabeth Gerry. Elizy was like another sister to the

Robbins daughters. Born in January 1814, she slipped into the Robbins family between Hannah Maria and Abigail. Having illustrious forbearers had not made life easier for Elizy. Like Julia's Grandfather Simonds, Elizy's maternal grandfather, John Bridge, was also in Captain Parker's Company. Selected as the representative to the Committee of Correspondence and Safety, he went on to fight at Bunker Hill and earned the rank of Major in the militia. After the war, he served Lexington for many years as an assessor, a magistrate, and a justice of the peace. Julia and Elizy not only had a heritage in common, but also years of close family friendships spanning generations. Elizy's father, Thomas Whitcomb, a physician and member of the Massachusetts Medical Society, was such a close friend of the Robbins family that his "riding out" with Aunt Caira after the marriages of Aunt Nabby Robbins Langdon and of Eli Robbins has been recorded in family history. Only family and the very best of friends accompanied newlyweds on the first part of their wedding journey. Elizy, who did not marry until she was thirty-five, had many years of shared adventures with the Robbins daughters, especially Julia and Ellen. Elizy knew not only the Robbins, but their friends and relations—from cousin George Simonds to the elusive Davison.

By the time Elizy married in 1849, her parents were deceased, leaving the Robbins as her surrogate family. It was a role they assumed for her newspaper correspondent husband, Harris Gerry, as well. Hannah Robbins had kept a bedside vigil when Harris's mother died years earlier. After Harris's marriage to Elizy, the couple moved to Washington, D.C., where Harris reported on Congressional debates and kept the Robbinses updated on the issues in the nation's capital. On February 7, 1850, he wrote Ellen Robbins about events there.

> *The slavery excitement has given a color to almost everything that has occurred. In fact, the dissolution of the Union has been the standard topic in almost every circle. In Congress, let what would be brought up, the slavery question would be sure to be dragged in. What the result will be it is difficult to foresee. All the leading men seem to be at a stand, not knowing what to do.*

Knowing that members of the Robbins family were assiduous newspaper readers, Harris did not describe the *"tumultuous scenes,"* beyond noting that when Henry Clay, known as the Great Compromiser for his ability to reach out to both sides in the growing debate over slavery, was scheduled to speak, the gallery was filled by 8:00 A.M. for a Senate session scheduled to start at noon. Instead, Harris wrote news of friends and relations visiting Washington, D.C.; these included the Robbins's Vermont cousins, George Langdon and his married sister, Caira, and Julia's special friend, Mary Plumer. In his letter to Ellen, Harris recounted some events of Mary's stay in the city.

> Last week Miss Plumer, with her father, and a Miss Baily arrived. They have made the most of their time. Miss Plumer, you are aware, is a politician, and, consequently, is just the person to enjoy a brief sojourn in Washington. She heard Mr. Clay, which, doubtless, she will consider an important event in her life. . . . Say to Julia that Miss Plumer made quite an imposing appearance, hanging upon the arm of Ex-Senator Evans, at the President's levee, last Friday evening.

Julia's friendship with the Gerrys was replenished when the couple returned to Boston, where Elizy, and sometimes, Harris, joined Julia for fairs, lectures, parties, and even an expedition to see the ruins left by the August 1851 tornado that devastated parts of West Cambridge.

After Harris found employment in New Hampshire, Elizy took over as correspondent, explaining that although Concord was *"a very pleasant old town,"* she missed *"the excitement of Washington St., the lectures, the amusements, &c &c."* Knowing Julia understood her interests, with a shared love for fashion, Elizy expressed surprise that even in Concord there were *"such good stores here, containing such stylish fashionable goods."*

When her niece Ellen was born in October 1854, Julia stole *"a few moments"* at work to share the news of her sister Ellen's dark blue-eyed, dark-haired daughter—*"the most **wonderful** of babies that ever was looked upon."* Julia commented to Elizy that Aunt Caira must have been pleased when visitors pronounced the baby's resemblance to her. Of Ellen, *"although she is so well,"* Julia noted that Dr. Currier had ordered three weeks of bed rest for the cautious new mother. Ever practical Julia, wondering who would do the extra laundry needed for the new arrival, added:

> The rest of our family are tolerably well, excepting Elira the [I]rishgirl, who took it into her head to have the typhoid fever right in the midst of the great occasion.

As Julia wrote this, frustrated over the constraints on her time, she concluded, *"I wish I could write longer but this will not finish my pattern."* When Elizy made a trip to Boston, stopping in East Lexington to call on Ellen and see the baby, she did not have time to visit Julia in Lowell. Today Julia vowed she would find time to write a proper letter to her friend.

What Julia really wanted was a visit with her friend, a chance to discuss the present predicament of Theodore Parker. Julia and Elizy, friends and admirers of Parker, frequently exchanged news of his lectures and writings. As ardent a supporter of Theodore Parker as Julia was, Elizy was even more passionate. Elizy expressed her concern to Julia about the indictment of Theodore Parker for inciting his listeners to attempt to rescue the fugitive slave, Anthony Burns, by an attack on the courthouse where he was held. The action failed and Parker, along with six others, was indicted by the grand jury. Elizy had written:

> *What will they do with Parker think you? Since he has had as he says "the honor to be indicted." Will it be an honor; it is honorable to anyone to have the honesty, the moral courage, the true **piety** to refuse obedience to a wicked law, what a noble, what a god-like stand Theodore takes, but I am dreadfully afraid that they will bring him in guilty and consequently imprison him! for six months! Imprison Theodore six months for speaking his honest sentiments for truth and right in 'Old Faneuil Hall' Well it seems to me a strange state of things but similar things have taken place before; there was once a man **crucified** for adhering to the right. After all, we need have no fears for Theodore Parker, for he will always come off victorious, if not in this misjudging world surely in another. But I should feel very badly to have him imprisoned. I have for a long time been anticipating his lecture here about the first of January; being deprived of the privilege of hearing him every Sunday I shall consider it a greater treat than ever to hear him lecture; he may possible stop here, and I may have the honor of seeing him, shaking hands with him, and catching something of that inspiration that is in him, and emanates from him; but enough enough. You will think me fanatical; I should not dare to write so to every one; but I know that **you** know how to take me; I am not "in love with the man," but I do respect nay more than respect him as the embodiment of greatness and goodness—as the truly great good man of America.*

Julia understood and shared her friend's concern.

Although they shared many confidences, Julia was undecided about sharing with Elizy a letter she had received from her cousin, Nathan Robbins. Nathan, sixteen years Julia's senior, was a successful Faneuil Hall meat merchant and banker with double ties to Julia. Nathan was a nephew of her beloved Grandfather Stephen Robbins; his wife, Eliza, was Hannah Robbins' niece—one of the local girls who picked up cut furs at Eli's mill to sew at home, making muffs and tippets, the fur edging for coats.

Were Elizy walking beside her, Julia might ask if her friend agreed with Nathan's assessment of herself. Even two months after receiving his letter, Julia still felt exposed by his analysis. It had started simply enough on her part. In thanking Nathan for his surprising gifts of a bracelet and a purse, given for no reason Julia could fathom, she had written, *"I cannot see why you should make such presents to me."* Nathan had seized on her remark and expressed his view that Julia

> *supposed there was not a being in this wide world that cared for your happiness or welfare or would like to be cherished in your pleasurable recollections.*

Was she really so alienated from family and friends or did this feeling surface occasionally? Nathan's words made her sound bitter and self-absorbed. If that were not sufficient, Nathan continued with a comparison of two Julias, *"the girl of the other days and the girl of mature life."* He added:

> *And I see and admire the energy and ambition, with which she seeks to stamp her maturer [sic] life; no[t] bending to adverse circumstances. On the other hand, a highly commendable determination to be independent. Would there were more such who bear the name of woman. . . . your history, or your contact with the world had been such, as to leave on your mind the impression, that all action was based entirely upon equivalents, or in other words, that all action originates in selfishness, that, alone, being the motive power of human action. When I reflect upon the past, I am not surprised that you should have come to that conclusion. Trace your history along back for a few years.*

Nathan then wrote about the selfishness, the bitterness, and the baseness that he saw in a person he identified, not by name, but only as *"your and my relative."* Explaining that not everyone was like this, he hoped his presents brought Julia pleasure and would convey his interest in her *"prosperity and happiness."* True, she did seek independence but she did not need his approval to do so! She was not one of his four daughters, unfortunately all deceased, but a thirty-six-year-old woman who had been working in Lowell for the past three years. Hadn't she and Ellen handled the family's legal tangles for the past several years? Was Nathan correct in ascribing to her the belief that selfishness determines all actions? Her work for Washington Goode and at the Anti-Slavery Bazaar certainly belied this. Julia was wary of his seemingly sudden interest and gifts, his hope of seeing her again and his wish of hearing from her. How differently he portrayed her from how she saw herself as the person who tried to follow Emerson's and Parker's instructions for a good life. Why did she not see at least some of Nathan's view when she observed herself in a mirror?

How could she put all this in a letter to Elizy? She still was sorting through her reactions to Nathan's bold comments. Nathan had written of two Julias. Who was the real Julia? As the Lowell Company entrance was just ahead, Julia pushed the thoughts of Elizy and Cousin Nathan from her mind. Today she was to begin a new pattern; already she had images of swirls of flowers and scrolls in mind.

An attack on Senator Sumner shocks his supporters
June 3, 1856

Both Julia and her friend Elizy Gerry were relieved to hear that Theodore Parker's indictment for his role in attempting to rescue a fugitive slave had been dismissed after a few weeks. There were, however, other worrying events reported in newspapers, lectures, and letters from family and friends—most notably, the news that arrived from the Gerrys, Parker Pillsbury, and Julia's sister. Now living in St. Louis, Ellen frequently relayed information that conveyed the mood from the middle of the increasingly divided country.

In the early evening light enhanced by an oil lamp to better illuminate her pattern, Julia pulled out Ellen's letter from St. Louis, written on Tuesday, May 27. There on the third page was the heart of Ellen's letter.

Poor Sumner, I hope Massachusetts is not to lose one of the noblest bravest son's [sic] of whom I always felt so proud of.

Ever since Julia had heard the news of the caning of Senator Sumner as he sat at his desk in the Senate on May 22, her thoughts kept wandering to the horrific event. Two days earlier, in Senate debate over opening Kansas to slavery, the Free Soil Senator from Massachusetts was only stating his beliefs when he declared that permitting slavery in the state would be a rape of Kansas. With his speech, Sumner had redeemed Massachusetts from the shame of Webster's support for the Compromise of 1850 with its hated Fugitive Slave Law. Many of Sumner's supporters, Julia and Ellen included, had justified Sumner's tirade against pro-slavery senators, Andrew Butler of South Carolina among them. Sumner had called slavery "Butler's mistress," and for this, he paid a heavy price. While Sumner sat at his Senate desk writing letters and signing copies of his Kansas speech, Butler's nephew, South Carolina Representative Preston Brooks, repeatedly and brutally struck Sumner with a heavy cane. Sumner was defenseless against the blows. In an effort to escape the vicious attack, Sumner used the strength of his thighs to rip his desk from the floor where it was bolted, finally falling bloody and unconscious. Sumner, the persistent voice against slavery and for freedom was silenced; for how long, no one knew.

The tangle of politics mirrored the tangle of threads on Julia's table. The Lowell Company produced not only carpets, but coarse cotton cloth that was sold to plantation owners to clothe their slaves. Sumner had seen and denounced the conspiracy of planters and mill owners almost a decade ago. He called one the lords of the lash; the other, the lords of the loom. Lowell was as divided as the rest of the country. Julia had her own struggle when she accepted the position at the Lowell Company. For her, independence trumped ideology. True, the mills of Lowell depended on slave labor for raw material, but the endless yards of cotton cloth vastly eased the lives and chores of countless women. Theodore Parker cited the mill cities of Lowell and Lawrence as "two enormous Old Testament women, spinning and weaving year out and in, day and night both." Julia was cheered when she heard that Amos A. Lawrence, textile industrialist of the family and city of that name, had offered the bachelor Sumner his home as a place for recuperation from the beating. Talk was also swirling about a recent visitor to the home of the former Lowell Company Director, William Appleton. The visitor was Georgia Senator Robert Toombs, who had stood by as Brooks assaulted Sumner.

None of the news was good; violence was spreading across the country. Ellen's letter also reported on the Southerners who were rushing into Kansas to counter the New Englanders supported by the Amos Lawrence-financed New England Emigrant Aid Society. The day before Sumner's beating, pro-slavers had raided the free-state town of Lawrence. Describing the Southerners heading to the fray, Ellen wrote:

> *There is a good deal of excitement regarding Kansas affairs hereabouts [T]wo hundred of the most fiendish piratical men from Lousania [sic], & South that ever was seen from all accounts of them I should think they were on their way to Kansas I should think that Wolves would run away from them.*

Who would now speak with as strong a voice as Sumner for Massachusetts and the causes the Commonwealth held dear? Who would now rail against the Fugitive Slave Law, the domestic slave trade, and the expansion of slavery into the territories? Julia had been so pleased when the deadlocked Senate election in the Massachusetts legislature was broken by individual towns' sending instructions to their representatives to vote for Sumner. When the news of his victory had reached East Lexington at the end of April 1851, she tried unsuccessfully to get candles to illuminate in celebration. Sumner began his term in the Senate that December with the hopes of all those against slavery resting in his powerful orations.

Julia perused the other three pages of Ellen's letter. Descriptions of beautiful St. Louis roses that Aunt Caira would love, of Horace Mann's efforts to establish a state normal school in the west, of the hot weather without the cool New England nights but with an abundance of mosquitoes, even of Ellen's idea to try manufacturing wines from their East Lexington grapes now that she had seen how this was done, did not eradicate Julia's single thought of "Poor Sumner" or her regret that she had not been one of the five thousand Bostonians at the Faneuil Hall rally for Sumner. Julia extinguished the oil lamp and hurried back to her room at Mrs. Adams' house, where she was now boarding, with her head aching and her heart heavy with thoughts of Bleeding Kansas and Bleeding Sumner.

A loss in Lexington; letters and visitors to Lowell
APRIL 24, 1857

Last June when Julia was upset over the attack on Senator Sumner, she little expected that three months later, in September 1856, she would join her family in grieving over the loss of their patriarch. Her father, Eli Robbins, died of apoplexy (a stroke in today's medical lexicon) a few months shy of his seventieth birthday.

When his father Stephen Robbins died a decade earlier, at age eighty-nine, he died "young" by his reckoning. Eli, after his seventy years, was old; a once ambitious and successful businessman, he was brought down by the Panic of 1837. Although court documents filed after his death listed him only as a "furrier," he had played a prominent role in the development of East Lexington. One local historian who knew him described him thus.

> Eli Robbins . . . [was one] of the most enterprising and energetic men this town ever had. Upon receiving the fur-dressing business from his father, he increased the facilities for manufacturing by substituting machinery for hand-labor, when practicable; yet, with this addition, a hundred or more hands were employed. Besides the fur business, he had a dry-good and grocery store, carried on a large farm, and was largely engaged in building. No one ever contributed more towards making Main Street [Massachusetts Avenue] in East Lexington what it is at the present time than he.
>
> Many of the large shade trees were set out by him, and many of the buildings he erected; his lands were always for sale at reasonable prices, and in every possible way he was ever ready to lend a helping hand to others. Strange as it may seem, amid all the demands upon his time, he for several years taught dancing in this and other towns in the vicinity; more, perhaps, for pleasure than for profit. Although he had no knowledge of music, he could play the violin quite skillfully, and was the only person I ever saw that could play and dance at the same time. The old adage so often exemplified, of having too many irons in the fire, soon brought reverses, which, with other circumstances, reduced his resources beyond revival.

After his reversal of fortune in the Panic of 1837, Eli's mill and shop were lost in a disastrous fire in August of 1848. The loss, not covered by insurance, totaled $1,800. This was at a time when the town's annual school bill was $1,838.57 and the expenditure on town roads amounted to $1,901.07. The fire was another blow for Eli who had lived for years by making do and doing without. The fact that he died without a will only compounded these problems for his family, especially Ellen and Julia. However, one obligation for the family ended early in 1856 with the death of Andrew C. Davison for whom Eli had provided a home.

It was of comfort to Julia that her father's death was noted in the *Liberator*: "DIED–At East Lexington, 7th inst., ELI ROBBINS, Esq., aged 69 years, 10 mos." Eli had outlived his older siblings—his brothers Stephen and Samuel who passed away in their mid-sixties, and his beloved sister Abby Langdon, the Vermonter-by-marriage who so welcomed his daughters—but was survived by two younger siblings: Lot, in residence at McLean Sanitarium, and Caira, a caring aunt to his offspring. Hannah, his wife of forty-seven years, lost her mainstay. His son and namesake Eli, who as a young man turned to New York City for his life and livelihood, had slipped from the family circle. Of his four daughters, two were married, Abigail Lothrop and Ellen Stone; two were single, Hannah Maria and Julia, his favorite. She had been his right-hand in arranging speakers for his hall and had taken his stance against slavery. Eli had been concerned for Julia, a spinster often at odds with her mother. How long could she survive at the Lowell Company? After a visit home, Ellen with her two and a half year old daughter would be rejoining her husband Abner in St. Louis at some point, precipitating Julia's return to East Lexington.

The year 1856 had not ended well for Julia; life in Lexington was difficult after the loss of her father. In November James Buchanan, a Democrat from Pennsylvania, was elected President of the United States. He followed New Hampshire Democrat Franklin Pierce who had won the presidency as a dark horse candidate in 1852. Little had been done in the last four years to address the country's tensions over slavery—little other than endless debating. Some say Pierce lost heart over the death of his third and only surviving son, eleven-year-old Benny, who was killed in a train accident two months prior to the inauguration. Like many other Northerners, Julia was bitterly disappointed when Pierce, in addition to endorsing strict enforcement of the Fugitive Slave Act, supported the Kansas-Nebraska Act, which permitted Kansas settlers to decide for themselves the issue of slavery in their state. Julia had few illusions that Buchanan, a Southern sympathizer, boded well for abolitionist interests. Her hopes had rested with John C. Fremont, known as the "Pathfinder" for his western explorations. The first national candidate of the new Republican Party, he ran on a platform of "Free soil, free speech and Fremont." Now the Democratic candidate was in the White House; time was slipping away and with it any hope of mediating the slavery conflict. Some days the wave of pessimism Julia experienced when thinking about the country extended to her own situation.

Julia was only a few months away from marking the fifth anniversary of her arrival at the Lowell Company. The five years of independence came at a cost of five years of exhaustion and some social isolation. She had no time for a diary and her letters frequently ended with *"In haste, Julia."* Although Julia never seemed to have the time to write as long a letter as she planned, she received letters with pleasure—most of the time. When she studied literature at Adams Female Academy had she come across the words of John Donne? That English poet wrote that ". . . more than kisses, letters mingle souls; For, thus friends absent speak." Did some of Julia's correspondents use letters to speak more intimately of what they dared not say in person? This was most likely not true for her female friends, Elizy Gerry and Mary Plumer, whose heart-to-heart talks were an important part of any visit, but her male correspondents were another story. There had been her cousin Nathan's letter two years earlier and one last year from another relative, Stillman Lothrop, her sister Abby's husband. Describing himself as an outcast, Lothrop had the temerity to write Julia at Lowell, saying:

> *I think I have some claim on you, however, not much, because you are "Sister in law" which goes but for little with Some people—but because when we feel desire for companionship & are interested in an individual, and esteem them, we consider that we have a right to their very good will in return. On this ground I offer you my friendship hoping that you have felt kindly interest in my welfare. I have felt a great deal more for you than was ever expressed & I will hope you have not been indifferent to me.*

How dare her brother-in-law, Reverend Lothrop, who had abandoned her sister Abigail, leaving her more dependent on her family, write to Julia in this manner? Lothrop continued his letter:

Being unmarried, you no doubt are anticipating the full fruition of a ten-
der sympathy with some congenial companion. You will indeed be fortunate
if you find such an [sic] one. I doubt if you ever found one of your own Sex.
. . . I believe you have a kind & good heart, and no doubt feel better towards
me than I think. But you have "avoided me" heretofore. I do not wish to
suppose this austerity of manner to have arisen from your heart. I presume
you thought it good policy. However I wish to love you sincerely and purely
whether you can return it or not.

Julia's sister Abigail may have some claim on her, as might Abigail's sons, her nephews Follen and George, but claims ended there. When things were tense at the Robbins homestead in 1855, Julia had stayed at various times with the Lothrops, but she always paid her way—there were no favors owed. Earlier discussions with Lothrop about Brook Farm and other topics did not justify his present interest. Julia's reply to Lothrop, if there was one, is nowhere to be found among the family papers.

The letters Julia most longed for—from Davison—were sparse. Was he oblivious to what attracted other men to Julia? Did his silences, the long stretches of time between letters, indicate his lack of interest?

Julia turned her attention to the letter that had arrived for her that morning. She had recognized the slanted handwriting of Parker Pillsbury on this four-sided missive. Thankfully, he did not try to save paper as did some of her other correspondents by writing in tiny script or in two directions on the same sheet. Poor Pillsbury! Ever inclined to gloom, a mood exacerbated by his poor health, he certainly didn't seem happy. In this letter he reverted to his assault on the institution of marriage.

I have long believed & said that we were too far gone to choose Marriage
partners; and that the Institution is scarcely worth preserving. For it is
doubtful whether it is productive of most happiness or Misery.

After expounding on the sad state of affairs in the world and a similar state for friendships, Pillsbury admitted to wishing to know of his friends—their joys, their grief. She read his depiction of her at work at the Lowell Company:

Your image, bending over that table, often comes up before me. I love to
think of your studio, with its colors & combinings, as the altar of Beauty,
and yourself as the Presiding Priestess of Ministration.

Surprised but pleased that the famed radical abolitionist had visited her at the Lowell Company, she was less sure of how pleased the mill agent had been to see Pillsbury in a mill that depended on slave labor for its raw material. Julia was beyond concerning herself with what most of the world thought of her, but she was convinced that only Pillsbury would think of her in such exalted terms. Would that Davison saw her in the same light!

Julia had other visitors as well. In her years at Lowell, she invited family and friends to call at the Lowell Company's Counting House. This two-story building in the Greek Revival style with its wide corner pilasters was easy to find in the mill complex. The Lowell Company, like the other mills of the city, was a major attraction for visitors ranging from office holders to personal friends and family as well as individuals interested in the new technology. With its ten major manufacturing companies and a host of smaller ones, Lowell produced 2,100,000 yards of cotton cloth and over 20,000 yards of woolen cloth each week. It was such a magnet that visitors were advised to have cards of introduction to gain entry to many of the mills. An 1848 visitor's handbook stated that for the Lowell carpet works, "cards are absolutely necessary." For Julia's visitors, her name was sufficient for access to the Lowell Company complex.

Julia's mother Hannah spent two days in the city in September of 1853 when Julia's work was still a novelty. Her sister Ellen came on more than one occasion, bringing clothes and food from home. The fruit that her cousin George Simonds brought when he came to visit was always appreciated. When a friend employed as a calico print designer in a Newburyport mill came calling, the conversation was technical; with Parker Pillsbury, talk ranged from family issues to the politics of abolition.

Julia took great satisfaction in guiding her visitors around the mill's ten acres, never losing her way in the sprawl of buildings. Unlike the other mills, the Lowell Company had no central mill yard providing a plan of order. She showed them not only the pattern designing and cutting rooms, but the enormous weaving room, illuminated by skylights and hundreds of oil lamps. To avoid smoke from the lamps, only the best whale oil— sperm whale oil at $1.27 a gallon—was used. When Julia took a visitor on tour, she never knew exactly what to expect. A loom might be under repair or in full operation under the watchful eye of a fireman, an engineer, or an overseer. There was always cause for amazement. Julia never had a thought that any untoward word might be spoken to her as a female. The Lowell Company had a strict policy that

> The COMPANY will not continue to employ any person who shall be wanting in proper respect to the females employed by the COMPANY or who shall smoke within the COMPANY'S premises, or be guilty of inebriety, or other improper conduct.

For Julia, a highlight of her tours was a visit to the dye house. She loved the swirl of colors in the open vats and the swish of the skeins of yarns as the dyers moved the wool with their long poles. Only after the yarn had dried and was wound on bobbins was it ready for weaving by the female operatives on the newly-installed power looms. Then the patterns would spring to life. Julia delighted in visitors who broke up the long days as, most of the time, contact with the world beyond the environs of the Lowell Company was limited to letters sent and received. Sometimes the letters were enclosed in parcels. To cousin George Simonds, for his interest in politics and causes, Julia sent a copy of *Vox Populi*, the local paper, which took a stand against the ruling establishment in the city of Lowell. A letter to Ellen might accompany Julia's laundry along with an explanation, as if one were needed: *"These things need a good **boiling** and so I send them home."* Letters to Ellen were part of an on-going dialog; some were written hastily at Julia's boarding house or in minutes stolen from working on a pattern.

> *I paint very industriously through the day and rest upon it as well as I can through the night, am generally very well. . . . Do not cough much now. . . . I tried your medicine three or four days as you recommended it, kept me sick all the time. It might have helped my cough but I concluded the remedy was worse than the disease.*

In her letters, Julia's pride in her association with the Lowell Company was obvious. She exulted:

> **We** *make 4,160 yards carpeting per day at our establishment.* ***Our designing department*** *cost is 18,000 doll[ar]s a year.*

With the pride there was also exhaustion: *"We have [a] good long evening to ourselves but [I] generally feel rather the worse for the **wear**."*

After five years in Lowell, Julia was tired of the noise, of the city itself, of traveling to the mill in Biddeford, Maine, for the Lowell Company. There were compensations—she was able to indulge a taste for oysters, to spend $9—over a week's wages—on a single silk dress, and to purchase a pair of India rubber boots for $2. At a time when coffee was 15 cents a pound and sugar 9 cents a pound, she had treated herself to Emerson's books at a cost of $2.40 and to Alcott's *Conversations* for $1. She had seized the opportunity to attend lectures by Emerson and others at the Lowell Anti-Slavery Festival.

Never free of her East Lexington responsibilities, Julia traveled home most weekends. It was Julia who paid almost half the taxes on the Lexington property with her share of this annual levy approximating a month's salary. Since the death of her father the previous September, home was a changed place.

In Lowell, Julia also wondered about her future. Parker Pillsbury, in his condolence letter on her father's death, had remarked that he had looked for Julia at the Medical School in Philadelphia. He remembered an earlier expressed aspiration of Julia's to go to medical school. What other hopes had she once entertained? Next month would mark her thirty-eighth birthday. In a world defined for women by family, she was still single. With evident weariness, she wrote to her family, *"My Dear Robbins,"* of her wishes:

> *I have no love for city life left but my old wish for a rural life is as strong as ever, a good garden—horse and cow, being the height of my ambition—but I want a Morgan horse, and a Jersey cow.*

In farm animals, as well as in fashion, Julia had excellent taste.

Julia feels alone against the world
MARCH 30, 1860

Julia's world was once more circumscribed by the borders of East Lexington with occasional ventures to anti-slavery lectures and other activities in Boston, Concord, and nearby towns. In October 1857, Julia had

Four years after the death of Eli Robbins, Ellen wrote her sister Julia, reminding her to take steps to preserve their father's photograph.

returned to live in East Lexington, her presence mandated by Ellen's move to St. Louis to be with her businessman husband, Abner Stone. Legal difficulties resulting from Julia's and Ellen's responsibility to provide for their mother and sister were exacerbated by the death of their father in the fall of 1856. When Eli's businesses failed in the Panic of 1837, his lands and properties were placed in trust with Julia and Ellen as overseers of mortgages, leases, and rentals. This prevented confiscation of Eli's estate during his lifetime. As the mortgages were held by second parties and the leases by third parties, ground was ripe for disagreements. Some of the resulting legal discord colored the relationship between Julia and her mother. Hannah, in her seventy-third year, was as set in her ways of running her household as she had been since her marriage a half-century earlier. Julia, tired but exhilarated from her years of independence, displayed her usual enterprise in dealing with the legal morass and problems at home. When Parker Pillsbury read the death notice for Eli Robbins in the *Liberator*, he wrote to Julia from Ohio. In addition to expressing his sympathy, Pillsbury suggested that surviving parents *"appear a sort of cover to us, like the front line in battlefield."* Without her father, life became a battlefield for Julia. Gone were her dreams of yesteryear, replaced with property disputes, squabbles over the farm lease, arguments with lawyers, and admonishments from those she depended on for friendship and support.

The events of those years are found in letters, telling only snatches of the story. In the draft of a letter seemingly intended for Parker Pillsbury, Julia wrote, *"The past winter has been a long dark season to me, the **darkest** of my life."* Pillsbury's letters to Julia give hints of her predicament as he wrote, *"I know not hardly which most grieved me, your sad state of affairs, or my own utter inability to aid in your extrication. . . ."*

Counseling patience with the courts of *"so-called justice,"* Pillsbury noted that seldom was there *"a more cruel & flagrant instance"* of injustice than that suffered by Julia. Even when there was *"seeming success,"* the legal proceedings exacted their toll.

> *To come in such collision with one's own Mother and sister, and family, is a calamity not to be compensated by a simple verdict of a Jury or ruling of a court, however favorable to our side of the controversy.*

From St. Louis, Ellen badgered Julia with demands for action: find the best management for the farm; have the fruit trees trimmed, using the fruit as payment; don't do anything that will forfeit her and Julia's role as trustees; follow their father's example and be a peacemaker; don't write in pencil, which is difficult to read as it gets rubbed in travel; find out the provisions of a new law on redeeming mortgages. Ellen scolded Julia *"You seem to be always in a great hurry when you write."* As if Julia had nothing else to do, she asked, *"P.S. Did you do anything towards getting the Photograph of father done! I am afraid it will fade out if not attended to."*

One letter from St. Louis noted that cousin George Simonds, who paid his way in the household, had sent young Ellen a *"pretty Antislavery present of needlebook & picture."* Julia was directed to thank George for this gift. When George moved out of the Robbins homestead, Julia was relieved, writing to Pillsbury:

> *George has taken his departure I am thankful to say. He became very disagreeable. I miss his books & papers . . . but that is nothing to the great **gain** by the absence of himself. . . .*

Ellen was furious. *"How came George to go off!"* she demanded, as if that, too, were Julia's fault. Occasionally, Ellen would soften her tone, invite Julia to St. Louis, send a birthday present of a fine French collar *"to wear with the square necked dresses,"* and assure her sister that *"You know you can have half of my loaf as long as it lasts."*

Julia defended her decisions.

*I have had to work very hard to accomplish **all** I have done **alone**. I have endeavored to proceed according to law—& you may thank me that I did. You talk about the decision of a Judge with regard to it. You seem to have **strangely enough forgotten** that every step I have taken this year has been **sifted** before two or three lawyers and a **Judge** and no fault found. . . . It certainly is your **duty** to take some care and responsibility. It is not right that I should be left to take the whole brunt of the battle alone. . . . I hardly look on any side that I do not see some **snake in the grass**. You ought to consider that to sit still out there in St. Louis, & think what might be done is a very different thing from being here and **doing it**. You do not seem to understand about things. . . . Here is this great farm which must not run to waste. Will you help to keep it in decent order or what will you do with it? It is in far better condition this year to yield an income than last year.*

Ellen shot back, declaring her responsibility for *"nobody's acts, sayings, doings, but **my own**."*

Ellen wasn't the only one to express her exasperation. The following month, on February 20, 1859, in a letter that filled all four sides of folded paper, with the ink seeping through the thin paper and with a postscript written in the opposite direction on the first page, Julia responded.

I received your letter of Jan. 27th. I was somewhat astonished at the contents. I will defy anybody to do any better than I did last year under the circumstances. Let me tell you I was fortunate to lease it at all, much more so [to] find as faithful a person as I did. If I had leased it to the angel Gabriel they would not have been pleased. . . . If you can do better than I have, what are you thinking about not to be about it. Is it your duty to stay in St. Louis with folded hands? I have been looking about for an opportunity to sell or to let but I find nobody hankering after it during legal difficulties. . . .

Also grating on Julia was the lack of help from her thirty-three-year-old brother Eli. A successful merchant, Eli could have solved their problems with the stroke of a pen, had he the inclination to do so, but he was removed from their monetary difficulties; after all, his name was not on the deed and the lease. Julia's tone is clear as she wrote to Ellen, "*Your* *brother Eli is, I **hear**, opening a great store on Broadway, New York, and mak-ing all the flourish that would indicate great riches."*

But, it seems, there were more than just the legal issues. In one let-ter, Julia wrote, *"If I had not been so **bothered** & **perplexed** in every way I should have had everything arranged fair & square at the end of this year."* By January of 1859, however, Hannah and Hannah Maria had moved out of the East Lexington home! In a letter dated January 7, 1859, Mary Plumer addressed Julia's situation.

> *How do your business matters come on? Has your Mother taken any new steps? I trust she will see her error & come quietly home, & peace be restored. What does Ellen write? Is she not coming home? I wish she would. . . .*

With this turn of events, Julia wrote to Ellen, *"The lawyers say the wisest course for us to pursue is to keep up the home for Mother & Hannah. If they choose to go off and leave it, it is not our fault."* Ellen, in contact with her mother, wrote Julia in January 1859.

> *All I gather from Mother is that she and Hannah want to live at home but not while you and Mr. Barrett is there. The condition of things seems to be unfortunate.*

This is the first mention of John Barrett in any of Julia's correspondence. No letter or diary entry proclaims Julia's first meeting with Barrett; no letters from him to Julia are in the collection of family papers. One won-ders if this rustic Concord farmer was the subject of Parker Pillsbury's criticism in November 1858. After noting Julia's abolitionist activities,

> *It gave me great pleasure to hear Mr. Emerson say what he did about you at his house, the other evening after you were gone.*

he continued,

> *It did not add to that pleasure however, to see you in company, whose com-plexion and carriage did not quite fill my eye, nor meet my wishes were he there in any other than a secular position & we thought he was.*

Who was Julia's escort that evening? Neither Emerson's *Journals* nor let-ters provide any clues. What right did Pillsbury have to express his disap-proval of Julia's companion for the evening? It hardly seems that he would be critical of the Harvard-educated Davison. Julia was weary of Pillsbury's negative tone. How could she forget what he had once written her?

You did not tell me to whom you "might be married sometime." Do not be hasty about it. Marriage is I fear a desperate Lottery. Not all blanks to be sure, but alas, too many.

But was it marriage to Davison at which Julia had hinted? Decades later, in February of 1907, Davison, by this point a long-time city engineer in Pensacola, Florida, wrote cryptically to a Harvard friend and classmate of the event that he claimed changed his life. In a letter tucked into the Harvard College Class of 1845 Secretary's File, Davison referred to

. . . my two disastrous years in Boston, 1858–60, which reduced me from a competence and a good prospect of ample wealth, to the foot of the ladder; all commencing with endorsing, (a mere form, you know,) and ending with my paying other people's debts at the cost of all that I had.

As the death of his blind invalid father in 1856 had ended any obligation Davison might have felt to call at the Robbins's homestead, we are left to wonder on whose behest Davison had acted before he disappeared from Julia's life. Was it on her behalf, or that of his *"unlucky brother,"* or even his college roommate, William Plumer, by then the father of five surviving children? And disappear Davison did, but not without a fight from Julia.

In a letter to Julia on September 29, 1858, Mary Plumer expressed her bewilderment at Julia's request to ask her brother, William, about Davison, his Harvard roommate, but not to share any of her letters with William. Defending her brother and his friendship with Davison, Mary cautioned,

Davison is his particular friend, as you are also. If there is any difficulty between you I think he would be not likely to do anything either way.

The *"difficulty"* mentioned in Mary's letter was in regards to another woman, Jeanie (Jean Cameron Dow), a Southern woman whom Quincy Dow had met, courted, and married when he was working in Pensacola, Florida. Now Quincy's widow, Jeanie was visiting her in-laws in Epping where she had met Davison at a gathering at the Plumer home. Julia was not likely to be consoled by Mary's stance on this matter. Mary advised Julia:

> *If D[avison] is forgetting off his engagements I should have too much pride to ask him back. . . . he still has the highest regard for you & respect. If he is negligent it is either some whim, or he is attracted to some one else. That is my opinion—has he never had things odd ways before! I had an idea he was odd & peculiar—I never thought him a desirable match for you. Or that you were likely to be particularly happy together—I'm afraid you were not well suited to each other. I did not know till your last letter that he did not call on you. Now that certainly you must have expected from his friendship—if for nothing else in this crisis in your affairs. I do not wonder you felt Lost & deeply wounded.*
>
> *I cannot account for it.*

Three weeks later there was a six-page letter from Mary dated October 21, 1858. On the thin pages one can, with concentration, make out Mary's recounting the news of her friends and plans for travel to Boston. There was an invitation to Epping and a reaffirmation of her friendship with Julia. Buried in the middle of the letter, came the news Julia suspected.

> *As for D[avison] and Jeanie I expect there is something between them. I think now that he must have been attracted towards her when he saw her at our house. Tho[ugh] it was the last thing I thought of then. I will tell you all my thoughts when I see you—be careful what you say & do; so as not to commit yourself & show y[ou]r feelings. It is of no use to multiply words about it. It is painful for me to think or write on the subject. Peace be between me and thee. . . . I received a letter from Jeanie. . . . In it she speaks freely to me of her engagement, the first time anything had past [sic] between us on the subject, [she] said her Mother & her friends in Florida had given their consent, & I suppose they will be married in the course of the year. . . . How entirely you misjudge William. It is really too bad. If I did not think you carried out of yourself & blinded just now, I should feel—well—I will say nothing about it. It is of no use—but it is hard because Davison has not fulfilled your expectations. That you should blame others instead of, & more than him—why can't you just face it to him, & then let it rest. It is between you & him—no one else that I am acquainted*

*with is to blame, of that I am well convinced. You write as if you expected
me to do something—for the life of me I cannot see what. . . .*

After reading this, Julia had most likely thrown herself across her bed,
blinded by hurt and fury. How clearly she remembered when she had
written Quincy inquiring about engineering prospects for her friend
Davison and her urging Davison to meet Quincy. Never had she anticipated this turn of events—Quincy deceased and Davison in love with his
widow, Jeanie. Mary explained:

*When D[avison] was in P[ensacola] he saw Jeanie. It looks as if they met
by agreement & understood each other. We will talk over all your letter,
everything in it when we meet.*
Till then yours ever in love, M.E.P.

Four weeks later, on November 20, 1858, Mary Plumer, just home
from a journey and immersed in preparations for Thanksgiving, took time
to write to Julia. Having learned that Jeanie was at the Dows, she paid a
social call, hoping to talk with her, but she was too late; Jeanie had already
left for Boston, en route to New York. Mary related her conversation at
the Dows.

*I think [I] made you & your case appear in a better light than it had pre-
viously done. One thing I found out, that it is of no use for you to lay your
plans or expect to induce Jeanie to give up Davison, by anything you or any
one else can say or do. She is a resolute, persevering little piece, tho' so quiet,
& so many of her friends this way advise her holding on that there is not
doubt she will.*

Noting that her extended family, friends, and neighbors were conversant
with Julia's displeasure, Mary continued without any indication how this
gossip had spread.

*It is very unpleasant for me to hear your affairs thus discussed,& your name
banded about. The whole seems like a dream—it is so unlike you & what
you have always liked. One thing provoked me, & that was that all seemed
to have got the impression that you intended to prosecute Davison for "breach
of promise." I indignantly repelled the idea, as so inconsistent with your
delicacy & refinement of character, & with all your notions of things, &*

Mrs. Dow said that she agreed with me. She had such an idea of you,& had defended you when the others made the charges. She had always thought you very refined & ladylike. I was gratified at the way she talked. Jeanie's family were opposed to her marrying & settling at the North, but they gave their consent to a Northerner before, & probably could again. . . . Jeanie seems to be very fascinating to gentlemen. It seems two other gentlemen were in love with her. So I am told here. I am truly sorry she has not chosen one of them. What a deal of trouble & unhappiness it would have saved!

Assuring Julia that she shared *"anxious & troubled hours"* over this, more *"than Davison or any other man"* deserved, Mary tried to console her friend *"that it is all for the best."* Promising to always speak a good word for Julia, Mary gave Julia this advice:

You see, dear Julia, that when a lady come[s] forward to claim a gentleman & persists in asserting her rights, when he as reasonably denies them, it puts her in a false position.& the world do not feel for her as they ought— do not blame him as they ought. It is always so—a man can do as he pleases—a woman has few rights & still fewer privileges to assert them. The opinion of the world does not countenance her in so doing. She is said to be running after a man, & all sorts of unpleasant things are said. It is outrageous & sad that it is so—but so it is. We poor women cannot alter it. We must submit in silence, or we shall inevitably find ourselves put in a false position & exposed to condemnation or ridicule.

Writing with affection, Mary pronounced her judgment: *"Davison is no great loss."* Weary of this whole business, Mary wrote Julia *"how vexed & tried"* she was when she heard that Julia confronted Jeanie as she was boarding a train for New York with the accusation that *"she had twice injured you—that she got Quincy away from you, & now Davison."*

Julia was increasingly isolated—from her long-time friend Mary Plumer, over the matter of Davison, from her family over the legal tangles involving property, from her sister Ellen in St. Louis who judged sternly from a distance, from Parker Pillsbury who scolded her about her unidentified companion at Emerson's home, from her once best friend, her cousin George. Some years earlier, when her sister Ellen was being courted by her future husband Abner Stone and by another visitor to the Robbins' homestead, referred to only as Quimby, Julia weighed in with her opinion. She advised Ellen that Abner was *"a stick to lean upon."* Now, as the turbulent last years of the decade gave way to 1860, Julia found her own *"stick to lean upon"*—John Barrett.

Julia's patience had been sorely tested the last three years over property squabbles and contract interpretations. John Barrett, it seemed, was the only one who took her side. However, some disapproved of this relationship. Even Aunt Caira had noted her displeasure, scribbling in annoyance that Julia and Barrett were *"very cross"* to Julia's mother, Hannah. When Barrett accompanied Julia to seek a writ to turn out a tenant, Aunt Caira scoffed, *"this is doing good for a Concord man—to do as he has no right."* When the new year and new decade—1860—dawned, Julia prayed that things would be different. This spring Julia had reason to cherish the small streak of optimism that ran deep in her soul; she had turned a corner with the last legal settlement, Ellen's husband had taken ownership of the homestead, and there was now the chance of reconciliation with her widowed mother. Julia looked out the window at the yard and what she hoped would be the last of the snow. Crossing to the table, she sat down and dipped her pen in the inkwell.

> *Dear Mother,*
>
> *I hope you are not staying away because I am here. I fully understand that I **am to** leave **when** you **come back** to stay. Mr. Stone says that I interfere with his leasing the house to you. I supposed you thought that I was going to stay until you came. I shall begin to move the few things I have **out** today **if** I can get help. I hope you will come back with Hannah I should like to see you again before I go."*

Julia signed and dated the letter *March 30th, 1860 E[ast]. Lex[ington].*

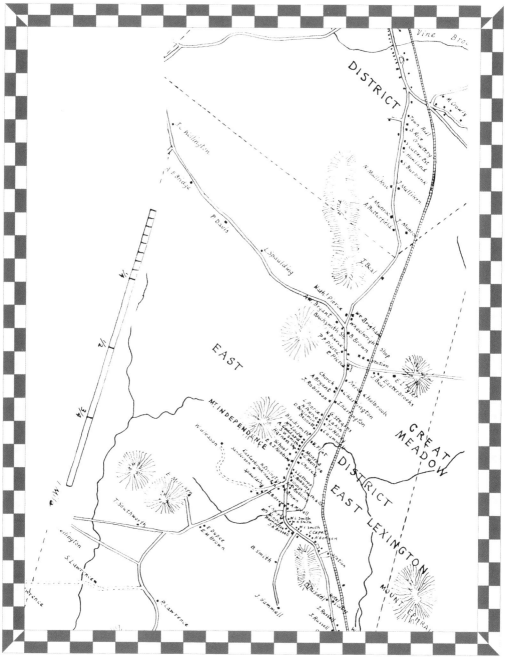

East Lexington: On this 1853 map of East Lexington, Ellen and Julia's property is just above the letters "ce" of Mt. Independence.

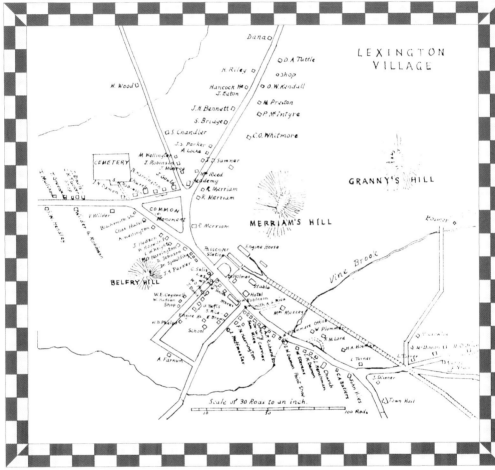

Lexington Village: An insert on the 1853 map of Lexington shows Lexington Village, today's Lexington Center. The monument noted on the Common is the Revolutionary War obelisk.

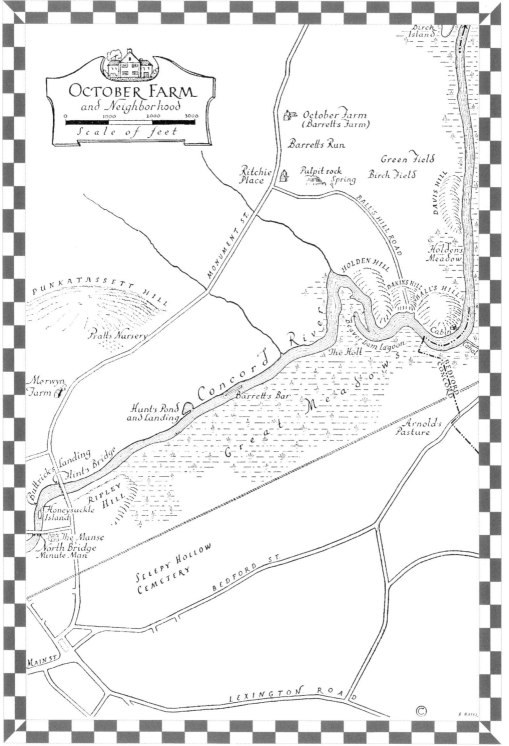

October Farm (Barrett's Farm): The Barrett Farm, later renamed October Farm, was on Monument Street, previously known as the River Road to Carlisle. By 1875 Julia and John owned 70 acres of land, some of which bordered the Concord River. In 1880 they bought the 11½ acre lot on Ball's Hill.

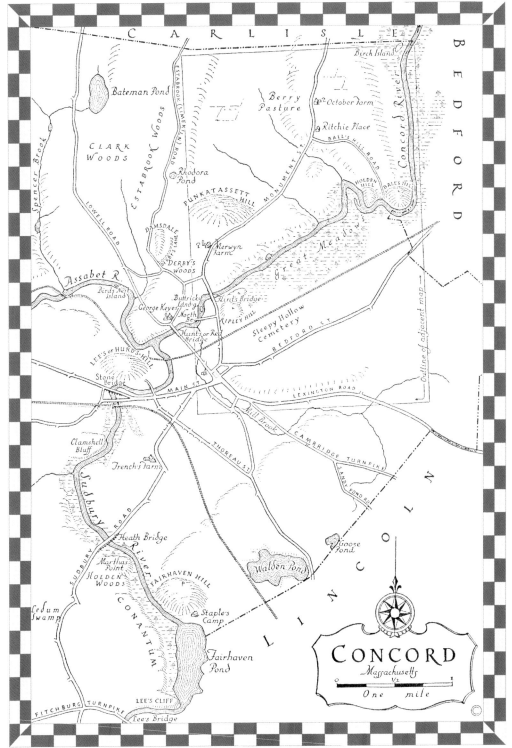

Town of Concord: After John's death in 1890, Julia remained on the farm for several years. Its new owner, William Brewster, a Harvard professor, ornithologist, and first president of the Massachusetts Audubon Society, called it October Farm. It was 2½ miles from the center of town.

CHAPTER 4

May 17, 1860: Farewell to the single life and the city

September 29, 1863: Concord, a town in time of war

March 12, 1874: Securing a farm and mourning a senator

July 18, 1883: The School of Philosophy—ideas for a summer day

November 23, 1886: A bazaar and petitions, this time for municipal suffrage

January 14, 1891: Life after two losses

Farewell to the single life and the city
MAY 17, 1860

For once, Julia's mood diverged from the country's; hers was the opposite of the nation's slide into pessimism. The Supreme Court's 1857 decision in the Dred Scott case had torn the country apart as the court ruled that the Missouri Compromise was unconstitutional. Now slavery could invade the previously free section of the Louisiana territory. Tension had been building between the Northern states and their Southern counterparts. Last fall, in October of 1859, the fiery abolitionist John Brown, with the financial support of some Massachusetts men, Theodore Parker among them, raided the federal arsenal at Harper's Ferry, Virginia, as a first step in a slave rebellion. Brown's hanging in December gave the North a martyr for the cause of abolition. Now the dispute raged in the political parties in this presidential election year.

Julia, who knew how differences and problems could tear apart a family, was not surprised that the Democrats were split over the issue of protecting slavery in the territories. Stephen A. Douglas emerged as the party's frontrunner on a platform of keeping the hands of Congress off the issue of slavery in the territories, of honoring Supreme Court decisions, and of acquiring Cuba. Two minority parties emerged—the Southern Democrats nominated John Breckinridge and the Constitutional Union Party picked a Massachusetts man, Edward Everett, as running mate to their presidential candidate, John Bell. Just the previous day, on May 16, 1860, the Republicans, who had participated in national elections for the first time only four years earlier, chose Abraham Lincoln as their presidential candidate. Lincoln had cemented his position on slavery a few months ago; at a speech at Cooper Union in New York City in February, he made clear "that no compromise with principle on the slavery extension issue was possible." Julia supported Lincoln and hoped for peace nationally and personally, even as prospects for keeping the Union together dimmed.

Personally, Julia had experienced a burst of optimism, finding her own stick to lean upon. Perhaps he wasn't the great love of her life as Davison had been for so many years, but Julia loved John Barrett for his companionship through her family squabbles and difficulties and for his quiet and undemanding presence. As of today, Thursday, the seventeenth of May, Julia and John were husband and wife, married by Reverend William Alger at the Bulfinch Street Church on Boston's Beacon Hill. Before beginning her life as the wife of a Concord farmer, Julia decided to show John the city of Boston as she said her farewell to the center of so much of her life—design school, lectures, walks and visits, bazaars and conventions.

John and Julia stood at their vantage point in the cupola of the Massachusetts State House, a popular viewing spot in Boston. From here, they were able to look down at the church where they had been married less than an hour ago. Tucked in between the brick townhouses lining Bulfinch Place, the church, with its gabled roof and brick exterior, was very different from Follen Church next to Julia's father's hall in East Lexington. Julia and John had signed the register at City Hall noting their ages, Julia forty and John thirty-three. Both recorded the names of their parents as well, Eli and Hannah S. Robbins for Julia, and Joel and Sarah R. Barrett for John. One wonders why Julia hadn't married in Follen Church in East Lexington where she and Hannah Maria had their own pew. Home in East Lexington was a difficult place for Julia now. Her father, who had always supported his favorite daughter's independent streak, was no longer living, and her mother, with whom Julia had perpetually clashed, was willing to disown her. Even if she had returned from St. Louis, Ellen's confinement with her second pregnancy would have prevented her attending her sister Julia's marriage. Ellen's second daughter, Mary, was born two months later, in July.

As John had supported Julia in her attempts to wade through the legal morass that was the Robbins' lot, her mother and even Aunt Caira took umbrage at him. Some of Julia's friends had raised eyebrows at her choice—a Concord farmer seven years her junior. Julia ignored them, not even bothering to remind them that East Lexington's beloved Charles Follen had married Eliza Cabot, a woman nine years his senior. Hadn't Transcendentalist Margaret Fuller's Italian nobleman been ten years her junior? Only the previous year John's neighbor William H. Hunt at age twenty had married a woman who was nine years older than he. There was talk at that time of Hunt's "attraction to a woman who was both more educated and cultivated than himself." Local gossips were sure to add the Barrett marriage with its similar comparison to their conversations. Julia would be untroubled by their comments, having learned from Emerson that "Character is higher than intellect."

Fortunately, the heat of the weekend before Julia's wedding was only a hint of summer, not a steady tenant as yet. Julia's silk dress from her last year in Lowell was perfect for this cool and fair Thursday in mid-May. Climbing the 168 winding steps to the cupola, John wondered how a photographer had ever lugged photographic equipment up here. Julia had told him of Hawes' panoramic photographs of the city and wanted John to see the scene for himself. From the four windows of the cupola there was an excellent view in all directions: north across Beacon Hill with its forest of brick chimneys and church steeples to the Bunker Hill Monument in Charlestown, southeast to the wharves crowded with sailing ships and to the islands sprinkled in Boston Harbor. Julia pointed out where she had heard Garrison ignite the crowd, where she had attended design school, and where she had volunteered at the Anti-Slavery Fair.

John's attention was captured by the view looking west; here at the edge of the Public Garden the city was "gaining ground." Beacon Street stretched west to where it met the mudflats of Back Bay and became Mill Dam. Railroad cars filled with gravel from Needham, a town to the southwest, dumped their loads onto marshes and mudflats to reclaim the area so the city would have room to grow. Indeed, the population was soaring, reaching 177,840 people, a thirty percent increase in only ten years. When the century began in 1800, the city had boasted of its 24,937 inhabitants; it was currently more than seven times that number. John realized that the entire population of the town of Concord—2,246 people—could fit into a few city blocks.

John looked at the water the city couldn't live with, the "polluted tidal estuary" that was the Charles River, and the water it couldn't live without, the Beacon Hill reservoir, a fortress-like structure behind the State House. John's thoughts turned to the water he knew best—the Concord River, which edged his farm and defined his life. John knew its meanderings and flows, its quiet refuge from his four sisters and his chores. Discipline had not been a strong suit with John's father who could not extend to his son what he himself did not possess. So John had grown up with time to explore, to learn the habits of the partridge and the snapping turtle, the muskrat and the heron. It was this world with tangles of columbines and fields of wild geraniums that he would show Julia. There were the apple orchards, now "domed masses of white and rose-tinted blossoms." In mid-summer there would be white water lilies afloat on the river and, at September's end, what never failed to surprise him, "the maple swamps ablaze with orange and scarlet."

Julia herself was lost in thought. For the last two years John had been her support, even going to the lawyer with her in the endless meetings over property, as she struggled with her family and her responsibilities. Julia would have liked nothing better than to have been married some weeks earlier when she moved out of her East Lexington home, but John had been too busy with his farm. While she waited for some slack time on the farm so John could leave his chores with a clear conscience, she had stayed with friends in Boston. Even this morning, when she was completing the marriage register, she had listed Boston, not East Lexington, as her residence.

Julia's reverie ended with the sound of John's voice. The Public Garden assumed its shape once again and she called John's attention to the distant side of the Garden, to Arlington Street where it intersected with the start of a "great central Avenue" 200 feet wide, which, according to city plans, was "destined at no distant day to be the finest thing of the kind in the world," matching the grand promenades of Paris and Berlin. They could see that this avenue was already graded for a block, as far as Berkeley Street. Julia had agreed with those in the city who thought that the intersection of the grand avenue and Arlington Street, the proposed location for a new City Hall, would be the ideal spot for an equestrian statue of George Washington. Julia pointed out the first house on Arlington

Street, on the corner of the great avenue. Its four stories of light gray free-stone from Nova Scotia were in the style of the Italian Renaissance, making it easily visible across the unfinished Garden. John looked again, thinking that building was large enough to be the city hall, not someone's house. Would Julia think of this house and its servants as she performed her housewife's work in his Concord farmhouse? Wouldn't his wife miss the energy and the excitement of the city? Ever since she was a young woman, the city had been an important component of Julia's life, its activities and lectures rescuing her from the humdrum of daily life. But Julia had assured John that she had had her fill of city life; Lowell had seen to that. Her dream now was of a good garden, a Morgan horse, and a Jersey cow.

At the Fitchburg Railroad Depot Mr. and Mrs. Barrett boarded the train to Concord. The town was a known entity to Julia in her role as a visitor to Emerson, to the Alcotts, to other friends, and as a business caller on Judge Hoar. Now she turned to Concord in the role of a wife whose husband was known for his cheerfulness, conviviality, and willingness to help out a neighbor in need. Julia thought of her wish for a rural life as the train pulled into the Concord station. John had left his horse and wagon in the yard of one of his dairy customers who lived near the depot.

John headed his horse north on the River Road to Carlisle. The horse, sensing the nearness of home, picked up its pace as they passed Punkatassett Hill. It was after sunset when Julia and John turned in the narrow way to the still-mortgaged Barrett farm. The farmhouse, standing for

The Barrett Farm had an abundance of wildflowers; lady's slippers are shown here in a photograph from the collection of the subsequent owner.

four generations with its side to the road, was in darkness. A new moon was three days away. A new chapter of Julia's life, a rural life, was beginning just as was a new chapter for the nation. The election of her candidate, the Republican, Abraham Lincoln, six months hence, would telegraph to the slave-holding states that the days of compromise were over. The South would have to choose to bow to Northern wishes or to secede. As the turbulence in Julia's life subsided, the agitation over states' rights and slavery grew violent. A woman and a country, so in synchrony in mood and outlook two decades earlier, were now the antithesis of each other. As the nation slipped toward war, Julia planned for days and months and years of a quiet peace in the Barrett homestead.

Concord, a town in time of war
SEPTEMBER 29, 1863

Julia and John had been married just short of a year when civil war broke out between the North and the South, the Union and the Confederacy. On April 12, 1861, Confederate General Pierre Beauregard ordered shore batteries to open fire on Union-held Fort Sumter in the harbor of Charleston, South Carolina. Did wars always begin on April days? Julia wondered. When President Lincoln issued a call for three-month volunteers, sixty-four men of Concord under the leadership of Captain George Prescott answered the president's call and left Concord on the April date synonymous with sacrifice—April 19. As was Julia, many people in town were grandchildren of Revolutionary War soldiers, with the ideals of that generation steadfast in their hearts. Indeed, the second part of the "Resolutions—War of '61" approved by Concord citizens read:

> RESOLVED that, as citizens of Concord, where was inaugurated the conflict which made us one people, we pledge our lives and fortunes to the support of the Union and the suppression of the Rebellion.

Julia thought that the good folk of Lexington might quibble over the use of "inaugurated" as the Lexington militia came under fire from the British regulars before their Concord brethren faced the same muskets.

A few weeks into the war, on May 1, 1861, women met at the town hall to organize their efforts for the soldiers. As summer approached and the Concord Artillery Company headed south, their wool uniforms added to their discomfort. The women thus set about to make lighter weight suits for the men. Local tailors helped cut out the pants, which were made from a new easy-to-make pattern, one without buttons. This version may have been easier for the women to sew, but it was not easier for the soldiers to don. The pants necessitated a special set of instructions to guide the soldiers in securing the straps and buckles. It is likely that Julia, with her talent for sewing and knowledge of operating a sewing machine, was part of this endeavor. Beginning these efforts in the town hall, the group of women later moved to the vestry of the Unitarian Church before finding a home in the Engine House; there, six sewing machines were in constant use.

In mid-summer 1861, Julia and John joined the rest of the town in welcoming home the Concord volunteers after their three-month enlistment. All were members of the Concord Artillery Company, which formed "the nucleus of Company G, Fifth Massachusetts Volunteers." Four members of the company had not returned; the Confederates held them as prisoners following the Union rout at the Battle of Bull Run on July 21.

The war went on month after month. As Louisa May Alcott wrote, the town had "[a]nxious faces, beating hearts, and busy minds." There were other calls for volunteers and finally a draft was instituted in 1862. Men from Concord fought for the Union cause but John Barrett was not among them. He was not too old for action, but he did not enlist or, from the available records, get drafted and find a substitute. Miss Alcott herself left to serve as a nurse at an army hospital in Washington, D.C., while the women who stayed home did their part for a victorious outcome.

As the war continued, the women also made articles for the United States Sanitary Commission. Foremost among these were bandages that even school children helped to roll. The supplies collected by the women also included sewn articles and cooked items including preserves. Some of the grape jelly that Julia was presently stirring was earmarked for the Sanitary Commission's distribution to the soldiers. This commission was formed to provide "medical care, supplies, and other comforts and necessities to soldiers in the field." How typical of the way government worked, Julia thought. Women, working to aid the soldiers, were already well organized with over 7,000 chapters of the Women's Central Association of Relief. The Sanitary Commission merely coordinated the work of the women's chapters and awarded official status to these groups. Men with social standing ran the commission, but it was still women like herself who worked in hot kitchens, went door-to-door for necessary items for the soldiers, and ran the fairs held across the North to raise funds for the organization. The roles assigned by gender seemed set in stone—men to direct, women to work. This was not the way things should be Julia reflected, but with a war on, she wasn't going to have that argument now.

As did other Northern women supporting the war and supplying items to the Sanitary Commission, Julia spent more hours in the kitchen. That's where she was at the moment, seeing to the jelly. Julia looked around her favorite room. It was truly her kitchen and her house now, hers and John's. Julia remembered her first weeks at the farm when she had waged war on the cobwebs and the dust in the old farmhouse. Now every closet had its bunch of dried herbs hanging inside. Her shawl table covers—one red, one green—brightened the parlor. With what her sister Ellen called her *"bump of order,"* Julia had put things to rights, but it had taken hard work and endless hours.

Since Julia and John were wed, John lost his unmarried sister, Caroline Augusta, and his widowed father, Joel. Both were buried next to his mother in Sleepy Hollow Cemetery in the center of town. John's three married sisters were well established in their own homes with growing families. When Julia married John, she knew her family would be a small one: the two of them, a few close friends, and some relatives.

Despite her long-standing role as a maiden aunt to her sisters' children—Abby's sons, Follen and George Lothrop, and Ellen's daughter—Julia had not had much experience with babies. She had never even dressed a baby until she was thirty-two. The visiting Pitman baby held this distinction, noted in her diary as the *"first baby I ever dressed."* One can deduce that Julia had little to do with the care of her younger brother Eli. In any case, Julia and John's hope or likelihood of children was not for public discussion. Julia's mother had been forty-three when the last of her seven children was born, but this infant daughter, Martha, lived only a few days. Julia's maternal grandmother Martha Simonds gave birth to her last and eighth child when she was forty-four; her paternal grandmother Abigail Robbins had the last of her eight children when she was thirty-five. All three women had begun their childbearing years in their twenties, quite unlike Ellen who was thirty-seven when her first child was born and forty-three for her second child. Julia was forty-four.

Even without children to feed, clothe, and otherwise provide for, Julia was busy with making do, as was everyone else in town. These were trying days with high prices on any available goods. The inflation rate was now around fifteen percent a year! Not only were the prices high, hard coin was non-existent in town. Julia calculated her small horde of Lyceum script, a paper currency that was used locally for exchange. Even if she had a fair amount, goods of any quality were in such short supply as to be non-existent in the town shops. Local described her world; it was rare to take a trip even to Lexington to visit Ellen now back in East Lexington with her husband and busy mothering nine-year-old Ellen and three-year-old Mary, the younger daughter named for Ellen and Julia's little sister who had died so suddenly when Julia was visiting her cousins in Vermont all those years ago. Julia's mother Hannah, nearing the end of her days, was assisted by Hannah Maria, with Ellen around to supervise.

Like most of the townsfolk, Mr. and Mrs. John Barrett settled in at their own place and used what they had or did without. In this regard, Julia was pleased with her latest accomplishment; just yesterday she finished turning one of her dresses from Lowell. For many women in her circumstances, turning a dress was a matter of necessity as fabric for a new one was so expensive. Turning a dress was simply a matter of taking a dress apart, turning the skirt upside down, and then re-stitching it. The fabric that had been gathered at the waist would look almost unworn in its new position at the bottom of the skirt; the worn edges of the hem would be concealed in the newly gathered waist.

In addition to the overlay of shortages and struggles brought on by the war, Concord had the usual problems of a nineteenth century New England town. Kerosene lamps provided illumination as well as the constant danger of conflagration. In an era when a spark from a railroad engine could ignite a blaze and when the ringing of a school bell or a church bell at an unscheduled time could strike fear in a Concordian's heart, fire was an omnipresent concern. Everyone was expected to do his or her part; the ladies had been commended for their role in fighting a fire at Hugh Cargill's place on the Mount Road. Another concern was sewage run-off that could contaminate streams and wells. Disease and vagrants were both frequent visitors despite serious efforts to curtail both. Irish immigrants, working as farm laborers, as servants, and as railroad repairmen, made up a fourth of the local population to the dismay of some townspeople who did not share either their religion or their customs.

Then there were the crises, the news of which spread as rapidly as wildfire and set hearts pounding. One of these occurred a year after Julia's marriage and move to Concord when the neighborhood was startled and saddened to hear of the death by suicide of twenty-three-year-old Ellen Hunt on April 8, 1861. Especially tragic, it was the second such death in her family; her sister Martha had similarly committed suicide at age nineteen in 1845.

Julia found that her previous acquaintance and friendship with some of Concord's notables eased her acceptance. She had happy memories of the September day in 1851, more than a decade earlier, when she and Mrs. Pitman rode up to Concord and called on the Emersons. Even though the sage was discussing *Margaret Fuller's Memoirs* with fellow author Ellery Channing, he welcomed Julia. On that occasion she even *"went to see his summer house."*

Julia was additionally acquainted with many Concordians through mutual friends who shared her sentiments and activities against slavery. Emerson extended his hospitality to fellow abolitionists Parker Pillsbury and Charles Sumner among others. Since 1859, Sumner had been seated in the United States Senate after taking three years to recover from the beating he had suffered there. Julia knew Mrs. Alcott whose brother, Reverend Samuel May, had preached at her father's hall in East Lexington; the Alcott daughters, younger than Julia, she had known for years. Louisa May Alcott, now thirty-one to Julia's forty-four, shared many of Julia's enthusiasms, admiring Senator Charles Sumner as well as Reverend Theodore Parker, a friend of both women. One of Julia's neighbors was Minot Pratt, one of the original members of the Brook Farm community. Every time Julia went to town, she passed the building that Marianne

Ripley used as a school. Marianne, the tall, thin sister of Brook Farm's founder, had shown Julia around on her first visit to the West Roxbury community. Julia felt at home in Concord.

Even so, there were some in town with whom Julia did not agree, not on a minor farm problem or local issue, but on the purpose of the war itself. While many of her neighbors believed, as did she and John, that ending slavery was as important as keeping the Union together, not all held this belief. The debate had raged anew last January as President Lincoln issued his Emancipation Proclamation freeing all the slaves in rebel-controlled areas. Ending slavery, ending someone else's bondage, was not seen as critical to some citizens of Concord. Fortunately for Julia, other Concord contemporaries were thoroughly committed, second-generation abolitionists, part of the town's long tradition of abolition. And who had better credentials to join this group than Julia: she was the daughter of an abolitionist father, she had written letters, arranged for speakers, circulated petitions, attended lectures and conventions, and worked at Boston's famed Anti-Slavery Bazaar. Even her husband did not know the full extent of her work. Busy with farm matters, John never questioned his wife's actions or looked disapprovingly on her ideas.

On this September day as Julia heard John's horse and wagon on the drive, she hurried outside. Her glance swept the yard. Most of the trees were still green, but the red maples had started to blaze crimson, heralding the coming parade of golden elms and multi-hued sugar maples. In the meadow there were too many crows to count, intent on finding food. Her attention was captured by the screaming of a red-shouldered hawk, reveling in the beauty of this spot at this season, oblivious to human concerns, of bloody battles raging in states and former states to the south.

As John descended the wagon, he handed Julia a note given to him as he made the rounds of his in-town customers. Addressed to Mrs. John Barrett and signed by Maria Pratt, the message was confined to two lines.

The Antislavery Society meet with us this afternoon.
Will you favor us with your presence?

How could she not go? The Concord Female Anti-Slavery Society, established in 1837, had a membership that read like a who's who list—Emersons, Thoreaus, and Alcotts among them. Even the indomitable founder,

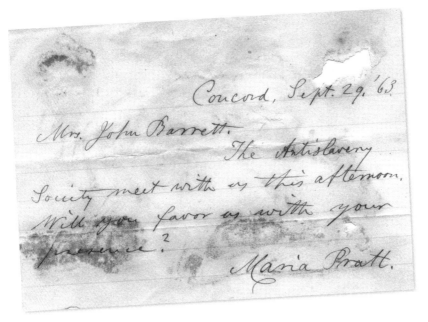

This letter to Mrs. John Barrett from Maria Pratt reads: "The Antislavery Society meet with us this afternoon. Will you favor us with your presence?"

Mary Merrick Brooks, was still involved with the group. Julia knew most of these individuals from attending anti-slavery gatherings and conventions, listening to speakers, and working to raise funds. As Julia made her way back to the kitchen with John a few steps behind, she listened to his account of the morning. That completed, she hurried to get dinner on the table. Her hired girl could be trusted to finish the jelly as she had worked with Julia on another batch a few days earlier.

As she set down the dish of meat and potatoes, the aroma of the food, complemented with herbs from Julia's garden, filled the air, eliciting a smile from John. Glancing over at his wife, he saw she too was smiling. Querying her seeming delight with the dinner, he found a more serious reason for her pleasure—her newly-turned dress would do just fine for this afternoon. With her turned dress and re-trimmed bonnet, Julia would be ready for the meeting. With more than twenty years of experience of arranging anti-slavery speakers, circulating petitions, working at bazaars, reading the *Liberator*, and discussing the problem of slavery with some of the abolitionist movement's leading figures like Pillsbury and Emerson, Julia was eager for the meeting.

Securing a farm and mourning a senator
MARCH 12, 1874

To Julia, the outdoors was more than the place outside the house; it was a refuge and solace, a place of beauty and adventure. John understood this as did the Concord naturalist Henry Thoreau who wondered:

> How womankind, who are confined to the house still more than men, stand it I do not know; but I have ground to suspect that most of them do not *stand* it at all.

Julia was always finding new reasons to agree with her now deceased acquaintance. It was almost three decades earlier that she had commended his work to her friend Mary Plumer.

Growing up in East Lexington, Julia had Mount Independence to climb when she was world-weary; at Adams Female Academy, there was a view to the distant mountain to ease a restless spirit. As the years of work in Lowell and attention to legal matters in Lexington left little time to revel in nature, living along the Concord River pleased her. Julia, standing in her south-facing front doorway, could survey the meadow and woods that comprised the farm she and John had secured. And stand there she frequently did, delighting in the scene before her, a sweep of New England landscape unmarred by the sight of another dwelling. She watched as the seasons changed, following the internal rhythms of the year. Weather was, of course, critical for a farmer as the seasons and the weather shaped the days and thus the life of the farmer—and that of his wife. Sometimes it seemed that the farm was more Julia's than John's. As of May 11, 1871, she was the one who was a member of the Massachusetts Agricultural Society.

In the year 1874, March was following its traditional pattern; one day had hints of spring, the next day was back in mid-winter. With the impending arrival of spring, the Concord farming community, including the Barretts, took stock of their financial situation, supplies, and equipment. After the noon meal was over this Thursday and the dishes had been cleared, Julia opened the box in which she stored the tax receipts and other papers of importance and spread them out on the kitchen table as she assessed their circumstances. John, more than willing to leave money matters to Julia, shared her dream of increasing their acreage.

However, he was more interested in learning the dates of the cattle show than the amount of the tax rate. In 1860 when John and Julia were married, John's mortgaged holdings amounted to fifty acres. In 1868 John and Julia bought two acres from the estate of Nathan Barrett. The parcel was located on the west side of the River Road, across the street and to the south of their farm. Perhaps they were looking for some higher—and drier—grazing land. The following year, 1869, they expanded their homestead by eighteen acres. Thus, in the first decade of married life, the Barretts had increased their holdings by forty percent.

As a dairy farmer, John Barrett was not a man of means. An article in the local paper made evident the fact that the life of a dairy farmer was not an easy or a profitable one. The piece by Waldo Flint titled "Producing Milk" asked the question, "What does it cost to raise a can of Milk, Summer and Winter?" Flint wrote that he had "for a long time been engaged in raising and selling milk" and that his six cows were valued at $65 apiece. The number of cans of milk sold varied monthly, from a low of 129 cans in April to a high of 276 cans in June, falling back to 222 cans in September. Adding the 91 cans consumed by his family, Flint's labors for six months resulted in a total of 1,429 cans of milk. For this time span, his expenses included hired labor for one-fourth of each of the 183 days, at a going rate of $2 per day or 50 cents for a quarter day. Also itemized as expenses were hay at $50, green fodder at $30, grain—his largest expense—at $140, as well as interest on money borrowed and taxes. From the cost of raising the milk, Flint deducted his profit on the sale of two commodities: calves for $30 and manure for $100. At the end of six months, there was a profit, or as Flint expressed it, a "balance in favor of milk," of $82.98. Flint added the caution that "The same cattle, in different hands, with the same feed, might give a different result."

It is not clear from the census data for the 1860s whether John had the expense, as well as the benefit, of hired help or whether he did all the work himself. A few months after their marriage, a census taker, S. H. Rhoades, visited the farm on July 23, 1860; John and Julia were recorded as the only residents. The state census of 1865 enumerated the household as John and Julia as well as Sarah A. Davis, a single white female born in Nova Scotia, and Anna Davis, aged two, born in Massachusetts. The United States census taken on July 13, 1870, listed only John Barett [*sic*] as a farmer and Julia as keeping house. More complete is the 1880 census, taken on June 7. Listed were John and Julia; Andrew C. Davison, aged sixty-one; Wyman Devans, John's twenty-two-year-old nephew; and Annie Davis, aged sixteen. The relationship and occupation for these three unmarried individuals are given: Davison as servant/farm laborer, Devans as boarder/student, and Davis as ward/housework. Andrew Davison was the older brother of William Davison, a.k.a. Benjamin Davison, who had jilted Julia and caused her such heartache. Remembering Andrew's condition as unbalanced, one wonders how much help this Davison was to John as he worked his farm. One hopes, in return for John and Julia's generosity in providing a home for Andrew, that he was not a burden to them. That he was part of their home, there is no doubt, but the date of his arrival and the extent of his value as a farm laborer are uncertain. Ellen, writing from East Lexington, often sent her regards to Mr. Barrett and to Davison. On one occasion, Ellen entered in her diary *"Mr. Davison here"* and detailed his help with the *"cutting of grain"* and moving things from one house to another.

Perhaps John hired local help as needed. In any event, with his cows assessed for only $35 apiece, unlike Flint's $65 cows, the yield of milk was probably less than what Flint outlined, lowering his profit margin. If John were as successful as Waldo Flint, he would have cleared less than $100 for six months of dairy work. Julia more than matched this income by picking seasonal berries that included blueberries, blackberries, raspberries, and especially strawberries. Strawberries were a notable Concord export; in 1874, the town produced 79,890 quarts/boxes of strawberries for a total amount of $13,702, averaging 17 cents a box. Julia sold her berries to her husband's customers in town, making as much as $100 a year. Julia would have had to pick 588 quarts/boxes to earn $100, assuming other kinds of berries sold for a price comparable to that of strawberries.

The $100 a summer that Julia earned represented a tremendous amount of work as well as a very solid amount of money. It was over three times the 1870 salary of W. H. Benjamin, the chief engineer for the Concord Fire Department and ten times the cost of repairing the roof of the Town House, the town hall. Totally incomprehensible to Concordians who followed the news in the myriad of papers that arrived in town each day was the figure of $75,000,000 to $200,000,000, the amount that

New York City's Tammany Hall boss, William Marcy Tweed, had stolen from the city treasury.

Local lore has credited Julia with helping pay off the mortgage as well as all the debts on the farm. In the Assessors' Records for the town of Concord for 1861 and 1862, it was recorded that John's assets included a single share of Fitchburg Railroad stock, valued for $80, then $85, a share. In 1864 there appeared in the Assessors' Records a one-time entry in the Taxable Cash Assets column: "money at interest belonging to wife $500." Where this money came from is unknown. Julia's mother had passed away on December 13 of that year. Given the debts and legal tangles associated with the Robbins' East Lexington property, it was unlikely the money came from Hannah. Was this money that Julia had squirreled away and finally deposited in the bank?

As Julia and John reviewed the financial status of the farm, they were mindful of their annual town tax bill. During the last taxable year, 1873, the sixty-eight acres of the homestead were valued at $25 an acre for a total value of $1700, while the two acres bought from the estate of Nathan Barrett had a value of $40. With the house and barn valued at $900, the total value of their real estate was $2640. On this real estate the town levied a tax of $25.34. There were other taxes as well. A personal property tax amounted to $2.50; the property assessed was the horse for $50 and the six cows for $210. A highway tax, an aggregate tax based on a percent of the poll, personal property, and real estate taxes, was an additional $7.54 and a poll tax of $2 was also levied. The Barretts' total tax bill of $37.38 was at least one-third, and probably more, of John's yearly profit from his dairy work, assuming he was as successful as Mr. Flint. Julia deserved much of the credit for careful planning and hard work as the Barretts solidified their financial standing. They would never be rich, but they were doing more than just getting along.

Julia knew that they would never be wealthy like her old acquaintance, Louisa May Alcott, whose writings turned a handsome profit; local gossips indicated her bank account held thousands of dollars. Julia remembered when the Robbins family of East Lexington was well-to-do and the Alcotts were the struggling family, but Julia was content with her lot. She had her husband and her health; Louisa, who never married, was, as she herself noted, "Ill a good deal."

John, sensing the discussion of taxes and finances over, was happy to escape to the barn where he was making needed repairs to his implements for spring planting. As Julia put the tax records and other papers back into the box, she noticed a small newspaper clipping from an issue of last September's Lexington paper at the bottom of the box. Even though she knew its contents by heart, she took it out and reread it.

> RUN OVER. Wednesday [September] the 24th ult', Mr. Joshua Hobart was called from his house by the report that a woman was lying in the road. He found upon proceeding thither that it was the body of Hannah Robbins, an elderly lady residing in the East Village. Nothing is known definitely in regard to the circumstances, of the accident, but it is presumed that she was run over by a passing team. She was very deaf, and thus would have been unconscious of its approach. Her face was badly cut and one arm was broken. She lingered until Saturday, the 27th ult, when death put an end to her sufferings.

Described as "elderly," Hannah Maria was then sixty-one years old.

Last September, for Hannah Maria's funeral, for the second time in as many weeks, Julia and John traveled to East Lexington for a burial in the Winship and Robbins family cemetery. Their first trip had been to bury Uncle Lot, Julia's father's younger brother, who had died September 14 at the age of eighty-three, at the McLean Asylum where he had spent the last forty-nine years of his life. Julia remembered the visits she had made to him there and his pleadings to go home; Lot lived a world apart from family and friends. A flood of memories had overwhelmed Julia as she surveyed the small burying place in East Lexington that was invaded by the noise and dust of Main Street. Here her parents rested as did her little sister Mary Lavinia. She and John stood witness on the two separate occasions as Lot and Hannah Maria were interred.

Hannah Maria's death was the first of the four Robbins sisters. As the eldest, it was not unusual it should be so, but the manner of her dying had shocked the family. Julia remembered that when she was sixteen and Hannah Maria was twenty-three there was a flurry of activity as legal papers were signed that released Hannah Maria's "right to dower." This helped to seal her sister's fate as a spinster, staying at home while Abby, Ellen, and Julia went off to Adams Female Academy, to lectures and parties, and eventually to married life. Hannah Maria had lived as a companion to her mother until the death of the widowed Hannah Senior nine years earlier at the age of seventy-eight. As for Julia's remaining sisters, Abby, Mrs. Stillman Lothrop, had been a widow for fifteen years. In the last years of her married life she had lived estranged from Stillman who died in the West Indies. Ellen, who lived in the old homestead, had joined her older sister in the state of widowhood two years ago after her husband Abner Stone had died of pneumonia. As for Julia, she proudly claimed her lot in life as mistress of the Barrett family farm on the River Road to Carlisle.

The death of Uncle Lot left only one member of her father's generation still alive, Aunt Caira. At seventy-nine, Caira Robbins still had her same spirit, talking about re-decorating her bedroom, having decided that a new carpet and new wallpaper were needed. Ellen kept an eye on her elderly aunt as Caira delighted in the company of her grandnieces. Ellen's daughters Ellen, twenty, and Mary, fourteen, loved visiting Great-aunt Caira, sometimes talking in the parlor, sometimes chatting in her upstairs bedroom warmed by the fireplace on chilly days. Julia and John visited East Lexington occasionally, never missing an important event such as Ellen's high school examination day.

Julia returned the clipping to the box and directed her thoughts to the present. Fortunately March of 1874 did not set the records for cold weather as was the case two years previous. The winter of 1872 had boasted the severest March cold in decades, even colder than last year when the thermometer recorded ten degrees below zero the first week in March. This winter was cold and snowy enough for Julia. It had begun early with the first snow of the season on Friday, November 14, followed by a severe coastal storm and gale. Like many early snows, this was more of a nuisance than a welcome change, as it didn't provide enough snow for sleighing. There was a respite of days above freezing in early January, but heavy snow and zero-degree temperatures reigned for the rest of the month. Last month, February, saw more snow and cold, enough cold to begin cutting the thirteen-inch thick ice on Fresh Pond. Now the flooding began.

March of 1874 was more ordinary. Even so, it still had moments of wonder. One morning when Julia was still busy in the kitchen with the remnants of breakfast, John had called to his wife to come quickly. Before

William Brewster described an incident of partridges devouring the new buds of an apple tree on the former Barrett farm.

leaving to deliver milk to his customers in town, he had noticed an unusual sight in the old apple tree about thirty yards from the barn. Julia had hurried to join her husband as he led the way around the barn. John had told her of his seeing such a sight before, but Julia had found it hard to believe. Now she was seeing it for herself and barely believing it. There were partridges in the apple tree! A few sat on the sturdy lower branches but the majority of the birds were in the upper, thinner branches. The birds, looking incongruous because of their size, were feeding on the tasty emerging buds of the still leafless tree. Ornithologist William Brewster, the next owner of the farm, would describe a similar scene:

> Those feeding near the ends of the slenderer branches maintained their foothold with no slight effort, jerking up their tails and fluttering their wings to preserve their balance as they stretched forward or even, for an instant, bent almost straight downward after the manner of Redpolls or Pine Siskins, picking off and swallowing the buds in rapid succession with much the same quick, bobbing motion of the head as that of a Hen picking up corn. The supply within reach (at least of such buds as they chose to take) seldom lasted more than a minute or two; when it became

exhausted, the Partridge would either work its way still farther out among the terminal twigs or fly to another part of the tree.

Julia and John watched the birds maneuver in the tree for several minutes, then as the birds flew off in several directions, they, too, went their own ways.

The thought of the partridges, just one of the constant wonders of their farm and woodlot, helped ease the gloom that remembering Hannah's death always evoked. Rising from the table, Julia returned the box to its rightful place on the top shelf in the pantry. Her reverie was broken by the surprising sound of hoof beats on the drive. The neighbors were usually busy with their own affairs. Fred Tarbell, their neighbor to the south, worked in Boston as a carpenter during the week, coming home only on Sundays. Of her neighbors to the north, Silas Conant ran his own farm, and did so very well, and Marshall Mason's work reflected his name; he was an excellent stonemason. Going out to the yard, she recognized the son of one of John's village customers with whom she was acquainted through the Anti-Slavery Society. The lad leaned down, thrust a newspaper into her outstretched hand, muttered that his mother thought she would want to see it, and was off. Julia subscribed to *The Woman's Journal*, a weekly paper, but not to one of the daily papers that came each morning and evening from Boston by train. Fighting a gust of wind that ruffled the unwieldy pages, Julia saw the news—"Sumner Dead." Indeed, two of the seven columns of the *Boston Globe* were devoted entirely to this story.

Hurrying back to the kitchen, Julia sat in the chair by the window. "The Great Statesman Gone To His Rest" was followed by "The Nation Mourns The Loss Of One Of Its Noblest Sons." The last news that Julia had heard of Sumner was from the previous December when she had read that he had been serenaded in Washington before making a speech to the black people of that city. Sumner had served continuously as U.S. Senator from Massachusetts since he had been first elected in 1851. Six years later he was honored with re-election by the Massachusetts legislature even though he was too unwell to serve in the Senate after his beating by South Carolina's Representative Brooks. In each subsequent election for that Senate seat, the Massachusetts legislature returned Sumner to the

Senate. However, in a misguided and unsuccessful attempt to help the nation recover from a bloody civil war, Sumner had proposed that battlefield names be dropped from the lists of soldiers' names in the Army Register. His idea was met with a torrent of opposition and the Massachusetts state legislature had entered a resolution of censure against Senator Sumner. Two days ago, on March 10, the U.S. Senate heard another resolution from the Massachusetts legislature, expunging the original censure resolution. This blemish was now removed from Senator Sumner's name, a name honored in Massachusetts by those who supported the causes of abolition and equal rights.

In the article recounting the time before Sumner's death, it was recorded that Sumner, despite some chest pain, had gone to the Senate as usual on Tuesday, March 10, where he seemed fine, looking well and in good spirits. In mid-afternoon, he left the Senate and entertained friends at dinner. Later in the evening, when "the paroxysm of pain returned," his physician was called. The best methods of the day for treating him were employed; he was given an injection of morphine and a footbath of mustard and hot salt water. When Sumner did not improve, friends and another doctor, the same one who had attended to President Lincoln, were summoned to his bedside. Sumner, resting more comfortably after additional morphine, and "a dose of brandy and ammonia," apologized for causing trouble. Sumner grew worse in the night; it was clear by morning that Sumner's hours were numbered. As recounted in the *Boston Globe*:

> The news of Mr. Sumner's illness spread rapidly through the city and hundreds of people, white and black, wended their way to his residence. The attendance of the negroes and the interest among them was particularly noticeable.

Julia hoped those in attendance told the senator, her senator, of the crowd's gathering. He would appreciate their presence. Sumner's support of equal suffrage for whites and blacks had been a constant in his life. When Judge E. Rockwood Hoar, famed son of Concord who had served as attorney general under President Grant, arrived at Sumner's deathbed, Sumner recognized him and urged that the Civil Rights bill not be lost. According to the article, about ten minutes before he died, Sumner had addressed Hoar:

"Tell Emerson I love and revere him." The Judge answered, "I will tell Emerson you love and revere him, for he has told me you had the whitest soul he ever knew."

Julia put down the paper, the print swimming before her eyes. The world seemed to collapse around her. Sumner was dead at sixty-three. Emerson, at seventy-one, had not been the same since the fire at his home almost two years earlier. Theodore Parker had died the youngest of all, at age fifty in 1860. These were the men who centered Julia's ideas, who supported her work for the abolitionist cause, who showed the way to a better world. But Julia was not alone in her sorrow. Upon the death of Sumner, the largest outpouring of grief and mourning since Lincoln's assassination would sweep the nation. Even Charleston, South Carolina, where secession was born, would lower its flags to half-staff. The walls and heat of the kitchen seemed to close in on her. Snatching her gray and white blanket shawl from its peg by the door, Julia hurried outside.

Julia followed the path to the river across the meadow with its patches of snow. She had to pick her way more carefully when she reached the ground under the trees where more sizeable remnants of the two feet of snow that fell the last week of February still lingered. With only a brightness behind the gray clouds that covered the sky, the river was a black mirror, reflecting the dark tree trunks and bare branches. Color seemed alien in this world of gray and black, fitting for the sad news she had heard. The red-winged blackbirds whose epaulettes would flash crimson had not yet returned. Their shrill screaming would have been fitting accompaniment for her mood. She walked the familiar paths, skirting snow and mud, memories flashing before her: searching for candles to celebrate Sumner's election to the Senate those many years ago, crying when the news of his attack by Bully Brooks reached her in Lowell, explaining his ideas and why they were right to John. Then she noticed that despite the lengthening days, now almost matching the nights in duration, with the absence of the sun, dark was falling early. Sunset wasn't until six but dusk was swirling around her. Julia bunched the shawl under her chin and turned toward home.

The School of Philosophy— ideas for a summer day
JULY 18, 1883

One of the highlights of Julia's year was attending the Concord School of Philosophy's four-week session held each summer. The School, founded in 1879 by local sage Bronson Alcott, began in the Alcott's home, known as Orchard House, and later convened in a structure of his design, Hillside Chapel, built on the hill behind Alcott's home. In addition to adult education and a defense of the branch of philosophy known as metaphysics, the school provided a look back at Transcendentalism, the intellectual movement that had fueled Brook Farm and other mid-century New England activities.

Julia reveled in the School's lectures. The topic for the morning of July 18, 1883 was typical—"Space and Time Considered; Basis of Kantian Philosophy, Ground of Certainty Deeper than Skepticism or Agnosticism." This topic was of no interest to her husband who accompanied her, not without protest, but Julia, who had been interested in Kant ever since her friend Theodore Parker had introduced her to the German philosophers decades ago, found the topic fascinating. Sadly, Parker had been dead now for almost a quarter of a century. His close friend, Ralph Waldo Emerson, whose house stood down the road from the Concord School of Philosophy, had died last year at seventy-nine. He had been one of the school's stars.

Some of the other luminaries at the school included Thomas Wentworth Higginson, an esteemed Boston editor, as well as Edna Dow Cheney, the founder of the Boston School of Design. In a previous session Cheney had spoken on the topics of "Color" and "Early American Art." Another woman who had graced the platform was Mrs. Julia Ward Howe. In a memorable lecture on "Modern Society" to an overflow crowd three years ago, she had condemned the search abroad by some wealthy American heiresses for a title in England and Europe and identified the problem of modern society as its abuse of the vast resources available to it; her presentation was acclaimed by critics as "the most brilliant effort of her public life." The educator Elizabeth Palmer Peabody was a key figure at the School as well, however, like John Barrett, she too had dozed through the hour and a half of this morning's lecture even though she was seated in the first row.

Julia stole a sideways glance at her husband and gently nudged his arm to wake him. He began his work at dawn, milking the six cows, picking vegetables, and making deliveries to his village customers. His regulars were especially pleased that he had brought along some of the raspberries that Julia had picked yesterday. Back home, he had rushed to change his clothes, and then he and Julia took the horse and wagon and hurried to the School of Philosophy for the opening lecture at 9:00. John was annoyed that he had to spend time indoors on such a day. When Julia elbowed him, he had been dreaming of his beloved river, its swirls and eddies, the white water lilies floating on its quiet stretches, the snapping turtles and painted tortoises lingering along the shady edges, the muskrat house as tall as he was. He opened his eyes. No wonder he was dreaming of the river. On the speaker's platform was a bowl of the very same water lilies, their fragrance filling the air.

The lengthy lectures were followed by an hour-long discussion. The audience, mainly women, delighted in this. John sighed and closed his eyes, clearly visualizing last night's scene of the bats, which nested in the shed near the house, wheeling through the evening sky. It had been cooler then, minus the heat that was stored for days in this Hillside Chapel. He had agreed whole-heartedly with an article Julia had read to him last summer on the Concord School of Philosophy in *The Woman's Journal*; speaking of the town and its weather, it noted, ". . . we do think it excels in tropic heat, more than any place we know of." Even the founder's daughter, Louisa May Alcott, with whom Julia was long acquainted, commented on the heat in a verse she wrote about the School: "Disciples devout both gaze and adore/As daily they listen and bake." While Julia looked cool in her gingham dress, John was sweltering in his wool suit, his collar irritating his neck. If asked, he would have vigorously defended the idea expressed in *The Woman's Journal* that "the school is for the few."

But John thought of the woman by his side, never able to stay annoyed with her for long. Mrs. Robbins Barrett she called herself. John was pleased she had not followed Lucy Stone's example and eschewed his name. He had never worked harder or been happier than he had been in the years since their marriage. To her credit, Julia was constantly there, working along with him. The berries that he delivered to his village customers in the morning were just a few of the many quart boxes Julia filled

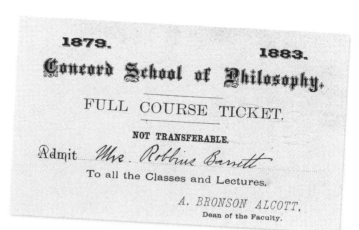

Julia purchased a ticket of admission to the Concord School of Philosophy each summer of its existence (1879–1888).

each summer. His debts were now paid and his farm now extended over seventy acres. Julia's berry money had made a huge difference in their lives. He certainly didn't mind that every year she bought a season ticket to the sessions at the School of Philosophy. It was her money; spending it as she wished was one way she could still assert her independence. This year's season ticket cost the considerable sum of $15. The individual tickets, like the one Julia purchased for her husband, were 50 cents apiece. Despite his suggestions, Julia was not interested in other ways she could spend those half-dollars.

The morning session over, Julia and her husband exchanged pleasantries with those seated near them. Not everyone present was a Concordian. Some people came to town for the daily sessions by train. An express train from the Fitchburg Railroad Depot left Boston at 8:00 A.M. to arrive in Concord in time for the 9:00 A.M. lectures. With the Fitchburg Railroad's nine daily trains from Boston and an equal number returning, it seemed everyone's wishes for transportation were met; the school's schedule was arranged so that evening lectures ended with time to catch a late return train.

Other visitors, like astronomy professor Maria Mitchell, the first person to discover a comet with the aid of a telescope, stayed in town with friends. A third group arranged for room and board in the village at $7 to $12 a week; the school's brochure listed seven names of local women from whom "lodgings with board may be obtained." As attendees were expected to actively study the topics presented, the Concord Free Public Library, with its collection of 17,500 volumes, became a popular place. John, like the local shopkeepers, did appreciate the increased sales when the town was abuzz with School of Philosophy activities. All the teas, parties, and receptions for visiting lecturers kept local notables busy entertaining; John was happy to fill their orders for cream and for Julia's berries.

As the dozens of attendees left the building, John looked for those he knew, and he knew almost everyone in Concord. With his friendly manner and willingness to do a good deed, John was a recognized figure in town; for years he had been singled out as the strongest man in town. Even women who were not among his village customers or members of the Unitarian church, where he attended meetings both religious and social, recognized him as he appeared at their farms to help with difficult jobs.

The Barretts left Hillside Chapel in an anticipatory mood, John for the freedom of the day ahead, Julia for the subsequent lectures in the School's summer session. She looked forward with particular interest to hearing Mrs. Cheney lecture on "A Study of Nirvana," Mrs. Howe on "Margaret Fuller," and Elizabeth Palmer Peabody on "Milton's *Paradise Lost.*" A local, Julian Hawthorne, seemed to have a less weighty topic planned with a presentation on "Novels." Since listening to the speakers in her father's hall years ago in East Lexington, Julia always liked hearing different opinions and ideas; all the speakers at the School of Philosophy this summer, she was certain, would prove most interesting. John knew that though the sessions seemed interminable, the summer had a way of slipping away as fast as river water ran through his open fingers.

A bazaar and petitions, this time for municipal suffrage
November 23, 1886

The years went by. There were springs when planting was delayed until the rains had ceased and the soil had dried sufficiently so the seed would not rot. There were summers when it seemed as if the rains would never come and autumns when dry, cool days blessed the harvesting. There were winter weeks when the Concord River was frosted with only a skim of ice and weeks when the surrounding marshes were frozen in time. There were days when Julia awoke to the east ablaze with the dawn and days when pounding rain hammered the rooftop. On winter days after a heavy snowfall when John joined other men of the town packing down the snow on the main streets, working in fading daylight, Julia dreamed of the light-filled days of early July when the first grass had been cut and bundled. Then possibilities and opportunities seemed endless. Julia glanced at the calendar hanging in her kitchen, noting that 1886 was almost over. Women still did not have the right to vote for president or even for local officials, excepting school committee members.

It had been twenty-one years since the Thirteenth Amendment, ratified in 1865 at the end of the Civil War, had accomplished the aim of the abolitionists and ended slavery in the United States. Five years later, in 1870, black men were enfranchised by the Fifteenth Amendment. That same year the woman suffrage newspaper, *The Woman's Journal*, began publication under the direction of Lucy Stone, her husband Henry Blackwell, and their daughter, Alice Stone Blackwell. On page one of every issue, the paper announced its purpose: "devoted to the interests of Woman, to her educational, industrial, legal, and political Equality, and especially to her right of Suffrage." Despite its name, however, it was not a typical woman's publication. It included excerpts from daily papers, presented book reviews, reported on the international as well as national achievements of women and on sessions in state legislatures, and cogently argued its case in its editorials.

Its writers included well-known figures such as Thomas Wentworth Higginson, whose column graced the front page of *The Woman's Journal* for fourteen years. An outspoken abolitionist, actively involved in the attempted rescues of fugitive slaves, Higginson had even traveled to Kansas to assist the Free Soilers there, allying himself with John Brown before serving as commander of the Union's first black regiment, the first South Carolina Volunteers. Higginson's name was a familiar one in the Barrett household as his second passion was woman suffrage. How often had John heard Julia quote Higginson on woman suffrage—women should vote "not because they are angels, but because they are one-half the human race"?

Julia's copy of *The Woman's Journal*, its $2.50 annual subscription price equaling fifteen boxes of boxes of carefully picked berries, was one of six sent to Concord each week. Other publications with six copies arriving weekly at the Concord Post Office included the *Sunday School Times*, *Harper's Bazaar*, and *Boston Commonwealth*.

Since Julia and her sister Ellen pored over each issue, it is likely that each would have seen the long retrospective piece by Ednah D. Cheney in the January 23, 1886 issue on Cheney's Boston School of Design for Women. Two weeks later in the February 6 issue there was a letter from Mrs. Cheney replying to an unknown correspondent. Mrs. Cheney noted Julia's employment as a carpet-designer and concluded:

> She gave up her position for strong family reasons, and having married a Concord farmer, has since been engaged mostly in other pursuits. She has, however, occasionally exhibited designs at county fairs for which she has received premiums.

The Woman's Journal additionally posted and reported on a plethora of town, county, state, and regional meetings, many of which Julia, Ellen, and, sometimes, John, attended. Eleven years ago, here in Concord, in May of 1875, Julia had heard William Lloyd Garrison as he addressed the Middlesex County Woman Suffrage Convention. This time-tested abolitionist and her father's friend, speaking on the occasion of the hundredth anniversary of the Battles of Lexington and Concord, invoked the ghosts of the Revolutionary War in the cause of woman suffrage. Exhorting his listeners to emulate their ancestors who fought for their rights a century earlier, he regretted that events at Lexington and Concord had the effect of freezing those places in history; now, he admonished them, they looked backward and not forward to the needed reforms of the late nineteenth century.

Others may have needed Garrison's reproof, but not Julia. Now sixty-seven, several years past the age when the Lexington newspaper had termed her sister Hannah as elderly, Julia and other supporters of the vote for women once again turned to the time-honored techniques that many of them as former abolitionists knew best—petitions and a bazaar—to rally support for their cause. Known as suffragists, these women recognized that they had a long and difficult struggle against the status quo;

conventional wisdom was deeply entrenched. In fact, in 1883, in a speech before the Massachusetts General Court, the state legislative branch, a Doctor Campbell from East Boston declared that political activity could be fatal for women who were pregnant or menopausal.

As was the case in the fight for the abolition of slavery, Massachusetts was in the forefront of the struggle for woman suffrage. The Massachusetts Woman Suffrage Association (MWSA) was created in 1870, the same year as *The Woman's Journal*. It was affiliated with the American Woman Suffrage Association (AWSA), which worked state by state for woman suffrage while also continuing to work for the rights of the black man. So widespread were the actions of the MWSA both within Massachusetts and beyond its borders that some considered woman suffrage a "Bostonism." In keeping with their belief that woman suffrage should be granted by the states, members of the Massachusetts group worked to gain local support to persuade the state legislature of the wisdom of granting women the right to vote.

In Massachusetts there was a softening in the resistance to woman suffrage. In 1874, in recognition of women's historic charge to raise the young as future citizens and to refine their character and morals, the Massachusetts legislature had guaranteed that women had a right to serve on local school committees. Elected by male voters, several women served in this manner. In 1879 the School Suffrage Act gave all women the right to vote for the local school committee. Most likely, Julia was one of the twenty intrepid women who exercised their right to vote for school committee at the Concord town meeting on March 29, 1880. In 1881, Ellen wrote to Julia of her daughter Ellen's election to the Lexington school committee with *"quite a number of votes."*

To many, school suffrage was a dangerous wedge. Woman suffrage became entangled in religion, education, politics, and temperance. In Boston, the Protestant establishment feared the vote of the Irish Catholic immigrant women, while the Roman Catholic Church took an anti-suffrage stand, condemning politics as an evil influence on family life. When the Women's Christian Temperance Union (WCTU) collected 10,000 signatures supporting a municipal woman suffrage bill, the liquor interests surmised that their businesses would suffer if women voted on the granting of liquor licenses. The MWSA, although happy to have the WCTU on their side, felt that temperance and suffrage issues should be separate. Linking these causes had produced unsatisfactory results in the 1870s.

For those women who had been engaged in abolition and temperance work as well as in nursing and relief work during the Civil War, voting solely for school committee did not suffice. They wanted to vote on all local issues and for all local officials; their goal was municipal suffrage, which Lucy Stone referred to as "enlarged housekeeping." Many considered women especially sensitive to moral issues and thus qualified to vote on solutions to contemporary problems: alcoholism, prostitution, the soaring number of foreign-born with their votes for sale for the price of the poll tax, and the reign of the political boss.

By 1880 Julia and other suffragists were hopeful of achieving municipal woman suffrage. As it required action only by the state legislature, it would be easier to attain than the passage of a federal constitutional amendment. Thanks to *The Woman's Journal*, its readers knew well that the required referendum for a constitutional amendment had been defeated in other states, in Kansas, Michigan, and Colorado. In Massachusetts, the alignment of political forces seemed favorable for municipal suffrage with support from all three branches of state government and from some of the leading citizens of the Commonwealth.

John, who attended countless suffrage meetings with Julia, recognized that the men in attendance were not brow-beaten husbands, commandeered by dominating wives, but some of the most distinguished citizens of the commonwealth. From the portrait that hung in an honored spot in the East Lexington home of his sister-in-law Ellen, John recognized William Lloyd Garrison, now eighty-one and a constant presence at these meetings. Joining Garrison were his sons, both Lexington residents, William Lloyd Garrison Jr., who handled the finances of the Massachusetts Woman Suffrage Association, and Francis Jackson Garrison.

Other familiar figures at suffrage meetings were the oft-quoted Higginson and William I. Bowditch, son of a famous navigator. Bowditch, who served a term as president of the MWSA, used his lawyer's talents to expound on the unjust taxation of women, who were taxed without the right to vote as the colonists had been under King George III in the previous century. Another distinguished Massachusetts man who also turned his attention to improving the legal status of women was Judge Samuel E. Sewall, descendent of a famous Puritan judge of the same name who publicly repented his role in the Salem Witchcraft trials two centuries earlier. The nineteenth century Sewall had been an unsuccessful candidate for governor, but was instrumental in drafting the Personal Liberty Laws for blacks in ante-bellum days. Such was her admiration for Sewall that Ellen Stone's actions received this notice in *The Woman's Journal*:

> In the [East Lexington] Library, Mrs. Stone, of Lexington, has placed Judge Samuel E. Sewall's bust with Hancock and Adams, with an appropriate tablet telling all who read [it] that he is doing to-day for women what they did for men in '76.

It should be noted that Sewall also represented the Robbins family in various legal issues over the decades.

Julia was acquainted with the MWSA's vice-presidents, prominent individuals who held an office with no formal duties, but whose written and spoken support helped the woman suffrage cause immeasurably. Among these were Mrs. Ralph Waldo Emerson, widowed in 1882, and Bronson Alcott, now eclipsed by his daughter Louisa. Also lending his voice to the campaign was abolitionist Wendell Phillips, long-admired by Julia; he had spoken out for woman suffrage at the Worcester Convention in 1850, the one Julia had hoped to attend only to have her hopes dashed by family responsibilities.

Women of means, such as Mrs. Fenno Tudor and Mrs. Sarah Shaw Russell, who favored municipal suffrage, opened their Beacon Hill homes to receptions for state legislators at which Lucy Stone, Julia Ward Howe, and other proponents of woman suffrage measures appealed to the senators and the representatives for their support. The suffragists, well versed in the rules of the legislature, knew that every qualifying petition was referred to a committee and given a public hearing. Thus the women worked to present petitions annually so their cause would be under constant consideration. Even the judicial branch had a positive view of the matter. In an advisory opinion, the Massachusetts Supreme Court had confirmed that the state legislature could enact woman suffrage for election of local officials as well as for voting in town meetings. Hence, a flurry of petitions for municipal suffrage ensued.

The January 23, 1886, edition of *The Woman's Journal* listed the Woman Suffrage Petitions presented to the General Court. The petition from Concord, noted on line 22, was sent by Julia A. R. Barrett.

SATURDAY, JANUARY 23, 1886.

MASSACHUSETTS WOMAN SUFFRAGE PETITIONS.

The following Petitions have been sent to the Massachusetts Legislature this week:

FOR MUNICIPAL SUFFRAGE.

TOWN.	NAME.	TOTAL.	MEN.	WOMEN.	REFERRED TO
Boston	Aasta Hansteen	And others 29	5	24	John O. Teele
"	Harriet A. Rogers	" 201	..	201	Michael J. McKetrick
"	Lucia T. Ames	" 19	13	6	Albert A. Woodward
"	Caroline Otis	" 22	3	19	Wm. A. Rust
"	Mrs. Geo. Clapp	" 25	4	21	Hazard Stevens
"	Cynthia P. Honer	" 27	5	22	Henry C. Allen
"	Evelina A. S. Smith	" 23	7	16	FrankE. Brigham
"	Mrs. J. M. Longstreet	" 11	3	8	Julius C. Chappelle
Uxbridge	Clarissa D. White	" 134	40	94	Jas. Daley
Waltham	Mrs. H. K. Parmenter	" 237	115	142	Erskine Warden
Mendon	Marie L. Bills	" 101	28	73	Jas. F.Stratton
Upton	H. W. Bradish	" 40	12	28	Henry E. Fales
North Dana	C. H. Mason	" 82	30	52	Jesse Allen
Hudson	Anne T. Wood	" 207	78	129	Edward R. Miles
Cambridge	Harriet M. Leonard	" 50	17	33	John W. Wilkinson
Lynn	Emma L. Olver	" 11	1	10	Amos Beckford
"	John W. Hutchinson	" 91	46	45	Edge e H. Goss
Worcester	Lucy M. Allen	" 32	6	26	Augustus N. Currier
"	Wm. H. Bartlett	" 35	10	25	Joseph Mason
Milford	Geo. F. Hoar	" 128	45	83	Henry M. Smith
Concord	Julia A. R. Barrett	" 10	2	8	Jas. K. Stratton
Cambridge	Laura S. Cheney	" 64	22	42	Henry Hosmer
South Hanson	Sarah R. Smith	" 20	2	18	George C. Bent
Lynn	Georgiana L. T. Luther	" 142	51	91	Miles Sampson
Boston	Mrs. M. J. Whitney	" 35	12	23	William A. Clark, Jr
North Abington	Marianna E. Clarke	" 22	2	20	J. Q. A. Brackett
Dedham	Jesse H. Jones	" 70	28	42	Wm. H. Gurney
Needham	Myra H. Gill	" 60	11	49	Frank A. Fales
Holyoke	Joanna B. Mills	" 320	97	223	Walter Hunnewel
Foxboro	Eliza Forsyth	" 164	86	78	Levi Perkins
Gardner	Josephine P. Holland	" 89	27	62	Benj. F. Boyden
Boston	John F. Ashley	" 222	108	114	Herbert S. Stratton
"	Annie E. Walcut	" 559	266	293	Eben C. Stratton (Senator)
"	S. R. Urbino	" 40	22	18	William A. Rust
Westboro'	Mrs. A. J. Snow	" 121	29	92	Horace F. Webster
"	L. M. Temple	" 6	2	4	
Dennis	Hannah H. Paddock	" 128	41	87	Geo. H. Loring
Acushnet	Sallie G. Wilbour	" 28	8	20	F. C. S. Bartlett
Haverhill	S. Amelia Newell	" 76	36	40	Ed. G. Frothingham
Holyoke	Hannah Wild	" 201	34	167	Jeremiah J. Keane
Brockton	Miley Estes	" 55	21	34	Chas. H. Carey
"	Elizabeth B. Battles	" 46	20	26	Patrick McCarthy
Granville	Mrs. C. A. Noble	" 111	46	65	Henry K. Herrick
Chelsea	Anna C. Lee	" 141	71	70	Geo. E. Morrill
Plymouth	Phebe R. Clifford	" 19	5	14	Arthur Lord
South Boston	Georgiana V. Robinson	" 37	6	31	Richard F. Tobin
Cambridge	C. L. F. Cooper	" 80	11	69	John W. Wilkinson
Brewster	Augusta T. Lincoln	" 120	44	76	Isaiah C. Young
Brockton	Sarah Packard	" 33	12	21	Patrick McCarthy
"	Olive D. Williams	" 91	44	47	Chas. H. Carey
"	"	" 87	42	45	" " "
"	"	" 87	41	46	" " "
West Newton	E. L. N. Walton	" 84	42	42	" " "
Boston	Eliz. S. Chadbourne	" 120	38	82	Elijah W. Wood
Lowell	Mrs. A. L. Richmond	" 29	5	24	Hazard Stevens
Worcester	Abby W. Wyman	" 85	26	59	Francis E. Shaw
Boston	Mary O. Ames	" 54	20	34	Henry S. Parker
Dorchester	Martha Clapp	" 64	14	50	William A. Rust
New Bedford	Wm. W. Crapo	" 93	40	53	Frank E. Brigham
Westboro	Sophia A. Forbes	" 769	333	434	Oliver P. Brightman
"	Calista A. Sturtevant	" 115	37	78	Horace F. Webster
Westvale	Annie E. Damon	" 33	13	20	
Raynham	Minot J. Lincoln	" 68	16	52	Henry J. Hosmer
		174	72	102	Melvin Wilbar

64 Petitions. Number of Petitioners: 6,497—2,375 Men and 4,122 Women.

When Julia undertook the task of collecting signatures on a petition for municipal woman suffrage, she knew it would be difficult. Concord, without a Woman Suffrage League, took a conservative position on the woman suffrage issue. Just last year Julia had been so discouraged over the lack of local support for a proposed suffrage meeting that she sent word to Mrs. Emerson: "I think I had better send back word to postpone it." Mrs. Emerson insisted that the suffragists meet in Concord, replying: "Do not send such a reply from Concord; appoint the meeting." Mrs. Emerson, who paid for the rental of the hall where the suffragists met, was rewarded when fifty individuals braved stormy weather to attend the meeting. Frank B. Sanborn, a former radical abolitionist, presided; the speaker, a Professor Harris, read his paper on "the need of woman's help in perfecting our development and civilization." Julia was heartened when those attending joined the cause as "avowed suffragists" and agreed to put *The Woman's Journal* in the town library.

Despite her age and the recurrence of the *"turns,"* the fainting spells of her girlhood, Julia did more than arrange and attend meetings. In January of 1886 Julia submitted a municipal suffrage petition with sixty-four signatures, a far cry from the four hundred signatures Thoreau had garnered on the 1849 Washington Goode petition from Concord. Julia had worn herself out, going from house to house and from farm to farm, getting the signatures of forty-two women and twenty-two men. Julia's activity was repeated by others across the state from Dorchester to Dennis, from Gardner to Worcester, for a total of sixty-four petitions with 6,497 petitioners—two-thirds women, one-third men. These petitions were submitted to the legislature by the third week in January. By the time the legislature voted on the issue, another fifty-seven petitions had been tallied, bring the number of petitioners to 10,511.

Julia's petition was referred to Henry J. Hosmer, himself a Concord resident, who represented the 26th Middlesex District of Acton, Carlisle, Concord, and Lincoln in the Massachusetts State House of Representatives. Hosmer, who was seated on the House Finance and the Joint Expenditures Committees, did not heed his petitioning neighbors. In April, he voted with the majority to defeat the municipal woman suffrage bill 132-77. The petitions from all corners of the Commonwealth had failed to convince the legislature of the merits of municipal woman suffrage.

In addition to Democrats, the Catholic Church, and the liquor lobbyists, there were some Republicans in opposition, their numbers increased as a younger generation of Harvard-educated, wealthy conservatives came of age. There were also the Antis, influential women who opposed woman suffrage of any kind. The Antis included the wives of some of the most prominent Bostonians: architect Randolph Coolidge, publisher Henry O. Houghton, philanthropist Robert Treat Paine, U.S. Senator Henry Cabot Lodge, State Senator George B. Crocker, and physician Charles Dudley Homans. Julia could never fathom how Mrs. Homans, known for her intelligence and graciousness, could serve on the State Board of Prison Commissioners and simultaneously be the leader of the Antis. This group of "Beacon Street silks," whose strong influence had defeated a municipal woman suffrage bill three years earlier, once again carried the day. Notable Bostonians who lent support to the Antis were orator Edward Everett Hale, author Richard H. Dana, and historian Francis Parkman. The latter felt that suffrage would bring harm not only to women and to family life, but to the state as well. Parkman wrote, "Women would be wily politicians, but, being women, would be immune from attack."

Julia and the thousands of other women in the rank and file of the campaign for municipal suffrage would not concede defeat. They persevered, using the tactics of petitioning and running a bazaar that they had honed in the fight against slavery. The last suffrage bazaar in Massachusetts had been held fifteen years ago, so the one scheduled for next month, in mid-December 1886, was eagerly anticipated. It seemed a lifetime ago that Julia had sold glassware at the Anti-Slavery Bazaar, and in many ways, it was, occurring before her studies at the Design School, her years of work in Lowell, the endless legal tangles, and her marriage. She had been married for over a quarter of a century! Settling into the routine of farm life, she yielded to the seasons and their calendar. Although she was still extending herself for a cause, she was more philosophical than she had been in her younger days regarding the amount of time needed for change. Years had dispelled some of the urgency she had felt when working for abolition. She was confident that women would someday be granted the right to vote. Although she herself may not live to cast a ballot for anyone other than school committee candidates, she believed her niece Ellen would one day vote for governor and even president.

It was after five o'clock when Julia looked up from her list-making to greet her husband as he came into the kitchen. A rush of November evening air and the sound of foxes barking in the woodlot followed him as he walked through the doorway. After he had finished milking the cows, John had walked to the riverbank to observe the muskrats. Since his youth, he had been intrigued by their building and swimming skills. With the sun setting about a minute earlier each day, today the almanac noted it at 4:16 P.M., the muskrats took advantage of the early darkness to emerge from their holes in the riverbank. A new moon was still two days away. Conscious of the animals and birds in his world, he looked for an old favorite, the tame little saw-whet owl. It was certainly more pleasant to have around than the great-horned owl whose raucous hooting had awakened him and Julia the previous night or the goshawk that sometimes invaded the poultry yards of the farms along the river. John thought he glimpsed a saw-whet in the distant leafless birches, so he replicated its double whistle of heu-heu and was rewarded with a returned greeting. In an earlier time Julia would have asked her husband about the other tasks he had planned to finish that afternoon, but that was not the case now. Ever since he had sustained severe injuries resulting from his fall under a load of sand, John found his chores a daily battle. The days of his winning cash payments for cranberries and apples at the Massachusetts Agricultural Society shows were over. Without John's participation, Julia no longer displayed her carpet designs and mats at the shows. Having had "the proud distinction of being the strongest man in town," he knew what was lost. And Julia put up a brave front even as her sister Ellen expressed dismay at John's weakened state.

John eased himself into the chair by the cast-iron stove, a chair he much preferred to the horsehair sofa in the parlor with its lace curtains and densely patterned carpet. He liked the kitchen with its well-worn floorboards; the light from the kerosene lamp dispelled the shadows, pushing them to the corner where the drying rack was hung with his still damp socks. He was delighted that the hired girl was preparing a favorite apple dish that Julia had taught her to make. As she flattened the dough into circles, then piled cut apples in the center of each circle, pulling up the edges to cover the fruit, John's thoughts strayed to this fall's apple picking. Nothing was better than an apple from one of his trees. John watched as each bundle of apples was wrapped in cloth, tied with string, and dropped into the large pot of water already boiling on the stove. John was looking forward to dessert.

In reply to John's query, Julia explained that she was checking her lists of friends and neighbors who had promised items for the suffrage bazaar. The scheduled speakers, the chorus of a hundred voices, even the special bazaar journal edited by Julia Ward Howe were all very well, but Julia knew the heart of any bazaar was the sales area. There were plans for thirty-five tables for "Sales of Christmas Goods, Useful and Fancy Articles." Donations were pouring in from other states, some, such as Minnesota and Colorado, hadn't even existed when Julia worked at the Anti-Slavery Bazaar in 1850. There were slippers and needlework, shell pincushions from Nantucket, fir-balsam pillows, pottery, paintings and photographs, wheat crackers, and homemade candies. Plans included selling slices of Centennial Pudding; the recipe, not the pudding, was over a century old. Local suffrage supporters had promised articles of needle-work and fancy items to the Concord Town Committee for this bazaar. The committee members were Frank B. Sanborn, Mr. & Mrs. John Barrett, Mrs. Anna B. Pratt, Rev. B. R. Bulkeley, Ann H. Bigelow, Prof. Wm. T. Harris, and Jane Hosmer. The inclusion of Julia's Unitarian minister, Reverend Bulkeley, was a firm rebuttal to the claims of the Antis; how could they say "only bad women would vote" with a member of the clergy supporting the cause? With funds desperately needed for organizing local suffrage groups, the goal for the bazaar was set at the astronomical amount of $5,000, about double the value of the entire Barrett homestead and seventy acres! Nothing could be left to chance. Tomorrow Julia would collect the promised items and send them by train to the city. John knew he would be commissioned to help. He didn't mind; if it was important to Julia, that was enough for him.

Julia once again expounded to John how she wished Concord had its own Woman Suffrage League! Every town with a suffrage group had a banner to display at the bazaar. She would have loved to help with the sewing of Concord's banner, with the design, the selection of colors, and the quotation. It would be more glorious than any of her carpet designs! The banner for the Boston League had a quote from her old friend Theodore Parker: "Justice is the key-note of the world, and all else is ever out of tune."

John studied his wife. How proud he was of her. When Julia announced a few years ago that she would accompany him to town meeting to vote for school committee, he was pleased. How different his reaction was from that of some of the other husbands in town! And last year, when the local historian in his chronicle of houses of Concord and their inhabitants had described Julia as "strong-minded," John had smiled as if he had won a blue ribbon at the county fair.

Life after two losses

As she went about her morning tasks, cooking, sewing and such, the nagging thought of this afternoon's meeting of the Concord Female Charitable Society gave Julia no peace. Should she attend? As it was the annual meeting—and she had missed only one of these in the last decade—she wanted to be there. But did she really want to face all those sympathetic friends and neighbors? Although her attendance at the monthly meetings was sporadic, an April meeting, a June meeting, maybe an October meeting, she was proud of her attendance at annual meetings. One moment she decided to stay home; the next moment she was considering what to wear. Her heavy black serge skirt, her black surah silk blouse with a belt, her fine black cashmere shawl with the crocheted edge would do nicely. With no time to spare, she made up her mind to join the other women, some friends, some nodding acquaintances, in the parlor of her church, the Unitarian church in Concord Center. She had pleasant memories of earlier meetings at the elegant Main Street home of Mrs. Ebenezer Rockwood Hoar where she had the opportunity to observe how the wealthy folk lived. All the times she had called on Judge Hoar for help in sorting through the legal tangles of the Robbins wills and estate provisions, she never had the leisure to gaze at her surroundings as she did while sewing at the monthly meetings held in his home.

Wasting no time in hitching up the horse, Julia climbed into the wagon and took the reins. Another wave of doubt swept over her. It wasn't until she reached Minot Pratt's huge elm tree, its bare branches silhouetted against the darkening winter sky, that she squared her shoulders and urged the horse forward. Perhaps some memory of the now-deceased Minot and the adventurous young woman she once had been when she met him on a visit to Brook Farm half a century ago urged her forward. She had felt alone in the world then, but not as alone as she felt now. At the last meeting she had attended on October 8 just three months earlier, she had no inkling of what lay ahead. That was an ordinary monthly meeting with only sixteen women in attendance, sewing, as usual, for the unfortunate children in town. Then, eleven days later, on Sunday, October 19, her husband, kind, helpful John, had a sudden attack and died; he was sixty-four.

John probably never thought he would pre-decease Julia. The Barrett men were long-lived; for six generations, only John's grandfather had died before he reached seventy, passing away at age sixty-seven. Two of his ancestors lived into their eighties, the prize going to great-great-great-grandfather Humphrey Barrett, Jr., who lived to age eighty-six. This was despite his birth in England in 1630, the same year the Massachusetts Bay Colony was established, coming to the New World with his father, and experiencing the deprivations and difficulties faced by early settlers. For one with such long-lived ancestors, death was not expected to pay an early call on John.

The local paper, *The Enterprise*, recorded John's passing.

The people of our town were greatly surprised and shocked on Monday morning to hear of the sudden death of Mr. John Barrett, a life long resident and much respected citizen. He was on the street on Saturday evening, in his usual good health and spirits, and on Sunday made no complaint, performing his usual duties. Late in the afternoon he went to to [*sic*] the barn to do his chores, and not returning, a search resulted in finding him dead, evidently from an attack of heart disease. In the death of Mr. Barrett the town loses one of its best known characters. A friend to every one, rich or poor, he was always ready and willing to do a kind act, and had always a cheerful greeting for all. For nearly half a century, he has borne the proud distinction of being the strongest man in town, and the story of his prowess and feats of strength would fill a book. Some years ago he fell under a load of sand, receiving severe injuries from which he never fully recovered and which undoubtedly hastened his death. A regular attendant of the Unitarian church he was always to be found at its meetings, whether religious or social. The funeral services were held at the church Wednesday afternoon, Rev. B. R. Bulkeley assisted by Rev. Mr. Holland, officiating. Mr. Barrett was sixty-four years old.

This obituary placed John in his world of Concord, but Julia was most comforted by the "In Memoriam" in *The Woman's Journal*, which identified John as "one of our number." Citing the cause of death as "heart failure," the piece continued:

His wife, Julia Robbins Barrette [*sic*], who has our heartfelt sympathy, is well known to many of the readers of the *Woman's Journal,* having been identified with the cause of liberty from youth. She and her family being foremost in the grand work of abolishing African slavery, as was natural she early identified herself with the "woman's cause." She found a ready helper in her husband, who voiced her sentiments most heartily, and was always constant in his attendance with her at our league meetings.

Somehow Julia got through the following days. After the service on Wednesday, the 22nd, John was buried with his parents, Sarah and Joel, and his unmarried sister, Caroline Augusta, in Concord's Sleepy Hollow Cemetery. His mother had died in 1859, at age sixty-three, the year before John married Julia; perhaps her passing had enabled John to change his domestic status and marry. Caroline and Joel had died a few years after John's marriage. Although there were three married sisters and their offspring, the Barrett name and lineage through Joel's only son ended with John.

Now in her seventy-first year, Julia felt old. Despite well-expressed concerns for her welfare, she had no intention of leaving the farm, which she and John had freed from mortgage and had even increased in size. There was now the homestead of fifty acres, the wood lot of twenty acres, and the Ball's Hill Lot of eleven and a half acres, the latter purchased in 1880. Their holdings were not the only things that had increased. In the thirty years since their marriage, the tax rate almost doubled from $5.70 to $10.80; the total town valuation did likewise, from $1,775,000 to $3,583,901. The livestock had been sold, but the Barrett farm in Concord's North Quarter was Julia's farm and she intended to keep it so. She was aware that things wouldn't always stay the same as inevitably the world was already changing around her. Even her road, the River Road to Carlisle, had a new name, Monument Street; local sculptor Daniel Chester French's statue of a militia man marked the site of the April 19 fight along the river.

The realization of John's death was just setting in when the second blow came on October 28. Ellen, who had been in poor health for almost a decade, died of pneumonia. The week after the "In Memoriam" honoring John appeared in *The Woman's Journal*, the paper printed an "In

Memoriam" for Ellen A. Stone. Julia's sister and partner in so many family and community affairs was praised for her support of equal rights for women, a passion she passed on to her surviving daughter Ellen, now enrolled at the Boston University Law School.

The death of Ellen's younger daughter Mary seven years earlier had exacerbated Ellen's penchant for worry—she became consumed with worry about Julia slipping on the ice, about John's weakened state. Julia had brushed aside her sister's concerns and kept her own counsel. Never one to worry about what others might say about her, Julia did as she thought best. True, there had been much about Julia to set tongues wagging: when she circulated the petition for Washington Goode, when she traveled to Boston to hear liberal, even radical, men preach about abolition and woman's rights, when she took employment at the Lowell Company, when she threatened to sue Davison over breach of promise, when she circulated the petition for municipal woman suffrage a few years ago. Just like her beloved friend Eliza Follen, Julia had also defied convention by marrying a man several years her junior. Julia was like Amy, the heroine in Eliza's book *Sketches of Married Life*; her opinions were always her own. Like Amy, Julia acted "with sense and feeling, and without asking what people will say." With her understanding husband who respected her opinions and actions, she had found a deep contentment. But now John was gone.

Julia was glad she had taken her black and white blanket shawl from the hook by the back door. Through her hooded cape, which covered even her black velvet bonnet, the January cold was reaching her bones; the shawl provided added warmth. Her gray squirrel muff, made in her father's fur mill in East Lexington, would have been a comfort, as much for the memories as for the piece itself, if she hadn't had to hold the reins. She urged the horse toward town thinking of past meetings, content with the time spent sewing petticoats and children's drawers and chemises, or stitching garments destined for a particularly unfortunate family. Sometimes the ladies worked on sheets, towels, and tablecloths for the town's Aged People's Home. The purpose of the society, duly noted in fine, spidery handwriting in a bound notebook graced with a marbleized paper cover, was "to relieve the wants of the indigent and stressed." Although at the July 1889 meeting, which Julia missed, "the ladies worked for the Johnstown sufferers," most of the group's efforts had local beneficiaries

Julia's name appeared twenty-six times on the attendance lists of the Concord Female Charitable Society between 1879 and 1893. Mrs. John Barrett is listed in the middle of the third column for the January 12, 1881, meeting.

with special attention reserved for the children of the poor. Monitoring the children's religion and morality and checking on their regular attendance at both Sunday meeting and at school was considered part of the charge of the Concord Female Charitable Society.

Even though a good crowd was expected for the afternoon's meeting, few items of clothing for the needy would probably be finished. The annual meeting agenda traditionally included a letter from the Children's Committee "showing how much the little folks appreciated the Christmas gifts distributed among them." Any vacancies that had occurred over the past twelve months would be filled, the treasurer's position among these. Julia had noticed that the acknowledgment for her 25 cent annual dues was from one of the other officers.

With a Lyceum lecture scheduled for this evening, the meeting would conclude with a supper served promptly at six. Gentlemen were invited to the supper and Julia expected several to be present. Had John been alive, she would have insisted on his escorting her and staying for the lecture. Tonight's speaker, Sergius Stepniak, intrigued her. Billed as "The Celebrated Leader of the Russian Revolutionary Party," his topic was "Siberian Exile." Stepniak, whose real name was Serge Kravchinsky, was "a man of great daring and physical strength" and "the darling of the revolutionary movement." After assassinating the head of the Russian political police, he escaped abroad, becoming the "leading interpreter in the west of the Russian revolutionary movement." The locals were pleased with their choice; this Russian author and nihilist had delivered his first lecture in Boston just eight days earlier. As heirs to the American Revolution, Julia and others in Concord welcomed Stepniak.

As Widow Barrett, she knew that the sympathetic looks cast her way would reopen the wounds of loss and loneliness. As she had been so many times in her life, she was again alone. Emerson had taught her to rely on herself, Parker had honed her ideals, and as Eli Robbins's daughter, she would face the unknown future as he did after the personally disastrous Panic of 1837—with hope in her heart. After tying the horse to a post in the churchyard, she turned as she heard her name called in the gathering dusk. A confident and neatly, even fashionably, attired Widow Barrett quickened her steps to join a friend.

EPILOGUE

Julia's last years
1892–1900

After John's death, Julia found herself looking at the farm from a different vantage point and what she saw emphasized her aloneness. She still delighted in the changing seasons, but each season had its own demands that threatened to overwhelm her. She knew it was time to sell the farm. In 1898, eight years after John's death, Julia sold her farm to William Brewster, a Harvard professor, ornithologist, and first president of the newly established Massachusetts Audubon Society. For the first time in its multi-generational history, the farm had an owner who was not a Barrett.

Julia packed her belongings and took leave of Concord, a place greatly changed since John had brought her there as a bride in 1860. Not only had the population doubled from 2,246 to 4,435 inhabitants, the town was a tourist attraction. It was site of the shot heard 'round the world, the homes of the philosophers Emerson and Thoreau, as well as the home of the little women who sprang to life from Louisa May Alcott's pen. Bicycles were everywhere, canoes plied the Assabet River, and local merchants delighted in sales of souvenirs and postcards. Thoreau would not have recognized the area surrounding Walden Pond as excursion boats and bathhouses, dining and dancing halls dotted the scene.

Back in East Lexington, Julia did not choose to live with either her sister Abby or her niece Ellen although the reasons for this are unknown. The federal census of 1900 recorded Julia as residing in Lexington with her former neighbors, the Dana family. Lexington, too, had drastically changed from the previous years in which Julia had lived there. The town buildings now had electric lights and $3,000 had been appropriated to convert the gas streetlights to electricity. In one of her last letters to Julia, Ellen had noted that the *"boom was in Upper Lexington,"* and she was right. Even though East Lexington claimed three of the four places in town where one could have a horse shod, the center of town was gaining on its once-and-still rival, the eastern part of town. Only ten of the twenty-three milk dealers, three of the eleven market gardeners, two of the six grocers, one of the three hairdressers, and one of the nine insurance brokers had East Lexington addresses. However, East Lexington had its compensations. The shade trees planted by Eli Robbins along Massachusetts Avenue (once Main Street) over half a century ago, coupled with the many houses on the street in the architectural style Eli favored (with five front windows on the second floor), made East Lexington "an attractive part of the town" according to the local business directory. East Lexington's bustling and noisy glory days of fur mills and teamster hotels were over. Julia's father's hall was now a branch of the town library, partly as a gift by Julia's niece Ellen. Julia, wanting her sister to receive her due, gave a portrait of the late Mrs. Ellen Stone for that building.

Lexington, then as now, celebrated its entry into history. Julia witnessed the commemoration of the 125th anniversary of April 19, 1775, the day that her maternal grandfather, Joshua Simonds, entered local legend for his action in saving the militia's gunpowder stored in the belfry. This was never just another day for her; it was the wellspring of her idealism.

A final glimpse of Julia, alive and in haste, was recorded by one of her Arlington cousins:

> Mrs. Barrett at 80 years of age is sprightly, and in full possession of all of her faculties, on occasion [she] prefers to walk for a mile or more rather than await conveyance; she resides 'mid the scenes of her childhood.

Julia died on October 5, 1900, in New England Hospital in Boston; she was 81 years, 4 months, and 11 days in age. Both Lexington and Boston registers noted the cause of her death: "Intestinal obstruction, old age, and hypostatic congestion of lungs."

A few days later a small funeral procession approached Sleepy Hollow Cemetery in the center of Concord, made its way through Authors' Gate, and stopped at the foot of the hill. To the right was a shady, slightly sloping plot marked by a white marble obelisk, the name Barrett clearly visible at the base. Julia was laid to rest beside John, joining his parents Sarah and Joel, and his sister Caroline. Carved on the left side of the obelisk was:

> John Barrett
> July 4. 1826
> October 16. 1890
> _____
> Julia A. Robbins
> His Wife
> May 6. 1819
> Oct. 5. 1900

A closer inspection of the 300 square foot plot reveals five small marble head stones sunken into the sparse grass and spreading moss indicating each individual member of the Barrett family buried there; the initials JARB are carved into one of them.

A true daughter of the nineteenth century, Julia participated in the reform movements that changed the country—abolition, temperance, and suffrage. She arranged anti-slavery speakers, circulated petitions, and volunteered at Boston's Anti-Slavery Bazaar at a time when so doing was considered radical. She was gratified when the Concord Woman Suffrage League was organized in June 1887. There appeared a seven-paragraph article on this event in *The Woman's Journal*, with an entire paragraph lauding Julia:

> Mrs. J. R. Barrett, who has always responded to every call made upon her from our headquarters, was present and expressed her delight at the success of the movement.

Schooled by Theodore Parker, Julia learned well a commitment to social action. On her death, *The Woman's Journal* noted, "Mrs. Barrett had a bright mind, and was a zealous Abolitionist and advocate of equal suffrage for women."

Julia did more than look on as the Industrial Revolution transformed the nation. When the Lowell mills were spewing forth enough cloth and carpet to encircle the globe, Julia's designing talents had contributed to the boom of industry. She was born when James Monroe of the Virginia dynasty was president, lived through twenty presidential administrations, and died when William McKinley was in the White House. Twenty-four states had joined the Union in Julia's lifetime, raising the tally to forty-five. She had reached adulthood before Texas, the Mexican Cession, and the Oregon Territory were acquired by the United States; lived through a bloody civil war; and died as the country was taking a place on the world stage, having acquired Cuba and the Philippine Islands after the Spanish-American War. When she was a young girl using Aunt Caira's pastels, John Singleton Copley's portraits set the standard for art. On trips to Boston in her years as a widow, she probably wondered about the new style of painting favored by Bostonians; daring for both style and color, it was labeled Impressionistic. She was a true citizen of her century; like her country, doing and going and becoming, always in haste.

When Lexington historian S. Lawrence Whipple described Julia's niece Ellen Stone as "a proud, intelligent, and independent woman, and one not easily daunted," he could have been referring to individuals from three generations of Robbins women; in addition to Julia's niece, Julia's Aunt Caira, Julia, and her sister Ellen all displayed this same strength of character. Yet Julia has been virtually forgotten, even more so than the other Robbins women. Aunt Caira Robbins' box of pastels is in Boston's Museum of Fine Arts, Ellen Robbins Stone's letters to the town disputing the cutting down of an elm tree on Massachusetts Avenue are local lore, and Ellen Stone is remembered as the first woman elected to the School Committee. For Julia Robbins Barrett, what remains is her name on petitions, as well as admission tickets to the Concord School of Philosophy, a diary, and some letters.

Nevertheless, today's women live in a society that Julia helped shape through her lifetime of work for causes that mattered. Hard-won rights come at a cost of time and energy, persistence and perseverance of prior generations. That Julia has been forgotten does not make her endeavors any less important or cancel our debt to her. As long as each generation is true to its ideals, as Julia was, her work will be honored even though her name is forgotten. That is how she would have wanted it.

Julia would concur with Whipple's judgment that "The Robbins-Stone families would have been right at home in today's activist world."

She would most likely still be at ease in East Lexington, attending another lecture in Eli's hall, sitting in her pew #35 at Follen Church, and walking briskly along Massachusetts Avenue, recognizing buildings now almost two centuries old. The changing seasons would still bring the same delights—the golden-hued palate of autumn, an early snow spread like wisps of cotton over the landscape, delicate showers of petals from the fruit trees in the spring, a clear summer day with a hawk wheeling over the field at Wilson Farm. Julia would find a way to express her ideals, indifferent to the century, committed to a cause that would extend respect and rights to those individuals still overlooked in our world.

Chapter 1

JULY 4, 1824

7   *The house*   Reinhardt and Grady, 23–35.

7   *A ruffled shirt*   Stone, 176.

LATE SUMMER 1832–SPRING 1833

13   *The fur mill*   "Reminiscences." *Proceedings*, 171–79; "Lexington Sixty Years Ago." *Proceedings*, 19–64.

14   *Caira's dress*   Stone, 74. This is also noted in Earle, 797–99. (These contradict Nylander, *The Art of Family*, 206, which refers to the salmon pink dress as the one Caira wore on Broadway.)

15   *box of English pastels*   Nylander, *The Art of Family*, 202–203.

15   *academy days and travels*   Stone, 62–80.

16   *Nabby*   Stone, 62–64.

17   *"I address . . . malignant fever"*   A. Robbins to A. Langdon, 19 November 1832.

17   *"on Wednesday"*   Hudson, Date of death as November 7, a Wednesday.

17   *quarantining passengers*   Rosenberg, 14.

17   *$50,000*   Ibid., 91.

17   *"festering manure . . . the disease"*   Ibid., 36.

17   *"[d]iarrhea . . . cramps"*   Ibid., 2.

17   *Stillman Spaulding*   Hudson, 555; 656.

18   *"As mother . . . Abby Robbins"*   Abby Robbins to Julia Robbins, 7 December 1832.

19   *"Having a few . . . the country"*   Ellen Robbins to Julia Robbins, 12 December 1832.

20   *met her father*   Julia Robbins to Caira Langdon, 21 April 1833.

21   *"Wash Monday . . . sweep carpets"*   Ellen Robbins' Diary, 1834.

21   *master builder*   Lexington architectural historians Reinhardt and Grady wrote "Master builder Issac Melvin must have come to East Lexington with copies of Asher Benjamin in his valise."

21   *"the prosperous . . . small businesses"*   Ibid.

22   *"J.A.H. . . . the Caryall [sic]"*   Ellen Robbins' Diary, 23 June 1833.

AUGUST 1835

23 *Adams Female Academy* Sklar, 191; Newell, 100–101.

24 *"All pupils . . . the Sabbath"* Catalogue Adams Female Academy, 1835–7.

24 *"so well contented"* Ellen Robbins (signed Adelia) to Julia Robbins, 19 August 1835.

JULY 1836

24 *"Bonnet $7.50"* Julia Robbins' Expense Account, 1836.

25 *evils of whispering* Julia Robbins' essay, 1836.

25 *Zilpah Grant* Green, 40–56.

25 *schedule . . . monitorial system* Catalogue Adams Female Academy; Green, 46.

26 *"Where the French . . . to follow"* Schiff, 166.

26 *"If we wish . . . to be profited"* Julia Robbins' essay, 1836.

27 *certificate* Adams Female Academy, 20 October 1835.

28 *town census* Hudson, 478.

28 *town budget* Town Report, 1835.

Chapter 2

Quotations from Buell are reprinted by permission of the publisher from *Emerson* by Lawrence Buell, Cambridge, Mass.: The Belknap Press of Harvard University Press, Copyright © 2003 by the President and Fellows of Harvard College.

FEBRUARY 1839

32 *Eli Robbins' businesses* Robbins-Stone Family Papers.

32 *"that we act . . . directs us"* Buell, 73.

33 *Emerson. . . . "perpendicular coffin"* height, weight, and manner of speaking, McAleer, 291–292 and lecture in East Lexington on the East Lexington Lyceum, 16 October 1983.

34 *"the sky and the woods"* Emerson, *Nature,* 21.

34 *"the charm. . . . of a January sunset"* Ibid., 22.

34 *"the graces of . . . summer"* Ibid., 23.

34 *"Build . . . world"* Ibid., 92.

34 *"inner spiritual experience"* Buell, 37.

34 *"I have been . . . read it"* Julia Robbins to Mary Plumer, 12 April 1839.

35 *"He spoke . . . I apprehended"* Stone, 71.

MARCH 25, 1844

35 *high tide for the Utopian communities* Walters, *American Reformers 1815–1860,* ix.

36 *Despite his history of troublemaking*   William Plumer, according to *Harvard Class Book 1845* was expelled with six others for the "gross act of insubordination," which was signing his name to a remonstrance against The Golden Branch Society. Plumer noted "In College, as in my former life, I have had few troubles and fewer friends . . . I have never known care."

36 *the railroad finally came*   The railroad's inaugural run was August 25, 1846. Kollen, *Lexington, Massachusetts Treasures from Historic Archives*, 100.

36 *another laundry day*   "Laundry" exhibit at National Heritage Museum, November 2005.

36 *commotion in the household*   Julia Robbins' Diary, 9 December 1850.

37 *"Since I last . . . deserted castle. . . ."*   Caira Robbins Langdon to Caira Robbins, 14 March 1844.

38 *"a barren place indeed"*   Julia Robbins to Caira Langdon and Ellen Robbins, 28 March 1843.

38 *"We had . . . enough of it"*   Ibid.

38 *"a truly mysterious subject"*   Ibid.

38 *the Phinneys*   Hudson II, 180–81.

38 *"did not . . . until afterwards"*   Julia Robbins to Caira Langdon and Ellen Robbins, 28 March 1843.

39 *Charles Follen*   Francke, *Dictionary of American Biography.*

40 *"beautiful wife"*   Ellen Robbins to Caira Robbins Langdon, 13 May 1839.

40 *"state of slavery"*   Ibid.

40 *Follen . . . once again relieved of a position*   "A Lot of History in Its Eight Corners," *Lexington Minuteman* (Lexington, MA), 30 December 1971, 30B+.

40 *on Robbins' land*   "Reminiscences," *Proceedings*, 176–77. The land was given by Stephen Robbins.

40 *On Monday evening*   Brayton, 9.

41 *despite their fund-raising . . . denied a vote*   Faith Ferguson e-mails, 27 and 29 May 2003. Ms. Ferguson expressed the idea that women doing the work and not being able to vote in parish affairs was a radicalizing experience for Julia.

41 *fair on Mt. Independence*   Notice for Fair 14 August 1839, Lexington Historical Society.

41 *"Two women . . . liberal minds"*   Note by one of the Robbins Women, UU Church Archives, attributed to Julia Robbins based on the handwriting.

42 *pews*   Hannah and Julia purchased pew #35, noted on Certificate #48, 15 January 1840; Stephen Robbins, pew #27, Certificate #5.

42 *chandelier*   Deming Jarves Invoice 1, 16 November 1844, UU Church Archives.

42 *Their mother Hannah*   Hannah also gave $5 to help meet the $350.78 cost of the church bell with its yoke and wheel. List—Contributions toward Bell undated UU Church Archives.

May 11, 1845

44 *Brook Farm*   Julia recorded visits to Brook Farm in her diary on two occasions; these entries provide the basis for this section. Julia Robbins' Diary, 2 May 1845 and 11 May 1845. Several works provide details of life here. See this section of the bibliography.

44 *white painted*   Swift, 27–8.

44 *the cent*   Ibid., 49.

44 *thousands of visitors*   Ibid., 203.

44 *charge its visitors for meals*   Delano, 53.

44 *"retrenchment"*   Dwight, 51.

44 *the Eyrie*   Swift, 30.

45 *the bespectacled Ripley*   Ibid., 144.

45 *Charles Fourier*   Gordon, 2; Haraszti, 28.

45 *"perfect order"*   Gordon, 2.

45 *George Ripley*   Adams, *Dictionary of American Biography*.

45 *his private library*   Ibid., 24.

45 *Sophia*   Bernardete, *Notable American Women*.

45 *many sent by Harvard*   Curtis, 69.

45 *checked domestic cotton dress*   Ibid., 66.

45 *laundry*   Swift, 50.

46 *ironing*   Curtis, 38.

46 *"Her Perpendicular Majesty"*   Ibid., 62.

46 *John Dwight*   Dobson, *Dictionary of American Biography*.

46 *Marianne Dwight*   Dwight.

46 *nursery duty*   Curtis, 183.

47 *sold locally*   Delano, 173.

47 *scarlet fever*   Ibid., 195.

47 *an amazing thirty dollars*   Ibid., 288.

47 *a good destination for a single man*   Delano, 82, 172.

47 *a sort of knickers . . . letting their hair fall loose*   Swift, 64.

47 *peas . . . potatoes*   Curtis, 56.

48 *Sale of berries*   Dwight, 28.

48 *the Phalanstery*   Swift, 34.

48 *"Whilst I see . . . for myself."*   Curtis, 50.

48 *Margaret Fuller*   Ibid., 114.

October 12, 1847

49 *Isabella grapevines . . . observatory*   "Reminiscences," *Proceedings,* 179.

49 *"Aunt Ca[ira] . . . of everything"*   Ellen Robbins' Diary, October 1847.

49 *a few coins*   "Give my thanks to Grandpapa for that money." Caira Langdon to Julia Robbins, 5 July 1829.

49   *his joking*   Julia Robbins to Ellen Robbins and Caira Robbins Langdon, 28 March 1843.

50   *he wouldn't be old*   "Reminiscences," *Proceedings,* 177.

50   *Julia took a mental inventory*   Hudson II, 577–81.

50   *Lexington tax records*   *Report of the Town of Lexington*, 1845.

51   *"particular attractions"*   Julia Robbins to Caira Robbins Langdon, 27 June 1844.

51   *"May morn . . . Henry"*   Letter from Henry Goodrich.

51   *"taken a contract . . . speculative"*   Ellen Robbins to George Simonds, 3 September 1847.

51   *"has learned . . . [Emerson's poems]"*   Henry Goodrich to Julia Robbins, 22 November 1847.

52   *an excursion to nearby Lincoln*   Ellen Robbins to George Simonds, 3 September 1847.

52   *"A letter . . . sent one"*   Ellen Robbins' Diary, 1847.

52   *Davison*   *Harvard College Class of 1845 Secretary's File*; *Harvard Class Book 1845.*

52   *"From my sixth year . . . unlearned"*   Ibid.

53   *Epitaph on a Goldfish*   Ellen Robbins' Diary, 1847.

54   *Lethe*   "In Greek mythology, a river in Hades whose water produced, in those who drank it, forgetfulness of the past." *OED*, 1570.

54   *"I have not been . . . all times"*   *Harvard Class Book 1845.*

54   *walked home with another*   Ellen Robbins' Diary, 10 January 1847.

54   *"he ought to be talked to"*   Ellen Robbins' Diary, 1847.

54   *a letter from his sister Nancy*   Nancy Svenson to Davison, 8 June 1846.

55   *their father, also named Andrew*   Petition of Andrew C. Davison.

55   *"two pedestrians"*   Ellen Robbins to George Simonds, 3 September 1847.

55   *"How long . . . three years"*   Benjamin R. Davison to Ellen Robbins, 29 July 1847.

55   *old memorandum book . . . turf ashes*   Caira Robbins Langdon to Caira Robbins, 11 March 1847.

SEPTEMBER 10, 1849

56   *Emerson had invited*   Buell, 247.

56   *"the Lord's chore boy"*   Mood, *Dictionary of American Biography.*

56   *A note from May*   Samuel May to Julia Robbins, Sunday noon, n. y.

56   *Dodge*   J. G. Dodge has remained elusive despite the author's checking graduates of divinity schools, church rosters, lists of abolitionists, and town directories.

56   *"universal brotherhood . . . of man"*   J. G. Dodge to Julia Robbins, 28 March 1849.

57   *to hear Brown*   J. G. Dodge to Julia Robbins, 17 April 1849.

57   *Dodge asked for*   Ibid.

57   *Washington Goode*   Articles in the *Liberator,* 30 March 1849 to 20 April 1849; *Council Files.*

58   *Women . . . petitions*   Bogin & Yellin, 17.

58   *"a political activity . . . suffrage"*   Van Brockhoven, 190.

59   *Goode petitions . . . Thoreau*   Wheeler, 161.

59   *398 signatures*   Jeffrey Cramer, Curator of the Henley Library at The Thoreau Institute at Walden Woods, letter to author, 5 June 2003.

59   *23,607 in all*   *Council Files.*

59   *Wendell Phillips*   In the following century, historian Richard Hofstadter described Phillips as the most impressive of the abolitionists and probably the most effective speaker of the era. 176–77, 181.

59   *people in the United States*   1850 census, *Historical Statistics,* Tables 91, 98, 119.

60   *"I hope . . . ungenerous manner"*   W. Q. Dow to Julia Robbins, 6 September 1849.

60   *valentine*   W. Q. Dow to Julia Robbins, 27 March 1848.

60   *"get a situation . . . a man"*   Ibid.

61   *108 pounds*   Julia Robbins' Diary, 17 January 1851.

61   *"new political . . . republic"*   Van Brockhoven, 193.

Chapter 3

Quotations from Porte are reprinted by permission of the publisher from *Emerson in His Journals,* selected and edited by Joel Porte, Cambridge, Mass.: The Belknap Press of Harvard University Press, Copyright © 1982 by the President and Fellows of Harvard College.

The first four episodes in this chapter rely heavily on Julia Robbins' Diary.

AUTUMN 1850

64   *tallied the Robbins' household*   1850 U.S. Census Lexington, Massachusetts, page 393 line 14.

66   *Julia began her reply*   Julia Robbins to Davison, October 1850.

DECEMBER 30, 1850

71   *Anti-Slavery Bazaar*   Julia Robbins' Diary, 14 December to 31 December 1850. Articles in the *Liberator,* 25 October 1850 to 31 January 1851.

71   *Without these fairs*   Ginzberg, 46.

71   *"The Union . . . Bazaar"*   "The Seventeenth National Anti-Slavery Bazaar," *Liberator,* 17 January 1851.

72   *speech last March 7th   Great Speeches*, 600–01.
72   *the abolition movement*   Kraditor, 3.
72   *"consigned his senator . . . of hell"*   Steward, 146.
72   *"Ichabod"*   Whittier, 186–87.
72   *"the divine Emerson"*   Julia Robbins' Diary, 1851.
72   *"Why did . . . For Sale"*   Porte, 437.
72   *"The fame . . . nasty law"*   Ibid., 422.
73   *"The air . . . in itself"*   Julia Robbins' Diary, 11 May 1851.
73   *"Garrisonians championed . . . on force"*   Harrold, 35–36. Quoted by
       permission.
73   *"exercised a strong personal influence . . . personified the religious beliefs of the
       group"*   Hersh, *The Slavery of Sex,* 144.
73   *Follen called abolition women's work*   Yellin, *Women and Sisters*, 60.
73   *Maria Weston Chapman*   Ibid., 49; Hersh, *The Slavery of Sex*, 11.
73   *This letter was critical*   Bogin & Yellin, "Introduction," 16.
73   *threat to the clergy's leadership*   Sklar, 32.
73   *two warring parties*   Hansen, *Strained Sisterhood,* 93. Hansen quoted Anne
       Warren Weston from the *Massachusetts Abolitionist,* 14 May 1840.
74   *In common with . . . feminist-abolitionists*   Hersh, *The Slavery of Sex*, 51.
74   *Liberty Bell*   1851 edition.
74   *All volunteers received*   Chambers-Schiller, 258.
74   *Foreward-dated*   Taylor, 88.
75   *explained . . . romanticized*   Ibid, 87–98.

February 1851

76   *the sun didn't rise*   Brown, *Brown's Almanac.*
77   *Grandmother . . . dress*   Nylander in Simons and Benes, 201–02; Earle,
       797–803.
77   *After an illness*   Ellen Robbins' Diary, 1847.
77   *Elizabeth and Martha*   Hudson II, 621.
77   *"bump of order"*   Ellen Robbins Stone to Julia Robbins, 19 October 1857.
78   *thousands upon thousands of stitches*   "As many as 20,000 stitches were
       needed to finish just one shirt." *Sewing Clothing.*
78   *a sewing machine*   Ibid. These machines were powered by a wheel turned
       by hand.
79   *Theodore Parker*   Christie, *Dictionary of American Biography;* Richardson,
       95–100, 204.
79   *"the miraculous . . . colleagues"*   Grodzins, "Chronology of *American Heretic.*"
79   *sit in church all day*   Julia Robbins' Diary fragment, 2 March n.y.
80   *"a perfect specimen of progress"*   Ellen Robbins' Diary, 1847.
80   *the weather*   Ludlum, *Country Journal*, 13–35.

December 1851

82   *events for 1851*   Julia Robbins' Diary throughout 1851, especially October and November. The entry for 10 October 1851 has an account of Parker's speech.

84   *a Miss Ednah Littlehale*   Ingerbritsen, *Notable American Women.*

86   *"the school . . . soon relinquished . . ."*   Cheney, "Schools of Design for Women," *The Woman's Journal,* 23 January 1886.

86   *"I am reminded . . . carpet-factory there"*   Cheney, "The School of Design," *The Woman's Journal,* 6 February 1886.

September 5, 1852

Details of Julia Robbins' life in Lowell—working hours, accommodations, supervisor, etc. are in letters to Ellen Robbins: 1 September 1852, 5 September 1852, 16 January 1853 and in her Expense Accounts for the years 1855, 1856, and 1857. Material quoted from Ewing and Norton: Reprinted by permission of the publisher from *Broadlooms and Businessmen: A History of the Bigelow-Stanford Carpet Company* by John S. Ewing and Nancy P. Norton, Cambridge, Mass.: Harvard University Press, Copyright © 1955 by the President and Fellows of Harvard College. Copyright © renewed 1983 by John Sinclair Ewing and Nancy Paine Norton.

87   *"We are . . . could design"*   Julia Robbins to Ellen Robbins, 1 September 1852.

87   *"largest . . . carpetings"*   Ewing and Norton, 7.

87   *business in ingrain carpets*   Ibid., 1.

87   *"an invention . . . with intellect"*   *Lowell Manufacturing Company: The Gateway to the Park,* 3.

87   *eighteen tons of wool*   Ewing and Norton, 20.

88   *a railroad spur*   Shepley, 15.

89   *Parker's view of women*   Parker, *A Sermon on the Public Function of Woman,* 5.

89   *Fontarire*   Julia Robbins to Ellen Robbins, 5 September 1852.

89   *his advice to them*   Ewing and Norton, 92.

89   *the rules posted*   Bigelow-Sanford Collection F-1, 1828–1858.

90   *"great blossoms . . . arranged"*   Ewing and Norton, 24.

90   *Nye's symmetrical patterns*   Ibid., 93.

90   *"have made every body at Lowell melancholly [sic]."*   Bigelow-Sanford Collection F-4, 115.

90   *"to eliminate . . . purposes"*   Ewing and Norton, 24.

90   *"the large, floriated scroll designs"*   Ibid., 24.

90   *Number 19 Kirk Street*   visit to Lowell, 24 March 2006.

90   *37½ cents*   Coolidge, 42.

91 *Parker* Parker, *A Sermon on the Public Function of Woman*, 12–16.

91 *a litigious lot* This was how S. Lawrence Whipple described the Robbins family in an interview with the author.

91 *"I told . . . the bill"* Julia Robbins to Ellen Robbins, 5 September 1852.

AUGUST 1854

93 *the first to preach abolition* Kollen, *Lexington From Liberty's Birthplace . . .* , 95.

93 *"brown, broad-shouldered . . . roots"* Lowell, 112.

94 *"gift from . . . presence"* Porte, 357.

94 *"a disruptive eccentric . . . authority"* Robertson, *Parker Pillsbury*, 2.

94 *"subverted . . . women"* Ibid., 3.

95 *"My Parker . . . Sarah A. Pillsbury"* Sarah Pillsbury to Julia Robbins, 26 March 1854.

95 *"call for . . . issues"* Robertson, *Parker Pillsbury*, 62.

95 *"of being noticed . . . women"* Ibid., 34.

95 *"to make the best of it"* Ibid., 29.

96 *"Often my dear . . . host"* Parker Pillsbury to Julia Robbins, 1 August 1853.

96 *"Your letter . . . a disappointment"* Parker Pillsbury to Julia Robbins, 18 September 1853.

97 *"One parting word . . . Affectionate P."* Parker Pillsbury to Julia Robbins, 1 June 1854.

97 *"My dear . . . be loved"* Parker Pillsbury to Julia Robbins, 30 July 1854.

MARCH 17, 1855

99 *Cold Tuesday* Ludlum, *Country Journal*, 67.

99 *breakfast* Food served in Lowell was part of the Lowell National Park Boarding House Exhibit visited 26 March 2006. Wendy George was the National Park guide who graciously answered my questions.

99 *$9 for a silk dress* Julia Robbins' Expense Account, 24 January 1855.

99 *bloomer costume* Julia Robbins' Diary, 25 July 1851.

99 *Elizy* Elizabeth Gerry was referred to as Elizy; she also is referred to as Sirrie.

100 *illustrious forebears* Hudson II, 745.

100 *"riding out"* Papers of Caira Robbins.

100 *"The slavery . . . to do"* N. H. Gerry to Ellen Robbins, Washington, D.C., 7 February 1850.

101 *"a very pleasant old town"* E. Gerry to Julia Robbins, Concord, 2 October 1854.

101 *"a few moments"* Julia Robbins to E. Gerry, 19 October 1854.

102 *the indictment of Theodore Parker* Christie, *Dictionary of American Biography*.

102 *"What will . . . America"*   E. Gerry to Julia Robbins, 3 December 1854.

103 *Nathan Robbins*   Family History unsigned, undated notes from the Lexington Historical Society Archives. Nathan Robbins was of the successful Arlington branch of the family. While still in his early twenties, he was proprietor of a stall in Boston's Quincy Market, selling poultry, game, and pork. Of Nathan it was noted: "A deserved reputation for sagacity and honesty was soon acquired; the patronage of the leading hotels and of the wealthy families was secured. . . . He was President of Faneuil Hall Bank for nearly 34 years. . . . To a discriminating judgement he joined a sympathetic, generous disposition; his charities were numerous but always unpretentious."

103 *one of the local girls*   Worthen, *Tracing the Past,* 81.

103 *"supposed there . . . recollections"*   N. P. Robbins to Julia Robbins, 17 January 1855.

JUNE 3, 1856

104 *Ellen's letter*   Ellen Stone to Julia Robbins, St. Louis, 27 May 1856.

105 *Senator Sumner*   Hayes, *Dictionary of American Biography.*

105 *Representative Preston Brooks*   Walmsley, *Dictionary of American Biography.*

105 *"two enormous . . . night both"*   Parker, *A Sermon of the Public Function of Woman,* 8.

105 *as a place for recuperation*   Josephson, 302.

105 *William Appleton*   Ewing and Norton, 11.

105 *visitor . . . Toombs*   Josephson, 302; Donald, 290.

106 *tried unsuccessfully to get candles*   Julia Robbins' Diary, 28 April 1851.

APRIL 24, 1857

107 *died of apoplexy*   *Report of the Auditors of the Town of Lexington for 1857,* 67.

107 *"furrier"*   Middlesex County Probate Court File Papers 40630, reel 487.

107 *"Eli Robbins . . . revival"*   "Lexington 60 Years Ago," *Proceedings,* 36.

107 *fire in August of 1848*   Ellen Stone to Abby Lothrop, 22 August 1848.

108 *died without a will*   Middlesex County Probate Court File Papers 40630, reel 487.

108 *death of Andrew C. Davison*   *Report of the Auditors of the Town of Lexington for 1857,* 67.

108 *noted in the Liberator*   Friday, 19 September 1856.

108 *outlived his older siblings*   Hudson II, 580–81.

108 *his third and only surviving son*   Gienapp, 223–24.

109 *"more than kisses . . . speak"*   Bartlett's, 230.

109 *"I think . . . to me"*   Stillman Lothrop to Julia Robbins, 11 April 1856.

110 *she always paid her way*   Julia Robbins' Expense Account, 1855.

110 *"I have long . . . Misery"*   Parker Pillsbury to Julia Robbins, 14 April 1857.

111 *in the Greek Revival style*   Shepley, 8.

111 *"cards are absolutely necessary"*   *Hand-Book*, 8.

111 *a calico print designer*   Margaret S. Carzon to Julia Robbins, 24 March n.y.

111 *illuminated by skylights*   Shepley, 7.

111 *oil lamps*   Ewing and Norton, 22.

111 *at $1.27 a gallon*   Bigelow-Sanford Collection F-4 Copies of Letters, Memo of Contract, 82.

112 *The Lowell Company had a strict policy*   Regulations Shepley, n. p.

112 *To Cousin George*   Julia Robbins to Ellen Robbins, 16 January 1853.

112 *Vox Populi*   Coolidge, 206.

112 *"These things . . . home"*   Julia Robbins to Ellen Robbins, 16 January 1853.

112 *"I paint . . . disease"*   Ibid.

112 *"We make . . . a year"*   Julia Robbins to Elizy Gerry, 19 October 1854.

113 *There were compensations*   Julia Robbins' Expense Accounts, 1855, 1856, 1857.

113 *in his condolence letter*   Parker Pillsbury to Julia Robbins, 24 October 1856.

113 *"I have . . . Jersey cow"*   Julia Robbins to the Robbins Family, 10 March n. y.

March 30, 1860

114 *surviving parents*   Parker Pillsbury to Julia Robbins, 24 October 1856.

115 *"The past winter . . . life"*   Julia Robbins undated paper.

115 *"I know . . . extrication. . . ."*   Parker Pillsbury to Julia Robbins, 3 June 1858.

115 *"so-called justice"*   Parker Pillsbury to Julia Robbins, 8 July 1858.

115 *"To come . . . controversy"*   Parker Pillsbury to Julia Robbins, 11 November 1858.

115 *Ellen badgered Julia*   letters from Ellen Stone to Julia Robbins, 1 January, 12 January, 2 February, 3 May 1858.

115 *"P.S. . . . attended to"*   Ellen Stone to Julia Robbins, 3 May 1858.

115 *"pretty Antislavery present of needlebook & picture"*   Ellen Stone to Julia Robbins, 12 January 1858.

115 *"George has taken"*   Julia Robbins undated paper.

115 *"How came George to go off!"*   Ellen Stone to Julia Robbins, 3 May 1858.

115 *soften her tone*   Ibid.

116 *"I have had . . . last year"*   Julia Robbins to Ellen Stone, 7 January 1859.

116 *"nobody's acts . . . **my own**"*   Ellen Stone to Julia Robbins, 21 January 1859.

117 *"If I had . . . this year"*   Julia Robbins to Ellen Stone, 7 January 1859.

117 *"How do . . . she would. . . ."* Mary Plumer to Julia Robbins, 17 January 1859.

117 *"The lawyers . . . our fault"* Julia Robbins to Ellen Stone, 20 February 1859.

118 *"You did . . . too many"* Parker Pillsbury to Julia Robbins, 10 January 1857.

118 *"my two . . . I had"* Davison to Harvard Class of 1845 Secretary, 19 February 1907.

118 *"unlucky brother"* Davison to Charles Folsom, 11 July 1892.

122 *"a stick to lean upon"* Ellen Robbins' Diary, 1852.

122 *"very cross"* Caira Robbins' Diary, 10 May 1858.

122 *"this is doing good . . . no right"* Ibid., 15 May 1858.

122 *"Dear Mother"* Julia Robbins to Hannah S. Robbins, 30 March 1860.

Chapter 4

Descriptions of flora and fauna on the Barrett farm are based on the observations of the ornithologist William Brewster, the subsequent owner. Brewster recorded these in his book *October Farm*. Quotations: Reprinted by permission of the publisher from *October Farm: From the Concord Journals and Diaries of William Brewster,* with an Introduction by Daniel Chester French, Cambridge, Mass.: Harvard University Press, pp. 170, 178, 187, Copyright © 1936 by the President and Fellows of Harvard College. Copyright © renewed 1964 by the President and Fellows of Harvard College.

MAY 17, 1860

124 *"that no compromise . . . possible"* Morris, 226.

124 *married by Reverend William Alger* City of Boston Registry of Marriages, *1861 Boston Directory*.

124 *with its gabled roof* Photo collection of the Boston Athenaeum.

124 *Julia forty* Julia, born on May 6, 1819, had turned forty-one eleven days earlier.

125 *"attraction . . . than himself"* Wilson, 2.

125 *"Character is higher than intellect."* "American Scholar," *Bartlett's*, 431.

125 *Hawes' panoramic photographs* Exhibit Boston University Art Gallery 2006. Pierce, "Gallery Talk," 2 March 2006; Kamplain, "A Photographic Portrait of Boston, 1840–1865."

125 *"gaining ground"* This is the title of Nancy Seasholes' book chronicling this work.

125 *Mill Dam* Seasholes, 126.

125 *the population was soaring* Search iBoston; Concord Special Collections "Population."

126　*"polluted tidal estuary"*　McNulty, 11.

126　*Beacon Hill reservoir*　Kay, 204–05.

126　*Discipline . . . strong suit*　Keyes, 10.

126　*"domed masses . . .blossoms"*　Brewster, 178.

126　*"the maple . . . scarlet"*　Ibid., 187.

126　*some slack time*　In the farmer's year, May, July, and December were noted as slack months.

126　*"great central Avenue"* "The Improvement of the Back Bay," *Boston Almanac 1860*, 34–38.

127　*a Morgan horse*　Julia Robbins to the Robbins Family, 10 March n. y.

127　*Fitchburg Railroad*　Wheeler, 178. Service to Concord was inaugurated in 1844.

127　*River Road*　This is now Monument Street.

September 29, 1863

128　*"Resolutions—War of '61"*　Gordon "Appendix" William Munroe Special Collections of the Concord Free Public Library. Quoted by permission.

129　*"the nucleus of Company G, Fifth Massachusetts Volunteers."*　Ibid., 3.

129　*"[a]nxious . . . minds"*　Myerson and Shealy, *Journals*, 109. Quoted by permission.

129　*did their part for a victorious outcome*　Gordon, 15–18. William Munroe Special Collections of the Concord Free Public Library. Quoted by permission.

129　*"medical care . . . the field"*　Marten.

130　*shawl table covers*　Julia A. R. Barrett Will and Inventory.

130　*"first baby I ever dressed"*　Julia Robbins' Diary, 5 September 1851.

131　*Lyceum script*　Scudder, 261.

131　*Turning a dress*　Pugliese.

132　*the ladies had been commended*　Chapin, *Entering Concord*, 163–64.

132　*Irish immigrants*　Nelson, 104–05.

132　*Ellen Hunt*　Wilson, 76.

132　*called on the Emersons*　Julia Robbins' Diary, 4 September 1851.

132　*Emerson . . . hospitality*　Petrulionis, *To Set This World Right;* to Charles Sumner 152; to Parker Pillsbury 126, 128.

133　*"The Antislavery Society . . . presence?"*　letter to Mrs. John Barrett, 29 September 1863. *Concord Ladies' Antislavery Society Records.* William Munroe Special Collections of the Concord Free Public Library. Quoted by permission.

March 12, 1874

135　*"How womankind . . . at all"*　Thoreau, *Walking,* 630.

135　*she had commended*　Mary Plumer to Julia Robbins, 12 May 1847.

135 *a member of the Massachusetts Agricultural Society* Massachusetts Agricultural Society membership diploma. *Massachusetts Agricultural Society Records*. William Munroe Special Collections of the Concord Free Public Library. Quoted by permission.

135 *Weather* Weather details in this section are from the *Boston Almanac, 1874* and 1875; Ludlum, *New England Weather Journal.*

135 *their financial situation* Information on the Barretts' real estate, personal property, and taxes was found in *Assessor's Records Town of Concord.*

136 *"Producing Milk"* Flint. William Munroe Special Collections of the Concord Free Public Library. Quoted by permission.

136 *census data* State Census 1865; Federal Census 1860, 1870, 1880.

137 *often sent her regards* E. A. Stone to Julia Barrett, 27 March 1883, 8 February 1888, 19 September 1889.

137 *"Mr. Davison here"* Mrs. Ellen A. Stone's Diary, 1882.

137 *a notable Concord export* Jarvis, *Traditions and Reminiscences*, 195–97.

137 *Julia sold her berries* Keyes, 10.

137 *salary of W. H. Benjamin* Chapin, *Entering Concord,* 163.

137 *the roof of the Town House* Ibid., 6.

138 *William Marcy Tweed* Morris, 250.

138 *Local lore* Keyes, 10.

138 *"Ill a good deal."* Myerson and Shealy, *Journals*, 193. Quoted by permission.

139 *"Run Over . . . sufferings"* undated newspaper clipping Robbins-Stone Papers.

139 *Uncle Lot* Mrs. Ellen A. Stone Acct. Book.

139 *"right to dower"* Robbins-Stone Papers.

140 *by the fireplace* Nylander in Simon and Benes, 205.

140 *Ellen's high school examination day* Ellen Stone to Abner Stone, 8 March 1871.

141 *"Those feeding . . . the tree"* Brewster, 170.

142 *"Sumner Dead"* *Boston Globe,* 12 March 1874.

142 *he had been serenaded* *Boston Almanac 1874.* Events of 1 December 1873.

142 *honored with re-election* U.S. senators were elected by state legislatures until the ratification of the Seventeenth Amendment in 1913. Sumner, first elected to the U.S. Senate in 1851, returned to the Senate in 1859 after his attack by Brooks in 1856.

143 *support of equal suffrage* Morris, 720.

144 *the largest outpouring of grief* Donald, 4.

JULY 18, 1883

Julia Robbins Barrett attended sessions at the Concord School of Philosophy; the tickets in the William Munroe Special Collections of the Concord Free Public

Library for each year from 1879, when it opened, through its final year, 1888, all have Julia's name on them. Quoted by permission.

145 *Transcendentalism*   Ronda, 321.
145 *Elizabeth Palmer Peabody*   Scudder, 284.
146 *John was annoyed*   Keyes, 10; Fenn, 33.
146 *he and Julia . . . to the School of Philosophy*   Wheeler, 176.
146 *a bowl of the very same water lilies*   Scudder, 284.
146 *an article . . . to him*   "Concord School of Philosophy," *The Woman's Journal,* 19 August 1882, 265.
146 *in a verse she wrote*   Scudder, 281.
146 *"the school is for the few"*   "Concord School of Philosophy," *The Woman's Journal,* 7 August 1880, 254.
147 *nine daily trains*   Jarvis, *Traditions and Reminiscences*, 141.
148 *his friendly manner*   "John Barrett" Obituary, *The Enterprise*, 24 October 1890. William Munroe Special Collections of the Concord Free Public Library. Quoted by permission.

NOVEMBER 23, 1886

In the 19th century, woman suffrage was the term used, replaced in the 20th century by women suffrage. As Julia used the singular, that is used throughout this work.

The abbreviation *TWJ* is used for *The Woman's Journal.*

The role of the Massachusetts Woman Suffrage Association and its parent organization, the American Woman Suffrage Association, has faded from memory as the history of the campaign for suffrage was written by the National Woman Suffrage Association (NWSA), the Stanton and Anthony camp. The National group, as its name implies, wanted national, not state, action to gain woman suffrage. There were other significant differences between the American and the National groups. The National group supported a variety of woman's issues; it even opposed the Fifteenth Amendment enfranchising black men as a distraction to their goal of woman suffrage. Stanton and Anthony also published a suffrage paper, *Revolution.* After two decades of competing for support, the American and the National groups joined forces in 1890. *Massachusetts and the Woman-Suffrage Movement* by Lois Merk details the suffrage campaign in this state. It was an enormous help in sorting through the details of activities, proponents, and opponents.

149 *not a typical woman's publication*   Merk, 26–27.
149 *Thomas Wentworth Higginson*   Howe, *Dictionary of American Biography*.
149 *"not because . . . human race"*   Merk, 16–17. Merk cited *TWJ,* 22 January 1870.

150 *one of six*   Jarvis, *Traditions and Reminiscences*, 242–43.

150 *pored over each issue*   Ellen Stone to Julia Barrett, 8 February 1888.

150 *the long retrospective piece*   "Schools of Design for Women," *TWJ*, 23 January 1886, 32.

150 *"She gave up . . . premiums"*   "The School of Design," *TWJ*, 6 February 1886, 44.

150 *Julia had heard William Lloyd Garrison*   "The Concord Middlesex County Woman Suffrage Convention," *TWJ*, 29 May 1875, 172.

151 *a Doctor Campbell*   "Address of Dr. Campbell," *TWJ*, 17 March 1883, 82.

151 *It was affiliated*   The New England Woman Suffrage Association shared headquarters with The Massachusetts Woman Suffrage and the American Woman Suffrage organizations.

151 *"Bostonism"*   Merk, ii.

151 *serve on local school committees*   Ibid., 45.

151 *the School Suffrage Act*   Ibid., 45. Two years later this act was amended, enabling women who owned taxable property to register to vote by presenting a sworn statement of their property's value as well as a receipt for the tax paid. Starting in 1881, in the Concord Assessor's records, Julia was no longer listed as "wife," but as Julia A. R., Julia A., or just Julia. Women without taxable property could register to vote by presenting proof of payment of a poll tax, set at 50 cents. As did the men, the women had to be able to read and write English. Satisfying these requirements, the women would find their names on women-only voting lists and would vote with a separate ballot.

151 *Julia . . . Concord town meeting*   Keyes, 10; Nelson, 99–101; Scudder, 280. Women attended town meeting for the first time on March 20, 1880.

151 *"quite a number of votes"*   Ellen Stone to Julia Barrett, 9 March 1881.

151 *immigrant women . . . the Roman Catholic Church*   Merk, 158–191.

151 *10,000 signatures*   Ibid., 107.

152 *issues should be separate*   Ibid., 141–42.

152 *Linking these causes*   Ibid., 57.

152 *"enlarged housekeeping"*   Ibid., 60.

152 *political forces seemed favorable*   Governor John D. Long supported woman suffrage, but in 1882 he was succeeded in office by the former Civil War general, Democrat Benjamin Butler. Butler had supported woman suffrage as a congressman but now was silent on the issue, not wanting to agitate his fellow Democrats. That political party historically opposed woman suffrage in deference to the liquor interests and to the immigrants' religious base, the Catholic Church. Ibid., 38, 84–85.

152 *the men in attendance*   Ibid., 9–23.

152 *From the portrait*   Fernald, 18B.

153 *"In the [East Lexington] . . . in '76"*   Pond, 36.

153 *represented the Robbins family*   S. E. Sewall to Mrs. Barrett, 17 April 1887.

153 *Women of means*   Merk, 36.

153 *the rules of the legislature*   Ibid., 33.

153 *In an advisory opinion*   Ibid., 59.

154 *a conservative position*   Ibid., 119.

154 *"I think . . . postpone it."*   Pond, 148.

155 *the recurrence of the "turns"*   Ellen Stone to Julia Barrett, 22 November 1884. In the 1880 Census, on the line where Julia is listed, there is a small check in the Health Column where it is asked if the person is "Critically ill? If so, specific." Did the enumerator, Alfred B. Warren, rest his pencil or record a fact?

155 *Julia submitted a municipal suffrage petition*   "Massachusetts Woman Suffrage Petitions," *TWJ*, 23 January 1886, 28; 1 May 1886, 139.

155 *he voted with the majority*   "The Vote of 1886," *TWJ*, 24 April 1886, 132. Massachusetts never passed a Municipal Woman Suffrage bill; women waited until the Nineteenth Amendment was ratified in 1920 to vote for local, state, and federal officials.

155 *a younger generation*   Merk, 54.

155 *the Antis*   Ibid., 65–75. The Antis were also known as the Boston Committee of Remonstrants.

155 *"Beacon Street silks"*   Ibid., 72.

156 *Parkman wrote*   Ibid., 92.

157 *his winning cash payments*   John received the following payments at Massachusetts Agricultural shows: 1874—Gratuity Cranberries $1, Apples $1; 1875—2nd Premium Wintersweet $1; 1876—Gratuity Cranberries $1.

157 *her carpet designs and mats*   Julia was paid $1.50 for Carpet Designs in 1874, 50 cents in the same category in 1875, and 25 cents for mats in 1878—all as gratuities. A Massachusetts Agricultural Society membership diploma for Mrs. Julia A. Barrett is dated May 11, 1871. *Massachusetts Agricultural Society Records*. William Munroe Special Collections of the Concord Free Public Library. Quoted by permission.

157 *"the proud distinction . . . in town"*   "John Barrett," *The Enterprise,* October 24, 1890. William Munroe Special Collections of the Concord Free Public Library. Quoted by permission.

157 *John's weakened state*   Ellen Stone to Julia Barrett, 8 June 1885.

157 *a favorite apple dish*   Jarvis, *Traditions and Reminiscences*, 63.

157 *the suffrage bazaar*   "Woman Suffrage Festival and Bazaar," *TWJ,* 4 December 1886, 388; 11 December 1886, 396; 18 December 1886, 404.

158 *"only bad women would vote"*   Merk, 113.

158 *the goal for the bazaar*   The bazaar realized $6,313 for the MWAS. Ibid., 124.

158 *banner for the Boston League* "The Woman Suffrage Bazaar," *TWJ*, 18 December 1886, 404.

158 *she would accompany* Scudder, 280. Women attended town meeting for the first time on March 20, 1880.

158 *"strong-minded"* Keyes, 10.

JANUARY 14, 1891

Information on the Concord Female Charitable Society is based on the *Concord Female Charitable Society Records 1869–1896*; *Annual and Semi-annual Reports 1869–1896*; *Presidents' Records 1888–1891*; *Presidents' Records 1891–1913*; *Reports of Monthly Meetings 1869–1881*; *Records of the Board of Directors, 1869–1891*; *Records of the Board of Directors 1882–1896*. When there were discrepancies in the attendance count between the Presidents' Records and those of the secretary, the author chose the secretary's figures. William Munroe Special Collections of the Concord Free Public Library. Quoted by permission.

159 *Concord Female Charitable Society* Wheeler, 164–68; Nelson, 46–48.

159 *what to wear* Julia's clothing is based on the Will and Inventory of Julia Robbins Barrett, Robbins-Stone Papers.

160 *Two of his ancestors* Barrett Family Genealogy Files. William Munroe Special Collections of the Concord Free Public Library. Quoted by permission.

160 *"The people . . . years old"* "John Barrett," *The Enterprise,* Friday, 24 October 1890. Newspaper clipping.

160 *"In Memoriam"* (John Barrett), *TWJ,* 8 November 1890, 357.

161 *the homestead of fifty acres* Concord Assessor's Record.

161 *tax rate . . . town valuation* Chapin, *Entering Concord*, 39.

162 *"In Memoriam"* (Ellen Stone), *TWJ,* 15 November 1890, 364.

162 *younger daughter Mary* "Deaths" newspaper clipping "In Colton, Cal., Feb. 26 [1884]. Mary B. (Stone) Oulton, of Lexington" Robbins-Stone Family Papers.

162 *Ellen's penchant for worry* Ellen Stone to Julia Barrett, 9 March 1881, 8 June 1885, 8 February 1888, 9 April 1890.

162 *the heroine in Eliza's book* Follen, *Married Life*.

162 *destined for a particularly unfortunate family* June 1888 meeting.

162 *"the ladies worked for the Johnstown sufferers"* In 1889, the Pennsylvania Steel Company of Johnston was hit by a devastating flood; over 2,200 lives were lost and many more were homeless. "A Roar Like Thunder . . ." http://www.johnstownpa.com/History/ hist19.html.

164 *Tonight's speaker* Concord Lyceum 1890–1891. William Munroe Special Collections of the Concord Free Public Library. Quoted by permission.

164 *"a man . . . strength"* Ulam, 294.

164 *"the darling of the revolutionary movement"* Siljak, 65–66.

164 *assassinating the head*   This was General Nicholas Mezentsev, Chief of the Third Department, the political police.

164 *"leading interpreter . . . movement"*   Ulam, 294–95.

Epilogue 1892–1900

165 *Julia sold her farm*   The Assessors Valuation List records "Barrett, Julia A. R." as owner of the 50 acre homestead, the 20 acre woodlot, and the 11½ (from 1895 noted as 12) acre lot near Ball's Hill through the year 1898.

165 *the population doubled*   "Concord Population."

165 *a tourist attraction*   Scudder, 294.

165 *surrounding Walden Pond*   Chapin, *Concord, Massachusetts*, 80.

165 *choose to live*   Exactly where Julia lived in East Lexington is not clear. The 1899 *Resident and Business Directory of Lexington and Bedford* listed Julia Barrett as living on Mass. Av. at the corner of Pleasant St. while her niece Ellen is recorded as living at Mass Av. near Pleasant St. The federal census taken on June 7, 1900, recorded Julia as residing with the Dana Family in East Lexington.

166 *electric lights*   Worthen, *Calendar History*, 91–92.

166 *"boom was in Upper Lexington"*   Ellen Stone to Julia Barrett, 9 April 1890.

166 *East Lexington claimed*   *Resident and Business Directory of Lexington and Bedford 1899.*

166 *"an attractive part of the town"*   "Other Points of Interest," Ibid.

166 *gave a portrait*   George E. Muzzey to Mrs. Julia R. Barrett, 21 May 1896.

166 *Mrs. Barrett . . . her childhood*   Robbins family history materials Robbins Library #7101-13.

166 *Julia died*   Deaths Registered in the Town of Lexington 1900; Deaths Registered in the City of Boston 1900.

167 *plot marked by a white marble obelisk*   The Barrett plot is #49 Glen Avenue. Patricia A. Hopkins, Town of Concord Cemetery Dept. Supervisor, letter to author May 20, 2003.

167 *"Mrs. J. R. Barrett"*   "Concord Woman Suffrage League," *TWJ,* 2 July 1887, 213.

167 *a commitment to social action*   Gura, 218.

167 *"Mrs. Barrett had . . . women"*   *TWJ,* 20 October 1900, 332.
     Parts of this column where the paper was folded have been obliterated. The obituary reads:
     "In Memoriam Mrs. Julia Robbins Barrett"
     Mrs. Barrett was the daughter of Eli and Hannah Simonds Robbins, and was born in Lexington, Mass., May 6, 1819. . . . was passed there. She belonged to a family of . . . , and her father was a man of activity

and enterprise, who did much for Lexington. He was interested in the formation of Follen Church, and by opening a hall in the building now occupied by the branch library, he, with others, secured noted preachers, like Emerson, Dwight, and Follen. Julia A. Robbins married John Barrett in 1860, and made her home on the old Barrett farm in Concord. For thirty years she was identified with its interests. After Mr. Barrett's death she remained at the old place. Two years since she sold it, and made her home with the Robbins in Boston. Mrs. Barrett had a bright mind, and was a zealous Abolitionist and advocate of equal suffrage for women. She belonged, also, to temperance organizations, and took great interest in the Horticultural Society. The past and present history of Concord and Lexington were household words to her. Her brother, Mr. Eli Robbins, and a sister, Mrs. Lothrop, survive her.

Information on Julia's staying in Concord and residence in Boston conflicts with census records.

168 *Aunt Caira's pastels* Nylander, *The Art of Family*, following page 202.

168 *"a proud . . . daunted"* Whipple, 18B.

LIST OF CORRESPONDENCE

Letters from Julia to . . .		Letters to Julia from . . .	
1829		July 5	Caira Langdon
1831		January 6	Mary C. Bean
1832		December 7	Abby Robbins
		December 12	Ellen Robbins
1833			
April 21	Caira Langdon		
1836		August 19	Ellen Robbins
		December 21	Ellen Robbins
1839			
April 12	Mary Plumer		
1840s		March 21 n. y.	Nancy Wellington
1841			
June 27	Caira Langdon	November 15	Mary Plumer
	(*added to Ellen's letter*)		
1843			
March 28	Ellen Robbins &	April 15	Ellen Robbins n.s.
	Caira Langdon		
1844		October 8	n.s.
		October 31	Ellen Robbins
1845		May	Henry
		September 2	lmt
1846		January 14	William Plumer
		February 15	William Plumer
1847		May 12	Mary Plumer
		November 22	Henry W. Goodrich
1848		March 27	William Quincy Dow
1849		March 27	J. G. Dodge
		March 28	J. G. Dodge
		April 17	J. G. Dodge
		September 6	William Quincy Dow
1850			
autumn	(Davison) n. d.		

Letters from Julia to . . .		Letters to Julia from . . .	
1851		July 30	Ellen Robbins
1852		July 13	Mary Plumer
September 1 (?)	Ellen Robbins	November 19	J. G. Dodge
September 5	Ellen Robbins	December 16	Ellen Robbins
1853			
January 16	Ellen Robbins	June 7	John Langdon
			(*also to Ellen*)
		August 1	Parker Pillsbury
		September 18	Parker Pillsbury
1854		January 1	Parker Pillsbury
		January 20	Ellen Robbins Stone
		February 21	Parker Pillsbury
		March 26	Sarah Pillsbury
		July 30	Parker Pillsbury
		October 2	Elizy Gerry
October 19	Elizy Gerry	November 7	Mary Plumer
		December 3	Elizy Gerry
		n.d., n.s.	Parker Pillsbury
1855		January 17	Nathan Robbins
		March 14	A. J.
		March 14	M. Curzon n. y.
March 17 n. y.	Ellen Robbins Stone		
July 28	Dear Friend (Davison)	November 18	Elizy Gerry
		December 24	Elizy Gerry
1856		February 3	Elizy Gerry
		April 11	S. L. Lothrop
		May 27	Ellen Robbins Stone
		June 9	Parker Pillsbury
		August 12	Parker Pillsbury
		October 24	Parker Pillsbury
1857		January 10	Parker Pillsbury
		January 28	Ellen Robbins Stone
		February 28	Parker Pillsbury
		April 14	Parker Pillsbury
		July 18	Parker Pillsbury
		September 7	Parker Pillsbury
		October 19	Ellen Robbins Stone
		December 1	Parker Pillsbury
		December 30	Parker Pillsbury

Letters from Julia to . . .		Letters to Julia from . . .	
1858		January 12	Ellen Robbins Stone
		February 2	Ellen Robbins Stone
		May 3	Ellen Robbins Stone
		June 3	Parker Pillsbury
		July 8	Parker Pillsbury
		September 19 n. y.	Mary Plumer
		September 21	Parker Pillsbury
		September 28	Ellen Robbins Stone
		October 4	Ellen Robbins Stone
		October 21	Mary Plumer
		November 11	Parker Pillsbury
		November 20	Mary Plumer
Parker Pillsbury n. d.		December 31	Ellen Robbins Stone
		n. d., n. s.	Parker Pillsbury
1859			
January 7	Ellen Robbins Stone	January 7	Mary Plumer
		January 17	Ellen Robbins Stone
February 20	Ellen Robbins Stone		
March 17	Ellen Robbins Stone	March 29	Ellen Robbins Stone
1860			
March 30	Hannah S. Robbins	April 4	J. G. Abbott
Early 1860s		n. d.	Ellen Robbins Stone
1880s		n. d.	Mary Mann
1881		March 9	Ellen Robbins Stone
1883		March 27	Ellen Robbins Stone
1884		November 22	Ellen Robbins Stone
1885		June 8	Ellen Robbins Stone
1887		April 17	S. Sewall
1888		February 8	Ellen Robbins Stone
1889		September 19	Ellen Robbins Stone
1890		April	Ellen Robbins Stone
1891		February 19	Miss Ellen Stone
1892		February 1	William Plumer
1896		May 21, 1896	Geo. E. Muzzey

Other correspondence

April 24, 1825	Hannah Penney to Hannah S. Robbins
July 6, 1828	Caira Robbins to Hannah S. Robbins
July 6, 1828	Caira Robbins to Stephen Robbins
November 19, 1832	Abby Robbins to Nabby Langdon
January 4, 1833	George Langdon, no salutation
March 8, 1835	Ralph Waldo Emerson to "My dear Sir"
January 14, 1837	Ellen Robbins to Caira Langdon
1837 (?)	Caira Robbins to Ellen Robbins
January 12, 1839	Ellen Robbins (n. s.) to Caira Langdon
May 13, 1839	Ellen Robbins to Caira Langdon
1840s n. d.	Ellen Robbins to Caira Langdon
March 11, 1840	Caira Langdon to Caira Robbins
June 27, 1841	Ellen Robbins to Caira Langdon
November 5, 1842	Ellen Robbins to Caira Langdon
March 4, 1844	Ellen Robbins to Caira Langdon
March 14, 1844	Caira Langdon to Caira Robbins
May 27, 1844	Ellen Robbins to Caira Langdon
March 5, 1845	Caira Langdon to Caira Robbins
October 21, 1846	Ellen Robbins to Caira Langdon
July 29, 1847	Benjamin R. Davison to Ellen Robbins
September 3, 1847	Ellen Robbins to George Simonds
August 22, 1848	Ellen Robbins to Abby Robbins Lothrop
February 7, 1850	N. H. Gerry to Ellen Robbins
April 4,1853	John Langdon to Hannah Robbins
February 16, 1854	Ellen Robbins Stone to Caira Robbins & Miss Page
December 26 , 1854	Ellen Robbins Stone to Abner Stone
January 22, 1855	Peter and Bridgit Cary to Ellen Robbins Stone
January 21, 1856	Hannah Robbins to Abby Robbins Lothrop
May 15, 1857	Ellen Robbins Stone to Abner Stone
August 24, 1857	Ellen Robbins Stone to Abner Stone
December 30, 1858	S. Sewall to C. Pike, Esq.
November 26, 1859	R. T. Smith to Abby Robbins Lothrop

December 1864	unsigned letter from E. Lexington
1870s	Ellen Robbins Stone to Eli Robbins
March 8, 1871	Ellen Robbins Stone to Abner Stone
March 17, 1873	Ellen Robbins Stone to Caira Langdon Nicholas
November 1883	Ellen Robbins Stone to Mr. Russell

Davison Family Correspondence in the Robbins-Stone Papers

To Benjamin R. Davison, later known as William H. Davison

August 29, December 17, 1838	J. M. Barnard
January 1, October 2, December 15, 1840	J. M. Barnard
February 13, August 15, 1841	J. M. Barnard
July 5, 1844	William Plumer
February 3, 1845	William Plumer
March 9, 1845	Nancy Davison Svenson
June 8, 1846	Nancy Davison Svenson

To Andrew C. Davison, Jr.

March 14, 1843	Nancy Davison Svenson
June 19, 1843	S. Willard
July 23, 1844	Nancy Davison Svenson
December 17,1 845	Nancy Davison Svenson
October 1, 1851	William H. Davison

General

Ahlstrom, Sydney E. *A Religious History of the American People*. New Haven: Yale University Press, 1972.

Boston Almanac 1839, 1847, 1854, 1855, 1860, 1861, 1874, 1875, 1880, 1883, 1884, 1886, 1887, 1888, 1890, 1891, 1892. Boston Athenaeum.

Boston Directory 1845, 1851.

Bowen, Catherine Drinker. *Adventures of a Biographer*. Boston: Little, Brown and Company, 1959.

———. *The Writing of Biography*. Boston: The Writer, Inc., 1951.

Brown's Almanac 1851, Number XIV. Concord, NH: John F. Brown.

Bruccoli, Matthew J. and Richard Layman, eds. *American Eras 1878–1899*. Detroit: Gale Research, 1997.

Bunting, Bainbridge. *Houses of Boston's Back Bay*. Cambridge: Belknap Press, 1967.

Burt, Christopher C. *Extreme Weather: A Guide & Record Book*. New York: W.W. Norton & Company, 2004.

Felt, Thomas E. *Researching, Writing, and Publishing Local History*. Nashville: American Association for State and Local History, 1976.

Ginzberg, Lori D. *Women and the Work of Benevolence: Morality, Politics, and Class in The Nineteenth-Century United States*. New Haven: Yale University Press, 1990.

Grunwald, Lisa & Stephen J. Adler, eds. *Women's Letters: America from the Revolutionary War to the Present*. New York: Dial Press, 2005.

Gura, Philip F. *American Transcendentalism: A History*. New York: Hill and Wang, 2007.

Hall, Donald. *New England's Disastrous Weather*. Camden, ME: Yankee Books, 1990.

Hansen, Karen V. *A Very Social Time Crafting Community in Antebellum New England*. Berkeley: University of California Press, 1994.

Hareven, Tamara K. "Family Time and Historical Time." *The Family*, edited by Alice S. Rossi, Jerome Kagan, Tamara K. Hareven, 57–70. New York: W. W. Norton & Company, 1979.

_____. *Themes in the History of the Family*. Worcester: American Antiquarian Society, 1978.

Historical Statistics of the United States. Bicentennial Ed. Washington, D.C.: U.S. Dept. of Commerce, 1975.

Kamplain, Anna Lee. "A Photographic Portrait of Boston, 1840–1865." Boston University Art Gallery, 10 February 2006–2 April 2006.

Kay, Jane Holtz. *Lost Boston*. Boston: Houghton Mifflin Company, 1980.

Knowles, Katharine with text by Thea Wheelwright. *Travels in New England*. Barre: Barre Publishers, 1972.

Kuklick, Bruce. *The Rise of American Philosophy*. New Haven: Yale University Press, 1977.

"Laundry." Exhibit at National Heritage Museum, Lexington, MA. Viewed November 2005.

Ludlum, David. *The American Weather Book*. Boston: American Meteorological Association, 1982.

_____. *The Country Journal New England Weather Book*. Boston: Houghton Mifflin Company, 1976.

_____. *Early American Winters 1821–1876*. Boston: American Meteorological Association, 1968.

Marten, James. "United States Sanitary Commission." *Encyclopedia of the American Civil War*. Santa Barbara: ABC-CLIO, 2000.

McCarthy, Molly. "A Pocketful of Days: Pocket Diaries and Daily Record Keeping Among Nineteenth-Century New England Women." *New England Quarterly* 73 (2000): 274–296.

McCusker, John. *How Much is That in Real Money?* Worcester: American Antiquarian Society, 1992.

McKillop, A. B. *The Spinster and the Prophet: H. G. Wells, Florence Deeks, and the Case of the Plagiarized Text*. New York: Four Walls Eight Windows, 2000.

McNulty, Elizabeth. *Boston, Then and Now*. San Diego: Thunder Bay Press, 1999.

Morris, Richard B. *Encyclopedia of American History*. New York: Harper & Brothers, 1953.

O'Connor, Thomas H. *Civil War Boston Home Front and Battlefield*. Boston: Northeastern University Press, 1997.

Pachter, Marc, ed. *Telling Lives The Biographer's Art*. Washington: New Republic Books, 1979.

Pierce, Sally. "Gallery Talk" for exhibit "A Photographic History of Boston, 1840–1865." Boston University Art Gallery, 2 March 2006.

Pugliese, Barbara. Gallery Talk for exhibit "Authentic Clothing of the Civil War." Tisch Library, Tufts University, 2 November 2005.

"Population Trends in Boston 1640–1990." *Boston History and Architecture*. iBoston. http://www.iboston.org/mcp.php?pid=popFig&laf=rg, accessed 22 March 2006.

Richardson, Peter Tufts. *The Boston Religion Unitarianism in its Capital City*. Rockland: Red Barn Publishing, 2003.

Seasholes, Nancy S. *Gaining Ground: A History of Landmaking in Boston*. Cambridge: The MIT Press, 2003.

Sewing Clothing. *Textiles in America exhibit*, American Textile Museum, Lowell, MA. 23 March 2006.

The New Shorter Oxford English Dictionary. Oxford: Clarendon Press, 1993.

Wilentz, Sean. *The Rise of American Democracy*. New York: W. W. Norton, 2005.

Zielinsky, Gregory A. & Barry D. Keim. *New England Weather, New England Climate*. Hanover: University of New Hampshire Press, 2003.

Zinsser, William. *Extraordinary Lives: The Art and Craft of American Biography*. Boston: Houghton Mifflin, 1988.

Individuals

Bacon, Margaret Hope. *Valiant Friend: The Life of Lucretia Mott*. New York: Walker and Company, 1980.

Baker, Kevin. "Capital Punishment." Biography Resource Center. http://galenet galegroup.com/servlet?BioRC, accessed 29 March 2005.

Bartlett, Irving N. "Daniel Webster as a Symbolic Hero." *New England Quarterly* 45 (December 1972).

Barton, Cynthia H. *Transcendental Wife: The Life of Abigail May Alcott*. New York: University Press of America, 1996.

Bates, Ernest Sutherland. "Alcott, Amos Bronson." *Dictionary of American Biography*.

Buell, Lawrence. *Emerson*. Cambridge: Belknap Press, 2003.

Bushman, Claudia L. *"A Good Poor Man's Wife": Being a Chronicle of Harriet Hanson Robinson and Her Family in Nineteenth Century New England*. Hanover: University Press of New England, 1981.

Carpenter, Delores Bird, ed. *The Selected Letters of Lidian Jackson Emerson*. Columbia: University of Missouri Press, 1987.

Cameron, Kenneth ed. *Concord Harvest, The Later Transcendentalists*. 2 vols. Hartford: Transcendental Books, 1970.

Christie, Francis A. "Parker, Theodore." *Dictionary of American Biography*.

Cole, Arthur C. "Webster, Daniel." *Dictionary of American Biography*.

Commager, Henry Steele. *Theodore Parker*. Boston: The Beacon Press, 1947.

Crothers, Samuel M. "William Ellery Channing." Biography Resource Center. http://galenet.galegroup.com/servlet/BioRC, accessed 4 May 2005.

Dalzell, Robert F. *Daniel Webster and the Trial of American Nationalism*. New York: Norton & Co., 1972.

Davison, Andrew. Petition of Andrew C. Davison for redress for sufferings & loss in consequence of confinement in the State Lunatic Asylum at Worcester. Catalog & Index Leave to Withdraw 10363. Massachusetts State Archives.

"Davison, Benjamin Rice/William Henry." *Class Book 1845* HUD 24.5.714. F. 81–83 and *Secretary's File Class of 1845* HUD 245.505. Harvard College.

Donald, David. *Charles Sumner and the Rights of Man.* New York: Alfred A. Knopf, 1970.

Donne, John. "Verse Letter." *Bartlett's Familiar Quotations*, 16th ed., Boston: Little, Brown and Company, 1992.

Emerson, Ralph Waldo. *Nature.* Boston: Beacon Press, 1985.

———. "Woman A Lecture Before the Woman's Rights Convention." *Against the Tide: Pro-Feminist Men in the United States, 1776–1900*, edited by Michael S. Kimmel and Thomas E. Mosmiller, 217–20. Boston: Beacon Press, 1992.

Fenton, Julie. "Miss Ellen A. Stone." Investigating Lexington's History Papers. Cary Library, Lexington, MA.

Follen, Eliza Lee Cabot. *Married Life.* Schlesinger Library Microfilm. Hollis 002637188. New Haven: Research Publications, 1975. (History of Women, Reel 164, no. 1053).

———. *Works of Charles Follen, with a Memoir of his Life.* 2 vols. Boston, 1842.

Francke, Kuno. "Follen, Charles." *Dictionary of American Biography.*

Fuess, Claude M. "Phillips, Wendell." *Dictionary of American Biography.*

Gienapp, William E. "Franklin Pierce." *The American Presidents,* Revised ed., Hackensack, N. J.: Salem Press, 2000.

Green, Elizabeth Alden. *Mary Lyon and Mount Holyoke.* Hanover: University Press of New England, 1979.

Grodzins, Dean. *American Heretic Theodore Parker and Transcendentalism.* Chapel Hill: University of North Carolina Press, 2002.

———. *Chronology of American Heretic*, lecture handout, Winter 2002.

Harvard Quinquennial Catalogue of the Officers and Graduates 1636–1930. Cambridge: Harvard, 1930.

Hayes, George H. "Sumner, Charles." *Dictionary of American Biography.*

Hedrick, Joan. D. *Harriet Beecher Stowe.* New York: Oxford University Press, 1994.

Hofstadter, Richard. "Wendell Phillips: The Patrician as Agitator." *The American Political Tradition and the Men Who Made It*, 176–77, 181. New York: Vintage Books, 1973.

Howe, M. A. DeWolfe. "Higginson, Thomas Wentworth." *Dictionary of American Biography.*

Ingebritsen, Shirley Phillips. "Cheney, Ednah Dow Littlehale." *Notable American Women.*

Johnson, David. "Assault in the Senate." Biography Resource Center http://galenet.galegroup.com/servlet?BioRC, accessed 29 March 2005.

Karcher, Carolyn L. *The First Woman in the Republic: A Cultural Biography of Lydia Maria Child.* Durham: Duke University Press, 1994.

Lippert, Joseph. *Life of Joseph Lippert*. Ms 1881–82 private collection.

Manual for the General Court Boston: 1886. Committees of Henry J. Hosmer.

Marshall, Megan. *The Peabody Sisters: Three Women Who Ignited American Romanticism*. Boston: Houghton Mifflin Company, 2005.

May, Samuel J. "Dr. Charles Follen." *Some Recollections of Our Antislavery Conflict*. Boston, 1869. Pamphlet.

McAleer, John. *Ralph Waldo Emerson: Days of Encounter*. Boston: Little, Brown and Company, 1984.

McFarland, Philip. *Hawthorne in Concord*. New York: Grove Press, 2004.

Messerli, Jonathan. "Mann, Mary Tyler Peabody." *Notable American Women*.

Mood, Fulmer. "May, Samuel Joseph." *Dictionary of American Biography*.

Moser, Harold D. *Daniel Webster: A Bibliography*. Westport, CT: Praeger, 2005.

Myerson, Joel and Daniel Shealy, eds. *The Journals of Louisa May Alcott*. Boston: Little, Brown and Company, 1989.

———. *The Selected Letters of Louisa May Alcott*. Boston: Little, Brown and Company, 1987.

Palmer, Beverly Wilson, ed. *Selected Letters of Lucretia Coffin Mott*. Urbana: University of Illinois Press, 2002.

Parker, Theodore. *A Sermon on the Public Function of Woman*. 27 March 1853 Leaflet Robbins-Stone Papers (name in pencil in top right corner: J A Robbins).

Perley, Sidney. *The Plumer Genealogy*. Salem: The Essex Institute, 1917.

"Plumer, William." *Biographical Directory of the United States Congress*. http://bioguide.congress.gov/scripts/biodisplay.pl?index+P000393, accessed 22 March 2006.

Porte, Joel, ed. *Emerson in His Journals*. Cambridge: Belknap Press, 1982.

Richardson, Robert D. Jr. *Emerson: The Mind on Fire*. Berkeley: University of California Press, 1995.

Robbins, Eli. Middlesex County Probate Court File Papers 40630, Reel 487.

Robbins family history materials. Robbins (Arlington, MA) Library, #7101-13.

Robbins, Stephen. "Purchase of Property," 8 November 1826. *Papers of Daniel Webster Correspondence,* vol. 2. Hanover: University Press of New England, 1976.

Robertson, Stacey M. *Parker Pillsbury: Radical Abolitionist, Male Feminist*. Ithaca: Cornell University Press, 2000.

Robinson, William A. "Plumer, William." *Dictionary of American Biography*.

Robinson, William S. *"Warrington" Pen-Portraits*. Boston, 1877.

Ronda, Bruce A., ed. *Letters of Elizabeth Palmer Peabody*. Middletown: Wesleyan University Press, 1984.

Rugoff, Milton. *The Beechers: An American Family in the Nineteenth Century*. New York: Harper & Row, 1981.

Sacks, Kenneth S. "'The American Scholar' and His Struggle for Self-Reliance." *Understanding Emerson*. Princeton: Princeton University Press, 2003.

Sanborn, Franklin B. and William Torrey Harris, eds. *The Genius and Character of Emerson*. Boston, 1884.

———. *Recollections of Seventy Years*. Boston: Badger, 1909.

Saxton, Martha. *Louisa May*. Boston: Houghton Mifflin Company, 1977.

Schlesinger, Elizabeth Bancroft. "Follen, Eliza Lee Cabot." *Notable American Women*.

Stange, Douglas C. "The Making of an Abolitionist Martyr: Harvard Professor Charles Theodore Christian Follen." *Harvard Library Bulletin* No. 1 (January 1976): 23.

Starr, Harris Elwood. "Follen, Eliza Lee Cabot." *Dictionary of American Biography*.

Stern, Madeleine. *Louisa May Alcott*. Norman: University of Oklahoma Press, 1950.

Stewart, James Brewer. *Wendell Phillips Liberty's Hero*. Baton Rouge: Louisiana State University Press, 1986.

Storey, Moorfield. *Charles Sumner*. American Statesmen Series. Boston: Houghton Mifflin and Company, 1900.

Sumner, Charles. Obituaries and accounts of his funeral. *Boston Daily Globe,* 12 March 1874, 17 March 1874. *New York Times,* 12 March, 14 March, 16 March 1874.

Tharp, Louise Hall. *Until Victory: Horace Mann and Mary Peabody*. Boston: Little, Brown and Company, 1953.

Van Doren, Mark. "Emerson, Ralph Waldo." *Dictionary of American Biography*.

Walmsley, James Elliott. "Brooks, Preston." *Dictionary of American Biography*.

Webster, Daniel. "Address Delivered in Faneuil Hall." 22 May 1852. *Speeches of Daniel Webster*. National Edition.

Webster, Daniel. "The Constitution and the Union." *The Great Speeches and Orations of Daniel Webster*, edited by Edwin M. Whipple. Boston, 1879.

Wheeler, Leslie, ed. *Loving Warriors Selected Letters of Lucy Stone and Henry B. Blackwell*. New York: The Dial Press, 1981.

Williams, Mary Wilhelmine. "Pillsbury, Parker," *Dictionary of American Biography*.

Lexington

Adams Female Academy. *A Catalogue of the Officers and Students of the Adams Female Academy*. Derry, New Hampshire. 1832.

Adams Female Academy. *A Catalogue of the Officers and Students of the Adams Female Academy*. Derry, New Hampshire 1835–7.

Adams Female Academy. "Report of Progress" for Miss E. Robbins September 1, 1832.

Adams Female Academy. "Testamonial" [*sic*] Julia A. Robbins Senior Class of 1836. Robbins-Stone papers.

"A Lot of History in Its Eight Corners," *Lexington Minuteman*, (Lexington, MA), 30 December 1971, 30B.

Atlas of the Towns of Watertown, Belmont, Arlington & Lexington Middlesex County, Massachusetts. 1898.

Brayton, Douglas Percy. *The History of Follen Church.* East Lexington Library, Pamphlet.

Brown, Abram English. *Beneath Old Roof Trees.* Boston, 1896.

Brown, Francis. H. *Lexington Epitaphs.* Lexington Historical Society, 1905.

Coburn, Frank Warren. *The Battle on Lexington Common April 19, 1775.* Lexington, 1921.

Collection of articles about the Stone Building, East Lexington, Mass. Lexington Room, Cary Library.

Cullen, Maurice R. Jr. *Battle Road.* (A Guide to Minute Man National Historical Park). Pamphlet.

Earle, Alice Morse. *Two Centuries of Costume in America,* vol. 2. New York: Macmillan, 1903.

East Lexington. Map. New York: Beers & Company, 1875.

East Lexington. Map. Lexington Historical Society, 1889.

Fernald, Helen Clark. "An Afternoon With Miss Ellen Stone." *Lexington Minuteman* (Lexington, MA), 30 December 1971.

Hinkle, Alice. "Eli Robbins sets store by bricks." *Lexington Minuteman* (Lexington, MA).

———. "Stone's walls make good neighbors," *Lexington Minuteman* (Lexington, MA), 26 August 1982.

———. "East Lexington, Center rivals during 1800s." *Lexington Minuteman* (Lexington, MA), 26 October 1989.

———. "Historic East Village: Bustling with vitality," *Lexington Minuteman* (Lexington, MA), 26 October 1989.

———. "Town's oldest building, with neighbor, in register." *Lexington Minuteman* (Lexington, MA), 27 May 1976.

Howell, William Dean. *Three Villages.* Boston, 1884.

Hudson, Charles. *History of the Town of Lexington with a Genealogical Register.* Boston: Wiggin & Lunt, 1868.

Hudson, Charles. *History of the Town of Lexington.* Bicentenary Ed., 2 vols. Boston: Houghton Mifflin Company, 1913.

Hurd D. H. *History of Middlesex County with biographical sketches.* Boston, 1890. *Insurance Map of Lexington.* Sanborn Map Company.

Kelley, Beverly Allison. *Lexington: A Century of Photographs.* Lexington, MA: Lexington Historical Society, 1980.

Kollen, Richard. *Lexington From Liberty's Birthplace to Progressive Suburb.* Charleston: Arcadia, 2004.

———. *Lexington, Massachusetts: Treasures from Historic Archives.* Charleston: History Press, 2006.

Kollen, Richard, Joo-Hee Chung, Heather-Marie Knight, and Kendra White-side. *Lexington*. Images of America Series. Charleston: Arcadia, 2001.

Lahikainen, D. T. *Lexington Portraits*. Lexington, MA: Lexington Historical Society, 1977.

Lainhart, Ann A. *1855 Massachusetts Census for Lexington*. Boston, 1991.

Lexington, Mass. *Annual Report of the town officers of Lexington* 1835, 1849–1854, 1857, 1860, 1900.

———. *Record of Births, Marriages and Deaths to January 1, 1898*. Boston, 1898.

———. *Reports of the Auditors and the School Committee 1847–51*.

———. *"Valuation of Real and Personal Estate 1849."*

———. *Map of the Town of Lexington*. Surveyed by Order of the Town. H. F. Walling, 1853.

———. Map. New York: Beers & Company, 1875.

———. Prints and Photographs. Collection at the Boston Athenaeum. Viewed 6 March 2006.

"Lexington Sixty Years Ago." *Proceedings of the Lexington Historical Society,* 19–64.

Lexington and Bedford Directory. 1887–8, 1894, 1899.

Neumann, Emily. "Stephen & Eli Robbins: East Lexington would not be the same without them." Investigating Lexington's History Papers. 2004–2005. Cary Library, Lexington, MA.

Newell, Harriet Chase. *Houses of the Double Range and East Derry, New Hampshire*. Littleton, N.H. 1954.

Nylander, Jane Cayford. "Preserving a Legacy." *The Art of Family*. D. Brenton Simons and Peter Benes. Boston: New England Historic Genealogical Society, 2002. 201–221.

Nylander, Jane. "Preserving a Legacy." *Historic New England Magazine,* (Fall 2002). http://www.historic newengland.org/NEHM/2002 Fall Page 06.htm, accessed 18 January 2007.

Plimpton, Oakes. *Robbins Farm Arlington, Massachusetts*. Camden, ME: Penobscot Press, 1995.

Reinhardt, Elizabeth W. and Anne A. Grady. "Asher Benjamin in East Lexington, Massachusetts." *Old-time New England* 67, Nos. 3–4 (1977): 23–35.

"Reminiscences of the Fur Industry." *Proceedings of the Lexington Historical Society,* vol. 2, 171–79.

Resident and Business Directory of Lexington and Bedford, Massachusetts 1899, N. Cambridge: Edward A. Jones.

Robbins-Stone Family Papers at the Lexington Historical Society Archives.
 Box 1 Account Books, Fur Books, Ellen Stone's notes on the life of Stephen Robbins.
 Box 2 Rental Properties.
 Box 3 Caira Robbins Letters, Papers, Diary.
 Box 4 Julia A. Robbins Letters and Papers.

Box 6 Ellen A. Robbins Stone Papers.

Box 7 Diaries.

Box 8 Newspaper clippings, art work of Caira Robbins and Hannah Simonds, photographs.

Box 9 Photographs.

Box 10 Scrapbook.

Box 11 Cookbooks Ellen A. Stone.

Books that belonged to Julia A. Robbins

An Epitome of History by J. E. Worcester Cambridge: Hilliard and Brown. 1827.

The Holy Bible inscribed "With the affectionate regards of M. W. Gale. Derry. Feb. 12, 1836." Concord: C.&A. Hoag, 1834.

Math exercise book 8 pages handsewn approx. 4×7.

A New Pocket Dictionary of the French and English Languages. 1830.

Scholar's Guide to Chirography, containing Writing-Book, Copies, Rules, and General Directions to the Art. Boston, 1830.

Rosenberg, Charles E. *The Cholera Years: The United States in 1832, 1849, and 1866.* Chicago: University of Chicago Press, 1962.

Schiff, Stacy. *A Great Improvisation.* New York: Henry Holt & Company, 2005.

Schlesinger, Elizabeth Bancroft. "Follen, Eliza Lee Cabot." *Notable American Women.*

Stone, Miss Ellen A. "Diary and Letters of Caira Robbins." *Proceedings of the Lexington Historical Society. Vol. IV.* 61–81.

[Stone, Mrs. Ellen A.] "In Memoriam." *The Woman's Journal,* 15 November 1890:364.

Unitarian Universalist Church Archives. Follen Church, Lexington, MA. Papers on church contributions, pews, and events.

Whipple, S. Lawrence. "Addendum" to "An Afternoon With Miss Ellen Stone." *Lexington Minuteman* (Lexington, MA), 30 December 1971.

Worthen, Edwin B. *A Calendar History of Lexington, Massachusetts 1620–1946.* Lexington: The Bank, 1946.

———. *Tracing the Past in Lexington, Massachusetts.* New York: Vantage Press, 1998.

Brook Farm

Adams, Raymond William. "Ripley, George." *Dictionary of American Biography.*

Benardete, Jane Johnson. "Ripley, Sophia Willard Dana." *Notable American Women.*

Bestor, Arthur Eugene Jr. *Brook Farm 1841–1847: An Exhibition to Commemorate the Centenary of Its Founding.* New York: Columbia, 1941.

"Brook Farm." *Columbia Encyclopedia*, 6th ed. http://www.bartleby.com/65/br/BrookFar.html, accessed 30 January 2006.

Curtis, Edith Roekler. *A Season in Utopia: The Story of Brook Farm*. New York: Russell & Russell, 1961.

Delano, Sterling F. *Brook Farm: The Dark Side of Utopia*. Cambridge: Harvard, 2004.

Dobson, Eleanor Robinette. "Dwight, John Sullivan." *Dictionary of American Biography*.

Dwight, Marianne. *Letters from Brook Farm 1844–1847*. Edited by Amy L. Ree. Poughkeepsie: Vassar, 1928.

"Fourier, Charles." *Columbia Encyclopedia,* 6th ed. http://www.bartleby.com/65/fo/FourierC.html, accessed 30 January 2006.

Francis, Richard. *Transcendental Utopias: Individual and Community at Brook Farm, Fruitlands, and Walden*. Ithaca: Cornell, 1977.

Gordon, Jessica. "Transcendental Ideas: Social Reform." http://www.vcuedu/engweb/trnscendentalism/ideas/brhistory.html, accessed 30 January 2006.

Haraszti, Zoltan. *The Idyll of Brook Farm as Revealed by Unpublished letters in the Boston Public Library*. Boston: Trustees of the Boston Public Library, 1940.

Raymond, Henrietta Dana. *Sophia Willard Dana Ripley: Co-Founder of Brook Farm*. Portsmouth: Randall, 1994.

Swift, Lindsay. *Brook Farm: Its Members, Scholars, and Visitors*. Secaucus: Citadel Press, 1961.

Abolition

Allegro, James J. "'Increasing and Strengthening the Country': Law, Politics and the Antislavery Movement in Early-Eighteenth-Century Massachusetts Bay." *New England Quarterly* 75 (2002): 5–23.

"Anti-Slavery Bazaar." *Liberator*. 25 October 1850 through January 1851.

Anti-Slavery Society News and Notices. *Liberator*. 30 March 1849, 6 April 1849.

Bacon, Margaret Hope. "By Moral Force Alone." *Abolitionist Sisterhood*, edited by Jean Fagan Yellin and John C. Van Horne, 275–97. Ithaca: Cornell University Press, 1994.

Blanck, Emily. "Seventeen Eighty-Three: The Turning Point in the Law of Slavery and Freedom in Massachusetts." *New England Quarterly*, 75 (2002): 24–51.

Bogin, Ruth and Jean Fagan Yellin. "Introduction." *Abolitionist Sisterhood*, edited by Jean Fagan Yellin and John C. Van Horne, 1–19. Ithaca: Cornell University Press.

Chambers-Schiller, Lee. "A Good Work among the People." *Abolitionist Sisterhood*, edited by Jean Fagan Yellin and John C. Van Horne, 249–74. Ithaca: Cornell University Press.

Dodge, J. G. Letters to Julia Robbins. 27 March 1849, 28 March 1849, 17 April 1849, 19 November 1852. Robbins-Stone Papers, Lexington Historical Society.

Friedman, Lawrence J. *Gregarious Saints: Self and Community in American Abolitionism, 1830–1870*. New York: Cambridge University Press, 1982.

Gara, Larry. "Crafts, Ellen." *Notable American Women*.

Ginzberg, Lori D. *Women and the Work of Benevolence: Morality, Politics, and Class in the Nineteenth-Century United States*. New Haven: Yale University Press, 1990.

Gougeon, Len and Joel Myerson, eds. *Emerson's Anti-Slavery Writings*. New Haven: Yale University Press, 1995.

Hansen, Debra Gold. "The Boston Female Anti-Slavery Society and the Limits of Gender Politics." *Abolitionist Sisterhood*, edited by Jean Fagan Yellin and John C. Van Horne, 45–65. Ithaca: Cornell University Press, 1994.

———. *Strained Sisterhood: Gender and Class in the Boston Female Anti-Slavery Society*. Amherst: University of Massachusetts Press, 1993.

Harrold, Stanley. *American Abolitionists*. Seminar Studies in History. Harlow, England: Pearson Education Limited. 2001.

Hersh, Blanche Glassman. "'Am I Not a Woman and a Sister?' Abolitionist Beginnings of Nineteenth-Century Feminism." *Antislavery Reconsidered*, edited by Lewis Perry and Michael Fellman, 252–83. Baton Rouge: Louisiana State University Press, 1979.

———. *The Slavery of Sex Feminist-Abolitionists in America*. Urbana: U of Illinois Press, 1978.

Hewitt, Nancy A. "On Their Own Terms." *Abolitionist Sisterhood*, edited by Jean Fagan Yellin and John C. Van Horne, 23–30. Ithaca: Cornell University Press, 1994.

Horton, Lois E. "Community Organization and Social Activism: Black Boston and the Antislavery Movement." *Abolitionism and Issues of Race and Gender*, edited by John R. McKivigan, 60–75. New York: Taylor and Francis, 1999.

Jeffrey, Julie Roy. *The Great Silent Army of Abolitionism: Ordinary Women in the Antislavery Movement*. Chapel Hill: University of North Carolina Press, 1998.

Johnson, Linck C. "'Liberty is Never Cheap': Emerson, 'The Fugitive Slave Law,' and the Antislavery Lecture Series at the Broadway Tabernacle." *New England Quarterly* 76 (2003): 550–592.

Kraditor, Aileen S. *Means and Ends in American Abolitionism: Garrison and His Critics on Strategy and Tactics, 1834–1850*. New York: Pantheon, 1969.

Lader, Lawrence. *The Bold Brahmins New England's War Against Slavery: 1831–1863*. New York: Dutton, 1961.

Lerner, Gerda. *The Grimke Sisters from South Carolina*. Boston: Houghton Mifflin Co., 1967.

————. "The Political Activity of Antislavery Women." *The Majority Finds Its Past*. New York: Oxford UP, 1979.

Lexington, Massachusetts. "Almshouse." *Auditor's Report*. 1849–50.

Liberty Bell. Publication of the National Anti-Slavery Bazaar. Boston, 1851, 1852, 1853.

Lowell, James Russell. "Letter From Boston" *The Complete Poetical Works of James Russell Lowell*, 111–13. Boston, 1890.

McKivigan, John R. ed. *Abolitionism and Issues of Race and Gender*. New York: Taylor and Francis, 1999.

————. *The War against Proslavery Religion Abolitionism and the Northern Churches, 1830–1865*. Ithaca: Cornell University Press, 1984.

May, Samuel J. Letter to Julia Robbins. Sunday noon. Robbins-Stone Papers. Lexington Historical Society.

————. *Some Recollections of our Antislavery Conflict*. Boston, 1869.

Mayer, Henry. *All On Fire: William Lloyd Garrison and the Abolition of Slavery*. New York: St. Martin's, 1998.

Mott, Lucretia Coffin. "To Roadside Family." 4 July 1865. *Selected Letters of Lucretia Coffin Mott*, edited by Beverly Wilson Palmer. Urbana: University of Illinois Press, 2002.

Perry, Lewis and Michael Fellman, eds. *Antislavery Reconsidered New Perspectives on the Abolitionists*. Baton Rouge: Louisiana State University Press, 1979.

Petrulionis, Sandra Harbert. "'Swelling That Great Tide of Humanity': The Concord, Massachusetts, Female Anti-Slavery Society." *New England Quarterly* 74 (2001) 385–418.

Pillsbury, Parker. "Intolerance." *Liberator* 20 April 1849.

————. Letters to Julia Robbins. 1 August 1853, 18 September 1853, 1 January 1854, 21 February 1854, 30 July 1854, 9 June 1856, 12 August 1856, 24 October 1856, 10 January 1857, 28 February 1857, 14 April 1857, 18 July 1857, 7 September 1857, 1 December 1857, 30 December 1857, 3 June 1858, 8 July 1858, 21 September 1858, 11 November 1858. Robbins-Stone Papers, Lexington Historical Society.

————. "The Morality of Nations." *Against the Tide: Pro-Feminist Men in the United States, 1776–1900*, edited by Michael S. Kimmel and Thomas E. Mosmiller, 221–223. Boston: Beacon Press, 1992.

Pillsbury, Sarah. Letter to Julia Robbins. 26 March 1854. Robbins-Stone Papers, Lexington Historical Society.

Robertson, Stacey M. "'A Hard, Cold, Stern Life': Parker Pillsbury and Grassroots Abolitionism 1840–1865." *New England Quarterly* 70 (1997) 179–210.

Sklar, Kathryn Kish. *Women's Rights Emerges within the Antislavery Movement,* The Bedford Series in History and Culture. Boston: St. Martin's, 2000.

Sterling, Dorothy. *Turning the World Upside Down: The Anti-Slavery Convention of American Women*. New York: Coalition of Publishers for Employment, 1987.

Stewart, James Brewer. *Holy Warriors: The Abolitionists and American Slavery.* American Century Series. New York: Hill and Wang, 1976.

Taylor, Clare. *Women of the Anti-Slavery Movement: The Weston Sisters.* New York: St. Martin's Press, 1995.

Van Brockhoven, Deborah Bingham. "Let Your Names Be Enrolled." *Abolitionist Sisterhood*, edited by Jean Fagan Yellin and John C. VanHorne, 179–199. Ithaca: Cornell University Press, 1994.

Walters, Ronald G. *American Reformers 1815–1860.* American Century Series. New York: Hill and Wang, 1978.

———. *The Antislavery Appeal: American Abolitionism after 1830.* Baltimore: The Johns Hopkins University Press, 1976.

Washington Goode. "Abstract of proceedings of the Executive Council in the Case of Washington Goode." *Council Files 1849 January–June.* Massachusetts State Archives.

———. *Liberator.* 30 March 1849, 6 April 1849, 13 April 1849, 20 April 1849.

Whittier, John Greenleaf. "Ichabod." *The Poetical Works of Whittier*, edited by Hyatt H. Waggoner. Boston: Houghton Mifflin, 1975.

Williams, Carolyn. "The Female Antislavery Movement." *Abolitionist Sisterhood*, edited by Jean Fagan Yellin and John C. Van Horne, 159–177. Ithaca: Cornell University Press, 1994.

Yellin, Jean Fagan. *Women and Sisters: The Antislavery Feminists in American Culture.* New Haven: Yale University Press, 1989.

Yellin, Jean Fagan and John C. Van Horne eds. *Abolitionist Sisterhood: Women's Political Culture in Antebellum America.* Ithaca: Cornell UP, 1994.

Lowell

Baldwin, David. "Larcom, Lucy." *Notable American Women.*

Baxandall, Rosalyln, Linda Gordon, and Susan Reverby, eds. *America's Working Women: A Documentary History—1600 to the Present.* New York: Random House, 1976.

Bigelow-Sanford Collections, F-1 Records 1818–1858, F-2 Records 1859–1899, F-4 Copies of Letters 1849–1873. Baker Library Harvard Graduate School of Business Administration

Blodget, Geoffrey. "Robinson, Harriet Jane Hanson." *Notable American Women.*

Butts, Miriam and Patricia Heard, compilers. *The Early Industrialization of America: "From Wharf to Waterfall."* Jackdaw No. A 32. New York: The Viking Press.

Coolidge, John. *Mill and Mansion: A Study of Architecture and Society in Lowell, Massachusetts 1820–1865.* New York: Russell & Russell, 1967.

Donald, David. *Charles Sumner and the Coming of the Civil War.* New York: Knopf, 1967.

Dublin, Thomas. *Women at Work: The Transformation of Work and Community in Lowell, Massachusetts, 1826–1860.* New York: Columbia University Press, 1979.

Dunwell, Steve. *The Run of the Mill.* Boston: Godine, 1978.

Eisler, Benita, ed. *The Lowell Offering: Writings by New England Mill Women 1840–1845.* New York: Lippincott, 1977.

Eno, Arthur L., ed. *Cotton Was King: A History of Lowell, Massachusetts.* Lowell Historical Society, 1976.

Ewing, John S. and Nancy P. Norton. *Broadlooms and Businessmen: A History of the Bigelow-Sanford Carpet Company.* Harvard Studies in Business History. Cambridge: Harvard University Press, 1955.

"Finishing Touches." Exhibit American Textile History Museum, Lowell, MA, visited 24 March 2006.

Hambourg, Serge. *Mills and Factories of New England.* New York: Abrams, 1988.

Hand-Book for the Visiter [sic] to Lowell 1848. Lowell Publishing Co., reprint 1982.

Hareven, Tamara K., and Randolph Langenbach. *Amoskeag Life and Work in an American Factory City.* New York: Pantheon, 1978.

Holcombe, Arthur N. "Lawrence, Abbott." *Dictionary of American Biography.*

————. "Lawrence, Amos." Ibid.

————. "Lawrence, Amos Abbott." Ibid.

Johnson, David E. "Assault in the Senate." *American History,* June 1999 v34 i2, p. 52 (7) 29. March 2005 URL Biography Resource Center.

Josephson, Hannah. *The Golden Threads New England's Mill Girls and Magnates.* New York: Duell, Sloan and Pearce, 1949.

"Lowell Manufacturing Company: The Gateway to the Park." *Milling Around* 1, 9 (October 1979): 3, 6.

Lowell. *Parts of Wards 1, 2, & 5 of Outline and Index Map Lowell, Massachusetts.*

————. *Map.* Lowell, 1879.

————. *Map.* Lowell, 1896. Lowell National Historic Park and Preservation Center.

Lowell Views. Lowell: Lowell Historical Society, 1985.

Macaulay, David. *Mill.* Boston: Houghton Mifflin, 1983.

Moran, William. *The Belles of New England: The Women of the Textile Mills and the Families Whose Wealth They Wove.* New York: St. Martin's, 2002.

National Park Service. *Lowell: The Story of an Industrial City.* 1992.

O'Connor, Thomas H. *Lords of the Loom.* New York: Charles Scribner's Sons, 1968.

Pendergast, John. *Lowell*, Images of America Series. Dover: Arcadia, 1996.

Robinson, Harriet Hanson. *Loom and Spindle or Life Among the Early Mill Girls.* Hawaii: Pacific Press, 1976.

Scoresby, William. *American Factories and Their Female Operatives.* New York: Burt Franklin, 1845, reprint 1968.

Shepley Bulfinch Richardson and Abbott. Lowell National Historic Park and Preservation District. Cultural Resources Inventory Volume 13 "Inventory Forms and Research Reports Industrial: Lowell Machine Shop Site through Massic Falls Industrial Site."

Taylor, George Rogers. "Bagley, Sarah G." *Notable American Women*.

Walmsley, James Elliott. "Preston Smith Brooks." *Dictionary of American Biography*; 29 March 2005 URL Biography Resource Center.

Wetherbee, Susan Moore. *The Diary of Susan Moore Wetherbee 1836–1841*. Ts. Mogan Cultural Center, Lowell, MA, n.d.

Wright, H. "The Uncommon Mill Girls of Lowell." *History Today* 33 (January 1973): 10–19.

Zimiles, Martha & Murray. *Early American Mills*. New York: Clarkson N. Potter, 1973.

Women's Rights

THEIR ROLE, RIGHTS, AND REFORMS, INCLUDING SUFFRAGE

Banner, Lois W. *Elizabeth Cady Stanton*. Boston: Little, Brown & Company, 1980.

Baxandall, Rosalyn, Linda Gordon, and Susan Reverby, eds. *America's Working Women: A Documentary History 1600 to the Present*. New York: Random House, 1975.

Berg, Barbara J. *The Remembered Gate: Origins of American Feminism*. New York: Oxford University Press, 1973.

Berkin, Carol Ruth and Mary Beth Norton eds. *Women of America: A History*. Boston: Houghton Mifflin Company, 1979.

Bernbaum, Ernest. *Anti-suffrage Essays by Massachusetts Women*. Boston: Forum Publications, 1916.

Bowditch, William I. *Taxation of Women in Massachusetts*. Cambridge, 1875.

Buhle, Mari Jo and Paul Buhle Eds. *The Concise History of Woman Suffrage*. Urbana: University of Illinois Press, 1978.

Chambers-Schiller, Lee. *Liberty, a Better Husband: Single Women in America, the Generations of 1780–1840*. New Haven: Yale University Press, 1984.

Collins, Gail. *America's Women: 400 Years of Dolls, Drudges, Helpmates, and Heroines*. New York: Harper Collins, 2003.

Concord Woman Suffrage Ephemera—William Munroe Special Collections of the Concord Free Public Library.

Cott, Nancy F. *The Bonds of Womanhood: "Woman's Sphere" in New England 1780–1835*. New Haven: Yale University Press, 1977.

———. ed. *No Small Courage: A History of Women in the United States*. New York: Oxford University Press, 2000.

———. *Public Vows: A History of Marriage and the Nation*. Cambridge: Harvard University Press, 2000.

Cott, Nancy F. and Elizabeth Pleck, eds. *A Heritage of Her Own: Toward a New Social History of American Women*. New York: Simon and Schuster, 1979.

Degler, Carl N. *At Odds: Women and the Family in America from the Revolution to the Present*. New York: Oxford University Press, 1980.

DuBois, Ellen Carol. *Feminism and Suffrage: The Emergence of an Independent Women's Movement in America, 1848–1869*. Ithaca: Cornell University Press, 1978.

D'Emilio, J. and Estelle B. Freedman. *Intimate Matters: A History of Sexuality in America,* Part II Divided Passions, 1780–1900. New York: Harper & Row, 1988.

Evans, Sara M. *Born for Liberty: A History of Women in America*. New York: Macmillan, 1989.

Fant, Louie J. Jr. "Fuller, Margaret." *Notable American Women.*

Flexner, Eleanor and Ellen Fitzpatrick. *Century of Struggle: The Woman's Rights Movement in the United States*. Cambridge: Belknap Press, 1975.

Frost, Elizabeth and Kathryn Cullen-DuPont. *Women's Suffrage in America*. New York: Facts on File, 1992.

Giesberg, Judith Ann. "Civil War Sister: The U.S. Sanitary Commission and Women's Politics in Transition." Program at the Schlesinger Library. 4 December 2000.

Gilbert, Armida. "Emerson in the Context of the Woman's Rights Movement." *A Historical Guide to Ralph Waldo Emerson*, edited by Joel Myerson. New York: Oxford University Press, 2000. 211–44.

Gordon, Ann D. "Elizabeth Cady Stanton and the Woman's Rights Movement." *Against the Tide: Women Reformers in American Society*, edited by Paul A. Cimbala and Randall M. Miller. Westport: Praeger, 1997. 41–53.

Gornick, Vivian. *The Solitude of Self: Thinking about Elizabeth Cady Stanton*. New York: Farrar, Straus and Giroux, 2005.

Green, Elizabeth Alden. *Mary Lyon and Mount Holyoke: Opening the Gates*. Hanover: UPNE, 1979.

Green, Harvey and Mary-Ellen Perry. *The Light of the Home: An Intimate View of the Lives of Women in Victorian America*. New York: Pantheon Books, 1983.

Hoar, Hon. George Frisbie. "Woman in the State." Woman Suffrage Pamphlet series. 1904.

Hoffert, Sylvia D. *When Hens Crow: The Woman's Rights Movement in Antebellum America*. Bloomington: Indiana University Press, 1995.

Kerber, Linda. *Women of the Republic*. Chapel Hill: University of North Carolina, 1980.

Kraditor, Aileen S. *The Ideas of the Woman Suffrage Movement, 1890–1920*. New York: Doubleday, 1971.

Lerner, Gerda. *The Majority Finds Its Past: Placing Women in History*. New York: Oxford University Press, 1979.

Lutz, Alma. *Created Equal: A Biography of Elizabeth Cady Stanton*. New York: The John Day Company, 1940.

Matson, Sally. "Susan B. Anthony: The Invincible." Presentation at Cary Memorial Library, Lexington, MA. 6 October 2005.

May, Samuel J. "The Rights and Condition of Women." *Against the Tide: Pro-Feminist Men in the United States, 1776–1900*, edited by Michael S. Kimmel and Thomas E. Mosmiller. Boston: Beacon Press, 1992. 94–97.

Merk, Lois Bannister. *Massachusetts and the Woman-Suffrage Movement*. Cambridge: General Microfilm Company, 1961. Schlesinger Library on the History of Women in America.

Norton, Mary Beth. *Liberty's Daughters: The Revolutionary Experience of American Women, 1750–1800*. Boston: Little, Brown and Company, 1980.

Osterud, Nancy Grey. "'She Helped Me Hay It as Good as a Man': Relations among Women and Men in an Agricultural Community." *"To Toil the Livelong Day": America's Women at Work, 1780–1980*, edited by Carol Groneman and Mary Beth Norton. Ithaca: Cornell University Press, 1987.

Parker, Theodore. *A Sermon of the Public Function of Woman*. 1853. Pamphlet. Robbins-Stone papers, Lexington Historical Society.

Pond, Cora Scott. "Suffrage Meeting at Lexington." *TWJ,* 9 May 1885, 148.

———. "Suffrage Meeting at Concord." Ibid.

Rich, Adrienne. "Heroines." *A Wild Patience Has Taken Me This Far*. New York: W. W. Norton, 1981.

Robbins, Julia A. Essay "If we wish to improve our minds," 1836.

———. "On the evils of whispering."

———. Expense Account, 1836.

———. Math exercise book, 8 pages, hand sewn, approx. 4×7.

Robbins-Stone Papers, Lexington Historical Society.

Robinson, Harriet. *Massachusetts in the Woman Suffrage Movement*. Boston, 1881.

Sherr, Lynn. *Failure Is Impossible: Susan B. Anthony in Her Own Words*. New York: Random House, 1995.

Silber, Nina. *Daughters of the Union: Northern Women Fight the Civil War*. Cambridge: Harvard University Press, 2005.

Sklar, Kathryn Kish. "The Founding of Mount Holyoke College" Berkin & Norton. *Women of America*, 177–210. Boston: Houghton Mifflin Co., 1979.

———. *Women's Rights Emerges within the Antislavery Movement, 1830–1870. A Brief History with Documents*. The Bedford Series in History and Culture. Boston: Bedford/St. Martin's, 2000.

Stolberg, Sheryl Gay. "Face Value at the Capitol." *New York Times*. 13 August 2003.

"The Woman's Journal." *International Encyclopedia of Women's Suffrage*, Santa Barbara: ABC-CLIO, 2000.

"Woman's Rights Convention." *The Liberator*. 11 October 1850 through 15 November 1850.

The Woman's Journal. 1875, 1880–1890. Schlesinger Library on the History of Women in America.

Concord

"Barrett Family." Genealogy Files. William Munroe Special Collections of the Concord Free Public Library.

[Barrett, John.] "In Memoriam." *The Woman's Journal,* 8 November 1890:359.

Bridgman, Raymond L., ed. *Concord Lectures on Philosophy*. Cambridge, 1883.

Brooks, Paul. *The People of Concord: One Year in the Flowering of New England*. Chester, CT: Globe Pequot Press, 1990.

Brewster, William. *Concord River: Selections from the Journals of William Brewster*. Ed. Smith O. Dexter. Cambridge: Harvard University Press, 1937.

———. *October Farm*. Cambridge: Harvard University Press, 1936.

Chapin, Sarah. *Concord Massachusetts*. Images of America Series. Dover, NH: Arcadia, 1997.

———. *Entering Concord: A History of Public Affairs 1850–2000*. Hollis, N.H.: Hollis Publishing Company, 2005.

Chapin, Sarah, Claiborne Dawes, and Alice Moulton. *Concord*. Then & Now Series. Charleston: Arcadia, 2001.

Cheever, Susan. *American Bloomsbury*. New York: Simon and Schuster, 2006.

Cheever, Susan. "Introduction," *Little Women*. By Louisa May Alcott. New York: Modern Library, 2000.

Concord. *Assessors' Records 1866–1892/93. Assessors Dept. Valuation List 1870–1877 Roll 010; 1887–1894 Roll 012; 1894 Roll 013*. William Munroe Special Collections of the Concord Free Public Library.

Concord Ladies' Antislavery Society Records. William Munroe Special Collections of the Concord Free Public Library.

Concord Lyceum 1890–1891 Course of Lectures and Entertainments. William Munroe Special Collections of the Concord Free Public Library.

Concord, Massachusetts. *Annual Reports of the Town Officers of Concord, Mass. From March 1, 1890, to March 1, 1891*. Boston, 1891. *Births, Marriages, and Deaths 1635–1850. Town Report* 1860. William Munroe Special Collections of the Concord Free Public Library.

———. Prints and Photographs. Boston Athenaeum. Viewed 6 March 2006.

———. Map. New York: Beers & Company, 1875. William Munroe Special Collections of the Concord Free Public Library.

———. *Reports of the Selectmen and Other Officers of the Town of Concord from March 5, 1860, to March 1, 1861*. Concord: Printed by Benjamin Tolman, 1861.

"Concord Days." *The Woman's Journal,* 29 August 1885:279.

Concord Events Scrapbooks Reel #1 Volumes 1 & 2. William Munroe Special Collections of the Concord Free Public Library.

Concord Female Charitable Society Records. Unit 1 Series 1. *Annual & Semi-Annual reports 1869–1896. President's Records 1888–1891. President's Book 1891–1913. Records of the Board of Directors, 1869–1881. Reports of Monthly Meetings 1869–1881. Reports of Monthly Meetings 1882–1896.* William Munroe Special Collections of the Concord Free Public Library.

Concord in the Mid-Nineteenth Century. Map. Compiled by Herbert W. Gleason for the 1906 edition of *Thoreau's Journal.* Frontispiece in Brooks.

Concord Ladies Anti-Slavery Society. William Munroe Special Collections of the Concord Free Public Library.

"Concord Population." William Munroe Special Collections of the Concord Free Public Library.

"Concord School of Philosophy." *The Woman's Journal,* 7 August 1880:254; 19 August 1882:265; 4 July 1885:213; 3 July 1886:212; 2 July 1887:211.

Concord Soldiers' Aid Society Records, 1861–1865. William Munroe Special Collections of the Concord Free Public Library.

"Concord Summer School of Philosophy." Pamphlet, n. d. William Munroe Special Collections of the Concord Free Public Library.

Events in Concord 1877–1916. William Munroe Special Collections of the Concord Free Public Library.

Fenn, Mary R. *Old Houses of Concord.* Old Concord Chapter DAR, 1974.

Fischer, David Hackett, ed. *Concord: The Social History of a New England Town 1750–1850.* Waltham: Brandeis, 1984.

Flint, Waldo. "Producing Milk." 1872 article. *Concord Farmers' Club Records, 1852–1883.* Series IV Clippings, 1854–1872. William Munroe Special Collections of the Concord Free Public Library.

French, Allen. *Old Concord.* Boston: Little, Brown & Company, 1915.

Gordon, Jayne K. "Concord and the Great Rebellion, 1861–1865." 1989 Concord Pamphlets 74-10. William Munroe Special Collections of the Concord Free Public Library.

"Guardians of a Dream." *Alcott NewsNotes.* Spring 2005. Alcott House publication.

Hosmer. Glass Plate Negatives—Images of Concord. Vault B5, Unit 5. William Munroe Special Collections of the Concord Free Public Library.

Jarvis, Edward. *Houses and People in Concord 1810 to 1870.* Annotated and references by Adams Tolman, 1915. William Munroe Special Collections of the Concord Free Public Library.

———. *Traditions and Reminiscences of Concord, Massachusetts 1779–1878.* William Munroe Special Collections of the Concord Free Public Library.

———. *Traditions and Reminiscences of Concord, Massachusetts 1779–1878,* edited by Sarah Chapin. Amherst: University of Massachusetts Press, 1993.

Keyes, John Shepard. *Houses & Owners or Occupants in Concord, 1885.* "River Road to Carlisle." Annotated by Adams Tolman. Collated by Marian B. Miller. 1–37. William Munroe Special Collections of the Concord Free Public Library.

Lainhart, Ann S. comp. *Massachusetts State Census for Concord 1855 and 1865.*

Littleton, Mass., Records *Births, Marriages, Deaths to 1850. Births and Deaths 1900.*

Lutyens, Elizabeth. *Concord Unfolded.* Concord: Marco Polo Guides, 1985.

Massachusetts Agricultural Society Records, 1803–1892. Series II. Item 6. Bound manuscript records, 1863–1882. Series III. Box 2. Item 2. Bound manuscript membership book, 1820–1888. Box 2. Folder 2. Engraved membership diploma for Mrs. Julia A. Barrett, 1871. Series V. Bound manuscript volume listing premium awards, 1847–1882. William Munroe Special Collections of the Concord Free Public Library.

Moore, Alex W. Jr. *Concord Authors.* Concord: Anaxagoras Publications, 1996.

Nelson, Liz. *Concord: Stories to Be Told.* Beverly: Commonwealth Editions, 2002.

Petrulionis, Sandra Harbert. *To Set This World Right: The Antislavery Movement in Thoreau's Concord.* Ithaca: Cornell University Press, 2006.

———. "'Swelling That Great Tide of Humanity': The Concord, Massachusetts, Female Anti-Slavery Society." *New England Quarterly* 74 (2001): 385–418.

Plan of the Town of Concord, Mass. In the County of Middlesex. Map. Surveyed by John G. Hales. Boston: Lemuel Shattuck, 1830.

Potter, Charles Edward, ed. *Old Families, Concord, Mass.* vol 1. Boston, 1887.

"Researching the Past: From the Female Point of View." Program, Concord Museum. 10 April 2003.

Richardson, Laurence Eaton. *Concord Chronicle 1865–1899.* 1967. William Munroe Special Collections of the Concord Free Public Library.

School of Philosophy materials in the William Munroe Special Collections of the Concord Free Public Library. Alcott Memorial Service "Remarks & Reminiscences" June 16, 1888. Barrett Collection of printed ephemera relating to sessions of the Concord School of Philosophy, Concord, Mass. 1879–1888.

Newspaper Clippings

Cooke, Geo. W. "The Concord School of Philosophy." *Christian Register,* August 21, 1880. *Events in Concord 1877–1916 Scrapbook.*

Mrs. Julia Ward Howe on "Modern Society." July 29, 1880 and from *The Herald,* July 30, 1880.

"The Sages at Concord." July 16, 1880.

Special Dispatch to *The Herald* on Mrs. Cheney July 28, 1884.

Programs of the School of Philosophy, 1879–1888.

Scudder, Townsend. *Concord: American Town*. Boston: Little, Brown, 1947.

Shattuck, Lemuel. *A History of the Town of Concord*. Boston, 1835.

Siljak, Ana. *Angel of Vengeance: The "Girl Assassin," the Governor of St. Petersburg, and Russia's Revolutionary World*. New York: St. Martin's Press, 2008.

Survey of Historical and Architectural Resources, Concord, Massachusetts, Volume III. Concord Historical Commission, 2002. William Munroe Special Collections of the Concord Free Public Library.

Thoreau, Henry D. "Autumnal Tints." *Excursions*, edited by Joseph J. Moldenhauer. Princeton: Princeton University Press, 2007.

———. "Walking." *Walden and Other Writings of Henry David Thoreau*, edited by Brooks Atkinson. N.Y.: Modern Library, 1992.

Ulam, Adam B. *In the Name of the People: Prophets and Conspirators in Prerevolutionary Russia*. New York: Viking Press, 1977.

Voye, Nancy. "Marriage in Concord: 1845 to 1855." Concord Pamphlets 74-12. William Munroe Special Collections of the Concord Free Public Library.

Weiner, Lynn. "Antebellum Temperance Reform in Concord, Massachusetts." Concord Pamphlets 74-11. William Munroe Special Collections of the Concord Free Public Library.

Wheeler, Ruth R. *Concord: Climate for Freedom*. Concord: Antiquarian Society, 1967.

The William Brewster Photographic Collection Vol. I: Images of Concord. Massachusetts Audubon Visual Arts Center, Canton, MA.

Wilson, Leslie Perrin. "A Concord Farmer Looks Back: The Reminiscences of William Henry Hunt." *Concord Saunterer* ns10 (2002): 65–124.

Wood, James Playsted. *The People of Concord*. New York: Seabury, 1970.

"A Wreath of Joy." Concord: Concord Free Public Library, 1996.

Zwinger, Ann, and Edwin Way Teale. *A Conscious Stillness: Two Naturalists on Thoreau's Rivers*. Amherst: University of Massachusetts Press, 1984.